Chinese Society in the Eighteenth Century

Chinese Society in the Eighteenth Century

SUSAN NAQUIN AND EVELYN S. RAWSKI

Yale University Press

New Haven and London

Designed by James J. Johnson and set in Bodoni types by The
Publishing Nexus Incorporated, Guilford, Connecticut.
Printed in the United States of America by Edwards Brothers,
Inc., Ann Arbor, Michigan.

Library of Congress Cataloging-in-Publication Data

Naquin, Susan.
    Chinese society in the eighteenth century.

    Bibliography: p.
    Includes index.
    1. China—History—Ch'ing dynasty, 1644–1912.
2. China—Politics and government—1644–1912.
3. China—Economic conditions—1644–1912.
4. China—Social conditions—1644–1912.   I. Rawski,
Evelyn Sakakida.   II. Title.
DS754.N4   1987   951'.03   86–29007
ISBN 0–300–03848–8 (cloth)
        0–300–04602–2 (pbk.)

The paper in this book meets the guidelines for perma-
nence and durability of the Committee on Production
Guidelines for Book Longevity of the Council on Library
Resources.

10 9 8 7 6 5 4 3 2

Contents

List of Plates, Tables, and Maps   vii

Preface   ix

Note on Chinese Terms   xiii

Qing Reign Periods   xviii

Part One: Qing Society   1

1. *Government Policies*   3
   Political Structures   4
   Social Policies   14
   Economic Rehabilitation   21
   Foreign Relations   27

2. *Social Relations*   33
   Kinship   33
   Residence and Community   39
   Economic Organizations   46
   Patronage   50

3. *Cultural Life*   55
   City Life   55
   Literati Culture   64
   Material Culture   72
   Life-Cycle Rituals   79
   Annual Festivals   83
   State Ritual   88
   Values and Beliefs   90

Part Two: Change and Diversity in
    Eighteenth-Century Society   95

4. *Social Change*   97
    Economic Diversity and Growth   97
    Demographic Trends   106
    Hereditary Statuses   114
    Social Mobility   123
    Assimilation of Minorities   127
    Frontier Society   130
    New Associations   133

5. *Regional Societies*   138
    North China   140
    Lower Yangtze   147
    Middle Yangtze   158
    Southeast Coast   167
    Lingnan   176
    Northwest China   184
    Upper Yangtze   195
    Southwest China   200
    Manchuria   205
    Taiwan   208
    Region and Nation   212

6. *The Eighteenth-Century Legacy*   217
    Dynastic Decline?   218
    Growth and Complexity   221
    The Opium War   232

Notes   237

Selected Reading   243

Index   265

Plates, Tables, and Maps

PLATES

PLATE 1. Potala Palace in Rehe   30
PLATE 2. Porcelain figure of the bodhisattva Guanyin   44
PLATE 3. *The Literary Gathering at a Yangzhou Garden* (detail)   70
PLATE 4. Cloisonné figurines of two women   76
PLATE 5. Snuff bottle   131
PLATE 6. *Barges of the Embassy Preparing to Pass Under a Bridge*   153
PLATE 7. Porcelain manufacturing at Jingdezhen   163
PLATE 8. A fortified Hakka house   175
PLATE 9. A resident of Hami   189

TABLES

TABLE 1. China's Population and Land Acreage, 1600–1850   25
TABLE 2. Index of Foreign Trade at Canton, 1719–1833   103
TABLE 3. Chinese Macroregions: Area, Estimated Populations, and Population Densities, 1843   214
TABLE 4. Major Domestic Uprisings and Rebellions, 1795–1840   229

MAPS

MAP 1. The Qing empire, showing macroregional systems   xiv
MAP 2. China's macroregions in relation to provinces   xvi

Preface

This book grew out of a collaboration on a chapter entitled "Chinese Society in the Eighteenth Century" for one of the (as yet unpublished) early Qing volumes of the *Cambridge History of China*. At first skeptical that there would be enough secondary material for a chapter about a century on which extensive research was just beginning, we soon realized that we had more than enough for a book.

We also realized that it might be useful to present current scholarly views on the society of this period for intermediate and advanced students, China scholars who work in other disciplines or eras, and historians of Europe, India, or Japan. The secondary literature on this topic has not been recently synthesized, and it is not readily accessible to those who do not read Chinese and Japanese. Moreover, general surveys of modern Chinese history cannot usually devote much space to an era before (supposedly) the real beginning of the modern period—conventionally dated from 1840, when China was defeated in the Opium War. While specialists may find interpretations here that are not part of the received wisdom, our book is aimed at those who do not concentrate on the Qing period.

The eighteenth century was one of the most dynamic periods in China's early modern era, a time when rulers of the newly established Qing dynasty (1644–1911) tried to harness the surge of economic growth and social change that had been interrupted by the transition from the previous dynasty. The Manchu armies, seeking to consolidate control over Inner Asian frontiers, created the largest empire China has ever known. Expansion by conquest was matched by internal migration into frontier regions, generating enduring conflicts between Han Chinese and non-Han peoples and demanding new efforts toward integration.

As China became part of an emerging world economy, foreign trade stimulated a new sequence in the process of economic development. Commercialization, urbanization, and increasing social and physical mobility encouraged the relaxation of fixed statuses and produced a more and more differentiated society, marked by intense competition for wealth, degrees, and other concomitants of elite status. Highly educated scholar-officials built on the intellectual achievements of the Ming dynasty (1368–1644) to secure the foundations for China's modern academic disciplines. Merchants helped knit the empire together with interregional trading networks and their own urban culture.

Western views of the eighteenth century were first shaped by reports from the Europeans who were missionaries at the court in Peking and traders on the fringes of the empire. European eyes, still innocent of the industrial revolution that was just beginning to take shape in England, were dazzled by Chinese sophistication and splendor. To these outsiders, the high Qing of the eighteenth century was the dynasty, perhaps even the civilization, at its peak.

From the vantage point of the nineteenth century, however, the eighteenth century appeared a good deal less admirable. Chinese literati of the Daoguang reign (1821–1850), stung by the depression induced by the opium trade and the humiliation of defeat by European powers, saw the preceding century as a time of corruption, extravagance, and irresponsibility. Late Qing thinkers such as Liang Qichao (1873–1929) identified the eighteenth century as an era of intellectual stagnation when the literati, mindful of the intense factionalism of the late Ming and fearful of state censorship, had retreated into historicism and philological research.

Chinese scholars today cannot forget China's failure, by comparison with Europe or Japan, to modernize rapidly. Many use Marxist models to show that Qing growth could not mature into a self-generating process of industrialization because it was not only stifled by the state and the ruling elites but also prevented by the conditions of Western imperialism. Thus, the failures of the late Qing were foreshadowed in the 1790s, when corruption, weakening central control, population growth, and a rising trade in opium became important and continuing problems.

It is against this backdrop of diverse interpretations, only in the last decade founded on extensive primary research, that we have turned to look again at the eighteenth century. We want to reexamine the major trends of the last four hundred years and reinterpret somewhat the ways in which the eighteenth century was connected to preceding and subsequent periods.

By "eighteenth century" we actually mean the early and middle

Qing; our emphasis on the fundamental social changes over what Fernand Braudel has called the "longue durée" makes the "long" century between about 1680 and 1820 the most natural period for analysis. We begin with the Qing conquest in the seventeenth century and conclude by considering the implications of eighteenth-century developments on nineteenth-century history. We have taken great care to disaggregate temporally the conclusions drawn by earlier historians about the entire Qing period. Our ambition is not merely to depict the "longue durée" but to fit long-term gradual processes of change into the complex concatenation of middle- and short-run events in which history is enacted.

To escape the often misleading generalizations necessary if one speaks of China as a whole, we have divided this vast empire into component macroregions (each easily comparable in size to a European nation) and show how imperial policies and specific local conditions produced very diverse social patterns. We have also been concerned with the characteristics of this society as a whole, in particular the institutions and mechanisms that knit it together.

The eighteenth century was not simply a painted backdrop to modern times. We have tried to provide more than a static picture of traditional Chinese society, to show instead the ways in which the society was changing in this period. Only by understanding the trends then already in motion may we appreciate their impact on later events. But precisely because mid-Qing society was part of a continuum, its characteristic trends were not always unique to it, and not all important developments were new ones. Although the sources rarely permit quantitative comparisons, we have tried to chart the direction of change, signal what is significant, and be judicious in the use of the word *new*. We invite historians of earlier centuries to help distinguish, for example, Song and Ming urbanization from Qing urbanization.

How does this work fit into the genre of social history? In our individual research, we have both been committed to "history from the bottom up"—i.e., to studying the perspectives and life experiences of ordinary Chinese people. The influence of the *Annales* school of social history on our work is obvious, but in this book we have departed in some significant ways from social history as defined by the *Annales* practitioners. Many social historians ignore political history; we have explicitly included a description of the Qing political system and of Qing policies (including foreign policy) because we believe that the state's actions affected the lives of even ordinary citizens. We have studied the entire social spectrum, from rulers and scholars to minorities and outcast groups. Because economic developments supplied the foundation and stimulus for many social changes, we have devoted space to the early Qing economy. Nevertheless, these other aspects of Qing history are introduced only as they affect social patterns and processes.

Although both of us have done primary research on eighteenth-century China, this book is built on the foundation of other people's work. We have shamelessly plundered the secondary literature on this period in Chinese, Japanese, and Western languages, including as much as possible of the flood of recent research based on Qing government archives opened in the 1970s and 1980s in Taiwan and in the People's Republic of China—though often drawing different conclusions. Despite our considerable debt to others, notes are few and acknowledge only rare or very specific information. The reader looking for further information should turn to the annotated bibliography for the best and most accessible sources in Chinese, Japanese, and Western languages.

We also refer to the provocative models for method and analysis provided by anthropology and modern European history. Of necessity, our conclusions are closer to hypotheses, and, writing as we do while the field expands around us, we fully expect our generalizations to be challenged and modified. At the same time, we believe that Chinese history needs to be set in a wide context and that the very dynamism of research in the early Qing calls for an occasional synthetic evaluation of past and current work, a look at what we know about Chinese society in the eighteenth century and at what we would like to know. If we can generate debate and stimulate further work on important topics, our efforts will have been well served.

This book is truly a joint effort: the entire manuscript has been thoroughly rewritten by both of us, many times. Such a close and satisfactory collaboration would not have been possible without computer technology, and we thank Robert Manson and Thomas G. Rawski for invaluable help on technical matters. We have been fortunate in receiving detailed comments from a number of colleagues at various stages in the writing of this manuscript. We would like to thank James Lee, Ramon Myers, William Rowe, Gilbert Rozman, G. W. Skinner, Jonathan Spence, James L. Watson, Pierre-Étienne Will, and R. Bin Wong for their advice. Jess Bell and Otto Bohlmann provided extremely useful suggestions for improvement of this manuscript. Many other colleagues have read parts of the manuscript or offered comments during colloquia at Berkeley, Columbia, Stanford, and York University; to them also we are most grateful. To Fred Wakeman, who dreamed up the topic and introduced us to one another, we are particularly indebted.

A Note on Chinese Terms

The Chinese terms and names in the text are rendered in Pinyin romanization, with the exception of Manchu names and some words that have long been standard English usage (Peking, Manchu, Taoism). For more on romanization, see p. 243. Macroregional names are taken with some modification from G. W. Skinner; the macroregions, depicted on maps 1 and 2, are based on maps in G. W. Skinner, "Regional Urbanization in Nineteenth-Century China," in *The City in Late Imperial China*, ed. G. W. Skinner (Stanford: Stanford University Press, 1977), pp. 214–15.

Our references to Qing rulers use their reign names, which are listed on p. xviii.

In the text, we refer to the Chinese acreage measure, the *mu*, which was not standardized during the Qing, and to the modern standard measure, the *shimu*, which was equivalent to .1647 acre or one-fifteenth of a hectare. We also refer to the Chinese measure of distance, the *li*, which was equivalent to .36 miles.

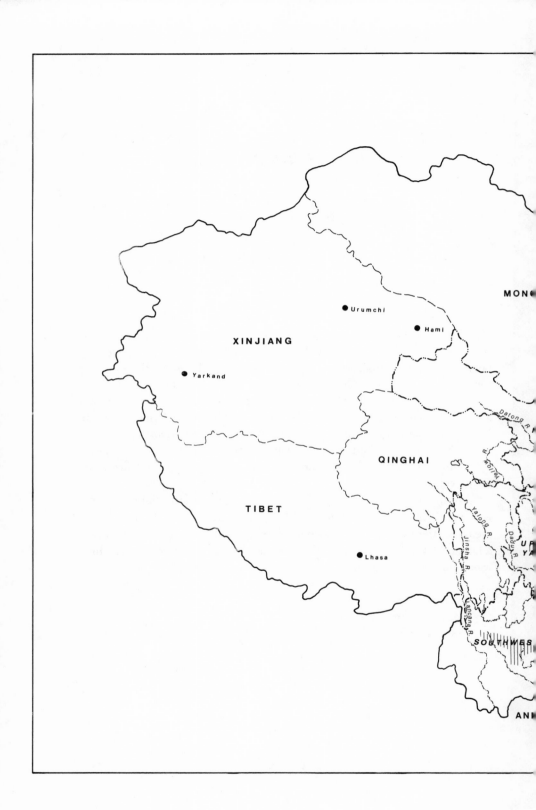

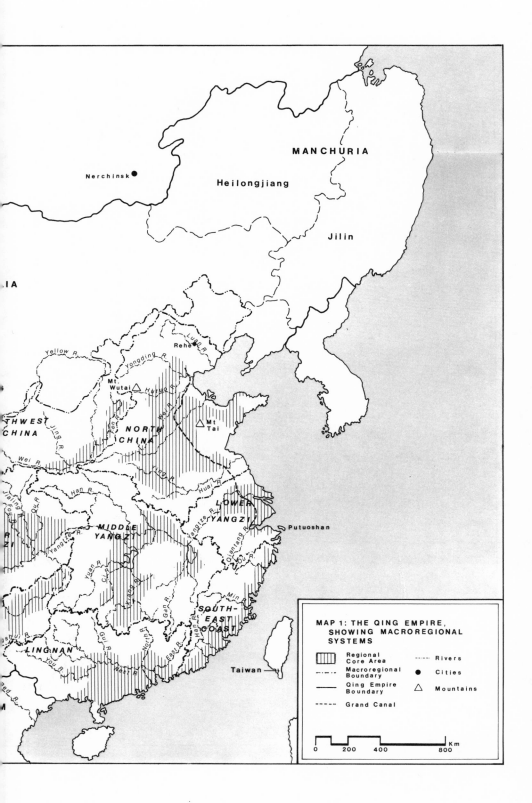

MAP 1: THE QING EMPIRE, SHOWING MACROREGIONAL SYSTEMS

Regional Core Area
Macroregional Boundary
Qing Empire Boundary
Grand Canal

Rivers
Cities
Mountains

0 200 400 800 Km

MANCHURIA

Heilongjiang

Jilin

Nerchinsk

Rehe

Mt. Wutai

Mt. Tai

NORTH CHINA

NORTHWEST CHINA

MIDDLE YANGZI

LOWER YANGZI

Putuoshan

SOUTH-EAST COAST

LINGNAN

Taiwan

Yellow R.

Yongding R.

Luan R.

Hutuo R.

Wei R.

Jing R.

Wei R.

Jialing R.

Qu R.

Han R.

Huai R.

Yangtze R.

Qiantang R.

Ou R.

Min R.

Yuan R.

Li R.

Yangtze R.

Xiang R.

Zi R.

Gan R.

Han R.

East R.

North R.

Gui R.

West R.

You R.

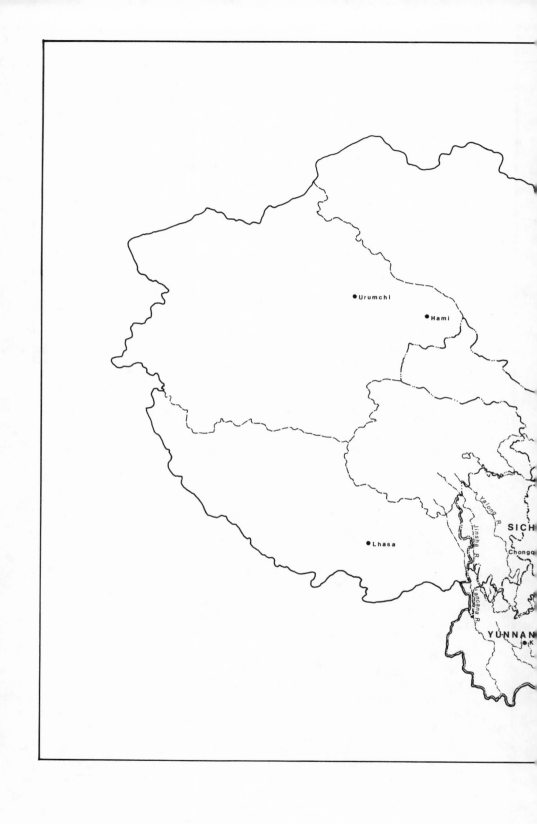

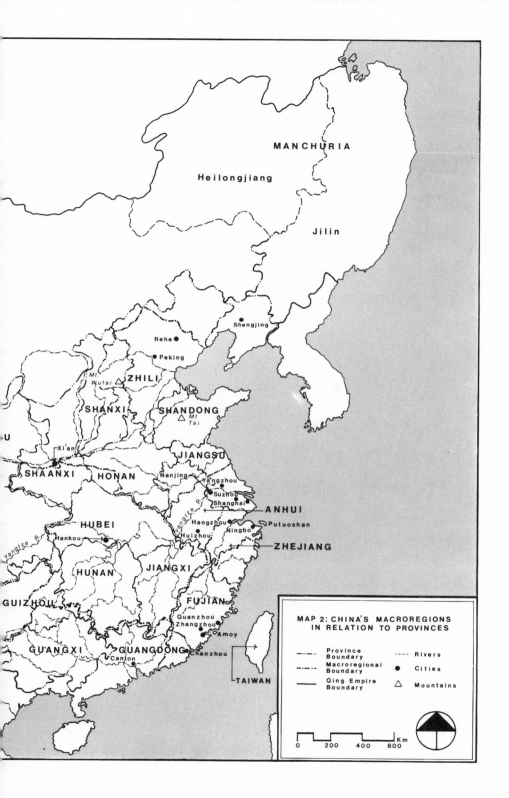

MANCHURIA

Heilongjiang

Jilin

Shengjing

Rehe

Peking

Mt Wutai ZHILI

SHANXI SHANDONG

Mt Tai

Xi'an

JIANGSU

SHAANXI HONAN Nanjing

Yangzhou

Suzhou

Shanghai

ANHUI

HUBEI Hangzhou

Hankou Huizhou Ningbo Putuoshan

ZHEJIANG

HUNAN JIANGXI

GUIZHOU

FUJIAN

Quanzhou

Zhangzhou

GUANGXI GUANGDONG Amoy

Canton Chaozhou

TAIWAN

MAP 2: CHINA'S MACROREGIONS
IN RELATION TO PROVINCES

- - - - - Province
           Boundary

- · - · - Macroregional
           Boundary

——————— Qing Empire
           Boundary

- - - -   Rivers

●   Cities

△   Mountains

0   200   400   600   Km

Qing Reign Periods

Reign Name	Years of Rule
Shunzhi	1644–1661
Kangxi	1662–1722
Yongzheng	1723–1735
Qianlong	1736–1795
Jiaqing	1796–1820
Daoguang	1821–1850
Xianfeng	1851–1861
Tongzhi	1862–1874
Guangxu	1875–1908
Xuantong	1909–1911

PART ONE

Qing Society

1

Government Policies

Few residents of the Middle Kingdom were unaware of the political system within which they lived. Like heaven, the emperor may have been far away, but people knew he was there; they could name the current dynasty and even numbered the years according to the length of each reign. A peasant did not have to understand the structure of the Qing bureaucracy to know that there were officials, somewhere, with the authority to make arrests, collect taxes, and lead armies. The precise impact of this state on its citizens is difficult to measure, however, and historians have probably assumed that it was more effective and more uniform than it in fact was. Nevertheless, the policies pursued by the Qing conquerors after 1683, when the first phase of conquest was completed, affected subsequent economic growth and social change, while certain political and military events shaped the context of eighteenth-century social life in crucial ways.

Just as Manchu innovations were grafted onto traditional institutions to reshape the mechanisms for governing this society, so some Qing decisions followed traditional precedents while others represented new solutions to both familiar and unfamiliar problems. Thus, while the eighteenth century witnessed the continuation of a number of long-term trends that had begun centuries before, Chinese society of the period also bore the imprint of the new dynasty that came to power in 1644.

We begin Part One with a look at the context provided by the state, specifically at early Qing attempts to restructure the polity, direct the society and economy, and regulate China's relations with her neighbors. Chapter 2 then introduces the basic institutions characteristic of eigh-

3

teenth-century society, and chapter 3 examines the range of both elite and popular culture in the period. In Part Two we look in more detail at how Qing society changed in the course of the eighteenth century. Chapter 4 deals with economic and demographic trends, stratification, and mobility. Then, having considered the empire as a whole, we try to describe the particular societies of each of China's regions. Finally, in chapter 6 we consider the linkages between this long eighteenth century and the rest of the dynasty.

POLITICAL STRUCTURES

The story of how the Manchus, a partially nomadic tribal people from the frontier lands of the northeast, became strong and well organized enough to oust the once glorious Ming dynasty (1368–1644) and rule all China is well known to Chinese historians. These descendants of the Tungus tribes who had ruled north China as the Jin dynasty in the twelfth century had long had extensive and regular contact with the Ming court, to whom they, like their neighboring tribes, paid regular tribute. An energetic chief called Nurgaci (1559–1626) and his son Hongtaiji (1592–1643) consolidated power among tribes to whom they gave the name Manchu in the Liaodong region beyond the Great Wall, the area we call Manchuria in their honor. With income from trade in valuable regional specialties like pearls and furs, the Manchus extended their control through warfare and alliances into Inner Mongolia and Korea. In 1644 they invaded and conquered China proper.

Aided by Mongol and Chinese advisers, Nurgaci created large, permanent, civil-military units called banners to replace the small hunting groups used in his early campaigns. A banner was composed of smaller companies, came to include some seventy-five hundred warriors and their households (including slaves), and was commanded by a chieftain who was a close supporter of Nurgaci (usually a son or nephew). Each banner was identified by a colored flag (yellow, white, blue, or red), plain or bordered. The banners became administrative units for registration, conscription, taxation, and mobilization of not only the Manchu population but also others who joined the Manchus before 1644. This efficient military force grew as new areas were conquered, and eventually, with Manchu, Mongol, and Chinese components, there came to be twenty-four banners (eight for each ethnic group). By 1648, fewer than 16 percent of the bannermen were actually of Manchu blood—a fact not well known at the time.

The Manchu conquest of China was thus accomplished by a multi-ethnic army, controlled and led by Manchu nobles and aided by the Chinese generals and their soldiers who had abandoned the Ming cause. The distinction between Han (ethnic Chinese) and Manchu, the formal legal barrier between bannermen (Manchu, Mongol, and Han) and non-bannermen, and the heightened concern with ethnicity generally all became special characteristics of Qing society.

As their armies expanded, the Manchus were simultaneously study-ing Chinese institutions and creating copies of Ming central-government organs in Shengjing (Mukden), the capital they established in 1625. Because the Manchu language had no written form, they devised a new written script for record keeping based on Mongolian. Remembering their Jin ancestors, Manchu rulers had from the outset supplemented their considerable military power with explicit claims to legitimacy. In 1635, victory over the Chahar Mongols brought the great seal of the Mongol khan to Hongtaiji, who could now also claim to be the heir of the mighty Chinggis Khan, founder of the Yuan dynasty that had ruled China and most of Asia in the fourteenth century. Once they entered Peking in 1644, the new conquerors, unlike the peasant rebels who had immediately preceded them, bid for Chinese allegiance by espousing Chinese ideals of government. The rulers observed the Confucian rituals and procedures treasured by the Chinese elite, called their dynasty Qing, meaning pure and unsullied, and adopted traditional imperial roles as son of heaven and moral exemplar. North China elites, exhausted from the decades of war and disorder that had attended the Ming collapse, were quick to give allegiance to these Manchu claimants to the throne and were in con-sequence rewarded with preference in government posts.

Several Ming generals were granted wide regional powers in south and southwest China in exchange for their vital assistance in quelling the loyalist opposition that persisted there for several decades. Three of these generals turned against the Qing in the 1670s when the Manchus attempted to check their power. During the resultant Rebellion of the Three Feudatories, the Qing not only acquired their own loyalist martyrs, Chinese bannermen who gave their lives for the new ruling house, but also began finally to win over the powerful elites of the Lower Yangtze region. (For a map showing China's component macroregions in the Qing, namely, North China, Lower Yangtze, Middle Yangtze, Southeast Coast, Lingnan, Northwest, Southwest, Manchuria, and Taiwan, see p. xiv.) The further courting of these southern literati at the expense of those from other regions was cemented with imperial patronage of scholarly projects and imperial visits to this area; by the early eighteenth century, the Lower Yangtze elites once more dominated the empire, as they had for centuries, both politically and culturally.

Manchu adaptation to the Chinese status quo was also reflected in the schools they established to educate princes, other members of the imperial clan, and able bannermen. The banner elites were taught Manchu and Chinese and trained to compete in the civil-service examinations that led to a prestigious career in government. By the middle of the eighteenth century, as the intimacy between conqueror and conquered deepened, it was no longer necessary for the throne to rely so exclusively on imperial bondservants (who were personal slaves of the rulers) and bannermen (who included Han Chinese as well as Manchus).

The collegial form of rule favored by the Manchus in their preconquest days was gradually replaced by the more autocratic imperial style of the Ming. The very formation of the Eight Banners under Nurgaci had shown the founder's adherence to joint rule by his sons and nephews who commanded those banners. Between the 1620s and the 1660s, actual leadership came as frequently from these commanders as from the nominal ruler. Though subsequent purges put three banners directly under the emperor, reliance on collective leadership during several regencies for child emperors after 1644 perpetuated the Manchu system. The young Kangxi emperor (r. 1662–1722) reasserted the imperial prerogative against his regents in 1669, but the consolidation of imperial power at the expense of the princes was not finally completed until the 1730s when the Yongzheng emperor (r. 1723–1735) destroyed the power base of rival princes by placing the remaining banners under bureaucratic supervision.

As Qing rulers tamed the potentially dangerous princes of imperial blood through Chinese institutions, they also used their talents. A few princes within each generation served in the bureaucracy, not merely to oversee their relatives by presiding over the Office of the Imperial Lineage but to advise the emperor as part of a special Council of Deliberative Officials, work in central-government ministries, perform diplomatic services, and lead military campaigns. Although the privileges granted them reinforced the loyalty of imperial kinsmen to the throne, the bureaucratization of the imperial lineage and the banners checked the tendency (already far weaker in China than in Europe) for a hereditary aristocracy with significant political power to emerge.

If the Manchus were quick to assimilate and adapt to Chinese bureaucratic forms of government, their Manchu experience also led them to modify and improve the political structure of the empire. The Imperial Household Department shows this Manchu influence quite clearly. This new institution, formally established in 1661, was explicitly intended to prevent the well-known usurpation of power by eunuchs that had characterized the courts of Ming and earlier dynasties. Eunuchs were still to be used, of course, to attend to the women of the imperial family, but they were to be directly supervised by officials of the Imperial Household. This institution was staffed by men from bondservant companies that had been formed of Han Chinese captured by the Manchus in the Liao River basin of Manchuria before 1644. Ideally suited to be brokers between conquerors and conquered, these Chinese bondservants were used as managers both of household affairs within the palace (the so-called Forbidden City in the center of Peking) and of the private income and property of the ruling family. During the late seventeenth and the eighteenth centuries, this department grew in size and function. Some sixteen hundred officials were employed by it in 1796, a figure that can be evaluated by remembering that county magistrates in charge of the basic territorial administrative units of the empire numbered, by contrast, fewer than thirteen hundred men.

In addition to providing for the emperor's food, clothing, and shelter, the Imperial Household engaged in a wide variety of activities extending far beyond the precincts of the Forbidden City. Its printing bureau published superb editions of scholarly works, and its agents managed the large landholdings confiscated in North China and reallocated to bannermen. Other units supervised various monopolies: the sale of ginseng, a rare root much prized for medicinal uses that grew in Manchuria, the early Qing trade with Japan in the copper needed for coins, the immensely lucrative salt monopoly, the imperial textile and porcelain manufactories in central China, and the customs bureaus throughout the empire. The Imperial Household lent its considerable capital to favored merchants and exchanged funds with the Board of Revenue, all the while remaining outside the control of the regular bureaucracy. Its importance in the early Qing period mirrored not only the general strength of the throne but also the tendency to create bureaucracies outside of (and on top of) bureaucracies.

But no great revolution in governance had accompanied the Manchu conquest. The regular Qing bureaucracy was patterned on Ming models and was outlined in repeated editions of the administrative codes of the dynasty. Government business was handled at the capital by the Six Boards, ministries that, together with the Censorate, formed the primary central government bureaus. The functions of the ministries were indicated in their names: Personnel, Revenue, Rites, War, Punishments, and Public Works. Located in Peking, these offices employed thousands of clerks and processed the increasingly large volume of government paperwork generated by the state.

Early Qing emperors consulted in Ming fashion with the heads of key metropolitan ministries and with a council of prominent Manchus. As in Ming times, a small group of grand secretaries helped process the government reports (called memorials) sent to the throne. After 1729, emperors relied more and more on a new organization, a Manchu innovation called the Grand Council. This group of six to ten high-ranking officials, half of whom were Manchus and half Chinese, met with the emperor daily, made recommendations on most important issues, and drafted imperial edicts.

China's many citizens, at least one hundred million of them at the beginning of the dynasty, were governed through eighteen provinces, three more than during the Ming. The lowest administrative units in the hierarchy were counties and departments (the latter created in strategic localities that demanded extra vigilance). By the end of the Qianlong reign (1736–1795), when the population had tripled, China had 1,281 counties and 221 departments, and the magistrate in charge of a county or department governed about 200,000 people. On average, seven to eight counties were under the jurisdiction of a prefecture, and from seven to thirteen prefectures made up a province. Field administration was organized to reflect the Chinese tradition of regulation through internal checks and balances, overlapping jurisdictions, an independent censorate, and deliberately vague bureaucratic boundaries. Most provinces were administered by a governor supervised by a governor-general who usually had several provinces under his jurisdiction, both bureaucratic layers newly formalized under the Qing. Some provinces were managed only by a governor, some only by a governor-general; there were constant adjustments at this level intended to achieve a suitable degree of supervision. Within provinces, censorate officials (organized in circuits) answered to another nearly independent vertical chain of command. Furthermore, three large new provincial-level bureaucracies were created, to take responsibility for the complex interprovincial grain traffic and waterway maintenance involving the Yellow River and the Grand Canal that linked it to the Yangtze. Military power had been recentralized, and, in addition to the banner forces stationed in Peking and at other strategic points in the empire, the Ming Army of the Green Standard was retained and used as a constabulary force.

Chinese officialdom was probably the most highly bureaucratized in the world at this time. Offices were ranked on an eighteen-point scale and staffed largely by civil servants recruited through regular examination. Thousands of men (these posts were not open to women) made this bureaucracy their career and lived with the constraints and opportunities of its many rules and regulations. Qing rulers modified the Ming system of personnel evaluation, reviving the use of a sliding scale of rewards and punishments predicated on an official's record in tax collection and criminal prosecution. It is believed that these improvements in personnel evaluation were a key factor in the increased efficiency of government during the early Qing. Manchu rulers also perpetuated, of course, the powerful traditional ideal of government service as the most desirable career for the educated man.

The framework of the examinations remained unchanged from the Ming: there was an elaborate tier of tests leading from the lowest, prefectural level *shengyuan* degree, to the *juren* degree on the provincial level, and to the *jinshi* degree on the national level. Winners of the prestigious national degree were ranked at an additional examination held in the palace in Peking, with the very best receiving special honors and very rapid advancement in the civil service. At each level, the number of degrees to be awarded was set in advance; quotas were used to guarantee a balanced representation among regions. (Despite these measures, men from one part of China, the Lower Yangtze, were still disproportionately represented among *jinshi*, for reasons we shall explore below.) Bannermen competed in a separate examination system that was more slowly freed of patronage and special privilege. Although the two highest degrees were supposed to be the prerequisite for office, in practice bannermen and even Chinese without these degrees did receive appointments. Another examination track requiring other skills supplied military officers for the Chinese army.

The civil-service examinations had been criticized in the Ming period for insisting on a highly artificial prose style and thus rewarding mediocrity and stifling talent. Although virtually no scholarly work has been done on the subject, the received wisdom is that the Qing examination system was also rigid in its traditionalism. However, although Manchu experiments with abolition of the stilted examination prose in the 1660s were halted because of conservative Chinese protests, in the late seventeenth century the examinations included essays on contemporary administrative problems, the writing of judgments in judicial cases, and discussions of Confucian texts with commentaries by the renowned twelfth-century scholar-official, Zhu Xi. For reasons not yet fully understood, a shift away from this practical orientation took place in 1757 and away from emphasis on the thought of Zhu Xi in 1799.

The long-term trend in Chinese history toward centralization of state power was continued and advanced under strong interventionist early Qing rulers, notably the Kangxi and Yongzheng emperors. Tightening up the Ming system, they brought important government decision making back into their own hands by reorganizing and streamlining the communi- cations system. Through deft placement of bondservants, who were out- side the civil-service bureaucracy and personally loyal to them, they were also able to check on official performance and supplement the information obtained through regular channels. A system of secret memorials sent direct to the emperor, bypassing the Grand Secretariat and Grand Coun- cil, came into being. By the early Qianlong reign, a new dual system of communications that sent routine business to the Six Boards and urgent items to the throne was in place.

But the streamlining of documentary flows to the emperor should not be taken (as it frequently has) as proof that the rulers had achieved despotic control over the bureaucracy. The continuing bureaucratization resulted in the would-be despot being engulfed in a sea of paperwork and procedural consultation. Nor did these centralizing reforms automatically make government more effective. The Qing system soon became so vast and complex that it was hard to carry out any policy at a distance. Detailed studies indicate that emperors and central-government ministers had to defer to and consult with powerful governors-general and governors if they wished particular policies to succeed. Success in some programs, for example the Qianlong "literary inquisition," depended also on the assistance of members of the elite. Emperors frequently took out their frustrations on individual officials (although the kind of personal abuse that was legendary in Ming times was not part of the Qing scene), but they could not remove the significant constraints to their personal power.

There is every evidence that Qing rulers were aware of their limited power. When his bondservant Cao Yin wanted to try to curb official corruption in the Liang-Huai salt bureau (see p. 26), the Kangxi emperor privately counseled him: "Stirring up trouble is not as good as preventing trouble occurring; just concentrate on matters of immediate concern. Otherwise I'm afraid that you'll get more than you bargained for and pile up difficulties for your successors. This sort of thing is not practicable on a long-term basis."[1] The assumption underlying the Kangxi emperor's remarks—namely, that the bureaucracy as a whole was resilient and powerful in resisting either imperial direction or internal reform—is a familiar one. China was perhaps unusual both in the sophistication of bureaucratic power and in the limits on it.

Another source of unresolved tension was the discrepancy between the state's desire to reach outside the bureaucracy and control localities directly and its inability to do so without the cooperation of local elites. The Qing had gone further than previous dynasties in formally restricting the privileges of degree-holders, officials, and their relatives. Local militias, which had often been led by local elites, were abolished or absorbed into the Army of the Green Standard, and officials were charged with supervising local elite management of community business such as irrigation, granaries, and welfare. The Yongzheng emperor made a particular effort to reform fiscal reporting and regain control of the delivery of taxes. But local elites, while siding with the state against local dissidents and playing an informal role in resolving disputes, effectively resisted official attempts at new land surveys and revisions of the tax records.

As time went by, furthermore, the Qing state began to have difficulty dealing with the growth that accompanied peace and prosperity. Limited by the existing communications technology and in some danger of collapsing under its own weight, the government was reluctant to expand and resisted making the revolutionary changes that would have involved local elites more formally in the extension of the bureaucracy at the subcounty and county levels. Instead, as we shall see, the tasks of government began to outstrip the staff and the budget, and, while officials turned to informal methods of obtaining funds, local elites took over more and more government functions.

Despite pronouncements that the new dynasty welcomed Chinese scholars into its service, the Manchu insistence on a system of dual appointments in the capital and the widespread use of bannermen in strategic provincial posts had put ambitious Chinese at a disadvantage in bureaucratic placement. The principle of dyarchy placed a Manchu and a Chinese at the head of each of the Six Boards and balanced one against the other at many other critical bureaucratic junctures. In 1667, after initially relying on Chinese bannermen (frequently with low qualifications) to staff the top provincial posts, the emperor opened these positions to the now more sinicized Manchus. The higher the office, the more likely it was to be filled by a Manchu. In the course of the entire dynasty, half of the powerful governors-general were Manchus, one-quarter were bannermen, and one-quarter were Han Chinese. The Court of Colonial Affairs (Lifan Yuan), which was in charge of Inner Asian matters, was staffed exclusively by

Mongols and Manchus. And, of course, the military forces of the Eight Banners were always commanded by bannermen.

The Manchus never relinquished their control of frontier policy, but Chinese were gradually able to enter government in greater numbers, while the creation of the Grand Council institutionalized a kind of Chinese-Manchu cooperation at the top that lasted until the twentieth century. The Hanlin Academy in Peking regained its traditional importance as the prestigious first step in the careers of the brightest degree-winners: its members advised the emperor, tutored princes, participated in official scholarly projects, and administered provincial and capital examinations. A separate quota guaranteed that Chinese bannermen, Manchus, and Mongols would also be represented in the Hanlin.

In the Kangxi and Yongzheng reigns, the examination system that fed the bureaucracy and created the symbols of local status was reestablished, and state-sponsored schools were set up in the provinces. Quotas allowed disadvantaged areas and minority groups to compete and promoted the social and political integration of the empire. They also helped equalize regional access to degrees (and hence to government posts), thus working against wealthy urban regions like the Lower Yangtze and in favor of the newly developing regions in the west and southwest.

General prosperity and population growth enlarged the size of the wealthy and educated classes and put pressure on the government to increase the number of degrees and posts. As a result, quotas for all three levels of degrees, which had been drastically reduced in the 1660s, experienced a persistent (but small) expansion.[2]

Two special examinations were held in 1679 and 1736 in order to bring eminent scholars into government, and other additional examinations for degrees and posts were given from time to time. In the course of the eighteenth century, extrastatutory competitions expanded the number of *jinshi* degrees by fully one-third. Although these exams tended to favor the more developed regions, they did increase the number of high degree-holders even as population growth continued to make this group a smaller percentage of the total populace. As the system became increasingly elaborate, qualifying examinations for each degree tightened competition while marking ever more refined levels of success and failure. The number of ranked posts in the formal bureaucracy also grew in the first three reigns, especially under Yongzheng. In the course of the century there was a 13 percent increase overall in the number of county-level units, as well as a regular upgrading of existing offices and an expansion of personnel.[3]

An unrelieved tension persisted between the formal criteria for success based on merit and the informal connections that were spun like webs through the examination and bureaucratic systems. Ambitious candidates for degrees found many ways of improving their chances for success in the face of steep odds. Licentiate-by-purchase (*jiansheng*) degrees, which qualified buyers for the provincial-level examinations, were sold more or less continuously. The *juren* examination given at Shuntian prefecture (Peking), for which any licentiate-by-purchase in the empire could register, thus became an important loophole in the system of provincial quotas. In the course of the eighteenth century, more men registered here received *jinshi* degrees than from any of seven other provinces in Lingnan, the Southwest, or the Northwest.[4] The sale of low-level posts and preferments was permitted to a very limited degree, in response, for example, to an urgent need for revenue and local loyalty caused by major disturbances such as the Three Feudatories (1673–1681) or White Lotus (1796–1805) rebellions.

Sharpened competition for degrees and office enhanced the importance of patronage and factional alliances to a man's career. The view from the throne was not sympathetic. An edict of 1729 explains:

> You people with the *jinshi* and *juren* degrees . . . like to form cliques to advance your own personal interests. In order to climb to high office you have given each other undue assistance and protection. . . . Since I have ascended the throne, many people have warned me not to trust officials with the two highest degrees. . . . Now, if you choose to continue [these] evil practices, as your emperor, I will not be able to give you an official position even if that is my wish.[5]

Imperial countermeasures strove to limit the power of personal connections by raising the qualifications for the post of examiner, introducing more frequent personnel reviews (from 1723), and multiplying the administrative regulations that governed behavior in office. Yet the problem could only be contained, not eliminated. The Yongzheng emperor was particularly active in drawing the line between public and private interest and in reducing the possibilities for corruption by officials, but his efforts did not long outlast his reign.

In the course of the eighteenth century, service in extrabureaucratic appointments and employment on scholarly projects became more readily available for educated men who had sought a regular career. From the *Ming History* project of the 1680s–1690s through the *Siku quanshu* ("Complete Library of the Four Treasuries") compilation of the 1770s–1780s, as we shall see, the state generated high-status opportunities that attracted hundreds of scholars. This patronage encouraged what became a quintessentially Qing elite life-style, in which holding office was only one of many career choices.

The political system that the Manchus put in place during the first half-century of their rule thus helped shape eighteenth-century Chinese society in important ways. The consciously multiethnic political institutions, present in the banner system from the outset, set the tone for an empire that would incorporate large numbers of non-Han peoples. Although relations between Manchu and Chinese were quite good during the period under study here, the ugly seventeenth-century legacy of hostility would resurface toward the end of the dynasty. The Qing state differed from its predecessor in a number of important ways. There was more of it: more officials, more layers, more structures, more paperwork. Imperial control over Manchu aristocrats, bureaucrats, and local elites was tightened, partially through new institutions and partially through the surge of confidence that a new dynasty had brought. Yet these changes were scarcely revolutionary. Indeed, it has been argued that Qing success in reinvesting the imperial system with vigor actually prevented China— by contrast with Europe—from moving in more innovative directions. From the point of view of Chinese society, however, the reconstructed Qing polity initially worked quite well. A bureaucratic career attracted able men, and a government that did its job made possible a century-and-a-half of nearly unbroken peace and prosperity.

SOCIAL POLICIES

The Manchus brought about no social revolution. With regard to Chinese society, as to state structure, they emphasized restoration of the established order—or a more ideal version of it. This order locked the throne into an interdependent relationship with wealthy and locally powerful families. The state offered the prestige and rewards of examination degrees and government office, and families with resources educated their sons for such service. In return and within limits, the government did not interfere with the local elites; in fact, it relied on them to supplement the resources of local officials. The Manchus did not change this system, they reinvigorated it. But they also attempted to modify it and to limit the power of local notables wherever possible. This conservative commitment, together with the inherent limits on state power in this period, gave the new rulers rather little room either to manipulate social processes or to adapt the system to changing social forces.

It should not be surprising that Qing attention was directed toward those elites on whom the state was most dependent. The eventual success of the Qing in winning over Han Chinese to its service involved both the carrot and the stick, and it was not achieved without some harsh measures to suppress those who appeared to express a preference for the fallen Ming. The spirited resistance that had been encountered in the conquest of the Lower Yangtze, a center of Ming culture, was no doubt a contributing factor in the famous Jiangnan tax case of 1661, a symbol of the antagonistic relations of this early period. The incident began when officials in a number of wealthy prefectures in southern Jiangsu province were promised promotions if they could make up the large tax arrears from these areas. Initial measures to collect the back taxes (many in arrears were degree-holders) brought protests from the local literati at the Confucian temple in Suzhou, protests that suggested rebellious intent to the Manchu regents in Peking. A nasty prosecution followed; eighteen scholars were executed, and more than eleven thousand literati were punished—moves that engendered bitter resentment toward the conquerors. In 1662, the already tense atmosphere was exacerbated by Manchu investigations in nearby Hangzhou, where a history of the fallen dynasty, the "Abbreviated Compilation on Ming History" that referred to the Qing as "barbarians," had been published. Those connected with this project were carefully tracked down (including even those who had merely purchased the book), and seventy individuals were put to death, their families exiled, their estates confiscated. The negative repercussions of this case extended, of course, to the entire scholarly community in the Lower Yangtze. These persecutions became the problematic legacy of the conquest decades; repeated for effect on a smaller scale from time to time in the eighteenth century, they were offset, slowly, by other more conciliatory gestures from the throne.

The Qing not only sought to cow the haughty elites of the Lower Yangtze; they moved—with care—to limit as well the power of local notables generally. The relationship of local elites to the state was an ambiguous one: educated men from wealthy families were both useful and dangerous. Their voluntary services as community leaders supplemented government action but could also usurp government functions. Though informal connections made through attendance at academies and examinations enabled individual officials to carry out their duties effectively, they also threatened the impartiality of the bureaucracy. Under the new dynasty, local-elite control over county-level appointments was virtually eliminated except in some frontier areas, while in 1657 the Qing narrowed degree-holders' exemptions from tax and corvée from the household to the individual. Both measures represented the elimination of significant sources of local power and privilege.

The state kept a particularly wary eye on those horizontal elite associations that could serve political functions. As we noted, not only were factions among officials denounced, but the formation of political associations by men outside of office was forbidden. In the early Qing, this ban seemed appropriate to many Han Chinese who remembered well the events of the late Ming. Then, weak emperors could not stop literati cliques formed around academies from extending their competition into the bureaucracy. Men associated with the Donglin Academy in Wuxi, a county seat in the Yangtze delta, had legitimized their political activity by defining it as a Confucian crusade to clean up widespread corruption at court. They mobilized men inside and outside government while trying to control critical appointments and eliminate their enemies from office. Their aggressiveness hardened factional lines and provoked a wave of purges and counterpurges that only further weakened the dynasty and promoted internal disorder. Reading this lesson of the past, Qing elites thus felt considerable ambivalence toward political associations outside government and acquiesced to imperial prohibitions; it was not until the nineteenth century that they returned to this arena.

The eighteenth century was a time of considerable social mobility, made possible by a variety of new sources of wealth. In general, the state was rather successful in luring those with new money into the examination and office channels that it could control. But, as we have already pointed out, they were almost too successful; although these systems were expanded in response to increased demand, not everyone could be formally accommodated. Sensitive themselves to the condescension of those elites with old money and extensive education, Qing rulers appear to have been quite comfortable with nouveau-riche merchants and other arrivistes. As outsiders, it was easier for them to welcome such families into the ranks of the Qing elite, and they did so enthusiastically.

The Qing state found it easier to regulate social mobility than to control the geographic mobility of their citizens. In theory, every household was registered with a local official. When corvée tax quotas were frozen at their 1711 level, the purpose of household registration shifted from taxation to census; in 1741, the *baojia* system became the primary vehicle for population registration. This was a system originally imposed by the government to promote mutual security: in theory, one hundred households were designated a *jia*, ten *jia* made up a *bao*, and the households within a *jia* were held responsible for the lawful behavior of all members. (In reality, it is unclear if the *baojia* ever functioned as it was supposed to.) Each household was supposed to update a door placard enumerating all members, and these placards became the basis for counting the population. As their reports reflect, officials complained about the difficulty of making this system work when they had to keep track of a population that was frequently on the move. During the eighteenth century, a series of regulations tried to deal with this problem (e.g., separating sojourners from permanent settlers by specifying the waiting time before a registration could be changed), but exceptions were continuously being made. Moving within and between regions was easy and increasingly commonplace for people at all social levels. In this case, as in many others that we will discuss, bureaucratic measures, however energetically implemented, could not keep up with the far-flung and growing population.

Qing emperors, because they themselves were not Han Chinese and because their reigns witnessed the incorporation of many tribal groups into the empire, took a greater interest in minority affairs than had their Ming counterparts. Their policies aimed at the somewhat contradictory goals of, on the one hand, integrating minorities into the polity and, on the other, protecting them from Han civilization. Institutions that encouraged assimilation were more appropriate, and thus more successful, in this era of expansive Han settlement.

The non-Han peoples who became part of the Qing empire—not just in name but also in fact—included numerous hill and mountain tribes of south and southwest China (the Miao, Yao, Lolo, and many other smaller groups) as well as the Tibetans, Uighurs, Muslims, Mongols, and Manchus of the far west, north, and northeast.[6] In the south and west, the Qing relied initially on the *tusi* (tribal headman) system, a traditional institution that allowed considerable autonomy for minority communities under the leadership of local chieftains whose power was simply confirmed by the throne. As migration into minority areas proceeded, however, the Yongzheng emperor began to convert the *tusi* territories into regular administrative units and to bureaucratize the positions of the remaining headmen. The state also forced many communities to accept Chinese colonists, and it promoted sinicization by constructing schools and temples.

In the far west, governance of the major cities along the Silk Road was put in the hands of prominent Muslim families, and Chinese colonists were fewer. Among the nomadic and seminomadic tribes of the north, a modified version of the banner system identified leaders, divided up existing tribes, and provided a framework for trade and tribute that was meant to channel contact with the Chinese world. The Qing court nevertheless encouraged (perhaps inadvertently) the trend toward a more sedentary and urbanized society on the steppes by actively promoting the monastic centers of Lamaist (Tibetan) Buddhism.

Backed up by the ready deployment of banner armies against the recalcitrant, these measures had the effect of tightening the administration of frontier areas, compromising indigenous leaders, and promoting trade and travel. It was perhaps in recognition of the vulnerability of frontier peoples that Qing rulers, as we shall discuss in more detail in chapter 4, attempted to segregate and protect minorities. But once border areas were peaceful, merchants and settlers were on their own. Government prohibitions on Han migration to Mongolia, Manchuria, and Taiwan were thus frequently ignored, while the ban on intermarriage between Han and non-Han was impossible to enforce. Despite the restrictions on frontier trade intended to slow the extension of the market economy, the Qing could not prevent tribal peoples from falling into debt to Chinese merchants, and the law against sale of tribal lands to Chinese was easily evaded through varieties of mortgage and permanent-tenancy arrangements.

Qing efforts to prevent the once martial bannermen now living in garrisons within China from adopting Chinese culture were even more vigorous. Banner soldiers made their homes in separate enclaves in cities; intermarriage with Han Chinese and any form of ordinary employment were forbidden. Yongzheng had succeeded in breaking the power of the Manchu clans; his son Qianlong soon worried that Manchus were becoming too sinicized. The basic traditional social unit, the clan, was becoming less important than the family, and Qianlong observed that some bannermen were adopting surnames like the Chinese (it had been customary for Manchus to use only personal names in public communications). Qianlong, frequently identified as a patron of Chinese arts and letters, was also the codifier of the Manchu tradition. Under his direction, Manchu genealogies that had begun to be compiled in his father's reign were published, a history of the Eight Banners was written, the Manchu shamanistic tradition was fixed in written form, and myths substantiating the origins of the imperial clan were elaborated. Qianlong corrected the Manchu used in written memorials and scolded bannermen who could not speak their native tongue. Qianlong was thus responsible for strengthening the foundations of Manchu identity at a time when Manchus were in danger of forgetting their roots. But the imperial payroll could not support the expanding banner population or screen out the attractions of Chinese culture. By the end of the century these all but fruitless attempts to prevent assimilation were abandoned.

Like all Chinese dynasties, the Qing government saw itself as the ultimate authority on personal and public morality. The first emperors followed the example of the Ming founder, whose hortatory Six Maxims had urged the populace to be filial to parents, respectful to elders, and amiable with neighbors, to instruct their children, remain in their place, and do no evil. In 1652, the Shunzhi emperor (r. 1644–1661) had these maxims carved in stone and posted in each prefecture. Kangxi issued his own Sixteen Injunctions in 1670, and Yongzheng amplified them in 1724. The Sacred Edict, as the injunctions were known, was to be read twice a month in every county of the empire. A great many other imperial pronouncements were issued to edify and instruct all segments of society, from bannermen (who were to preserve their Manchu virtues) to *shengyuan* and other lower degree-holders (who were to promote local law and order) to the common people (who were to avoid geomancy, pilgrimages, and heterodox religion). Nearly impossible to enforce, these pronouncements usually went unheeded: Manchu culture became a memory, lower degree-holders threw their weight around, and ordinary people went right on visiting sacred mountains and consulting geomancers about where to put houses and graves.

Nevertheless, ever optimistic about the power of the normative ideal, both emperors and elites took advantage of the expansion of the publishing industry to write books aimed at popular moral improvement. Chen Hongmou, for example, an eminent provincial official of the Qianlong reign, wrote a set of five books discussing not only proper official behavior but also community life, the raising of children, and the education of women. Though these didactic efforts were part of a venerable tradition, they were also specific responses to the geographic mobility and social change of this period. Frequent imperial injunctions about frugality and rationality naturally had a hollow ring in light of the extravagant rituals, unfilial sons, and fondness for pleasure typical of eighteenth-century court life.

In their policy toward religion, Qing rulers also combined Chinese tradition with a non-Han perspective. In principle, they tried to be impartial and to tolerate diversity. Certain Manchu shamanistic rituals were kept alive within the privacy of the Forbidden City, while Tibetan Lamaist Buddhism was adopted as a kind of imperial cult and promoted as an important facet of foreign relations with Central Asia. Within China,

Islam was given protection and Buddhism, Taoism, and most popular cults were encouraged.

The Kangxi, Yongzheng, and Qianlong emperors actively patronized Buddhism inside China. A "Dragon Edition" of the enormous Buddhist Canon was reprinted in 1738 under imperial sponsorship and then translated into Manchu in 1790. The emperors visited famous pilgrimage mountains such as Wutaishan in Shanxi (dedicated to the bodhisattva of wisdom) and showered the monasteries with gifts. Imperial calligraphy graced temples of the popular religion at famous sites like Mount Tai in Shandong and shrines dedicated to deities such as Guanyin, Tianhou (Empress of Heaven), or Guandi (God of War). They not only maintained the official cult but enlarged it, providing funds for designated deities in the budgets of officials from the emperor down to the county magistrate so that temples could be maintained and regular offerings provided. This kind of support both enhanced the prestige of selected temples and sites and created an atmosphere favorable for the growth of popular religious institutions generally.

There was, however, considerable imperial suspicion of religious voluntary organizations, which embraced temple fairs and pilgrimages. Following Ming precedent, the government also firmly outlawed sects they perceived as heterodox. Here, as in other instances where popular behavior ran counter to government wishes, enforcement could only be selective. Sectarians were singled out for particular attention, but although the throne usually called for harsh punishments according to the letter of the law, local officials looked the other way if sectarian activity was not disruptive. Repression was more uniformly implemented during the series of small millenarian uprisings that took place in different parts of north China late in the eighteenth century and were seen as military emergencies. Qing policy toward Christian missionaries was two stranded. Jesuits had been at the court in Peking since the sixteenth century, and some were permitted to remain as artists and consultants on condition that they refrain from preaching their religion. Those who tried to proselytize—and a small but persistent group of Catholic missionaries led hunted lives in order to minister to converts—were punished, when they were caught, with the same strictness as others who followed "deviant paths."

Despite its large and sophisticated bureaucracy, the Qing state's capacity to deal with social problems was actually quite limited. The traditional system worked because as long as the ideal of government service remained attractive and the Neo-Confucian philosophy on which

the examinations were based remained convincing, the state could manipulate the symbols and the avenues to power and could use them to shape
the behavior of would-be members of the elite. This symbiotic relationship
with wealthy and learned families, renewed with each generation through
the exams, assured a commitment to a loosely defined orthodoxy by the
most powerful groups in this society. Standards dictated by the throne
could thus be imposed with some hope of success upon those who sought
degrees and office.

Aided by these elites, and with no church or aristocracy to rival its
influence, the Chinese state could also define right and wrong for the
society at large and could use both laws and moral suasion to enforce these
norms. Emperors and elites found exhortation a congenial method for
promoting right behavior among citizens, even though the results were not
always discernible. The army was at hand, of course, to give muscle to the
law, but even laws rested on some degree of social consensus. Whatever
the statutes said, a county magistrate with a small staff found it quite
difficult to deal with large social problems or to alter widely accepted
behavior. It was one thing to arrest burglars or murderers, quite another to
prevent changes in residence, restrict trade, eliminate ethnic hostility, or
put an end to popular religious festivals. Thus, while many Qing social
policies were quite distinctive, they were most successful when riding
with, not against, developments that were largely outside their control.

ECONOMIC REHABILITATION

The health of this huge and diverse economy was obviously a critical
concern to early Manchu rulers—and of fundamental importance to the
health of society in general. In 1644 the Manchus found much to be done,
but the initial stages of recovery were rather easy to promote.

Any new dynasty was expected to provide relief from the harsh
corvée and taxes that accompanied the last decades of the preceding
government. These were welcome responses to the general cry for relief
and redress and to the devastation of localities involved in rebellions and
wars of conquest. In the 1640s and 1650s, the Manchus abolished late
Ming surtaxes whenever possible and granted tax exemptions to areas
damaged by fighting, but remissions were eliminated by the urgent need
for funds to finance the conquest. Attempts to recompile the tax registers
were frustrated, and eventually registers based on inaccurate sixteenth-
century quotas had to be used. In order to make sure that people paid and
that officials relayed the monies, various decrees spelled out the con-

sequences for local magistrates who failed to collect their tax quotas. A sliding scale of punishments for gentry, degree-holders, and yamen (government office) personnel who consistently failed to pay their own taxes was institutionalized in 1658. The laws could be selectively enforced, as they were during the 1661 Jiangnan tax case, a clear demonstration of the state's willingness to attack gentry prerogatives to obtain tax funds.

It was not until the 1680s, after the Ming loyalist and Three Feudatories uprisings had been quelled, that the Qing began to permit tax remissions on a significant scale. By 1711, the tide was running the other way and total tax remissions exceeded one hundred million taels (ounces of silver), more than the annual central-government revenues.[7] The *ding* (corvée) and land taxes were merged into a single tax that was collected in silver and thus easier to assess and administer; this reform promoted the general transition from payment in kind, typical of the Ming, to payment in money. As many scholars have noted, the shift from registering people to registering land was a sensible adaptation to the long-run trend toward an increasingly commercialized and fluid society. The permanent freezing of the corvée tax quotas in 1713, hailed as a new symbol of imperial benevolence, not only reflected the government's inability to rehaul the tax system but also blocked future increases.

In this huge agrarian economy the land tax was the largest single source of revenue for the government. Fiscal motives and the ideological priority long accorded to agriculture had prompted the Manchus to make early efforts to put abandoned plots back into production. Because about two hundred million *mu*, or more than a quarter of the total cultivated acreage ca. 1600, had slipped off government rolls by 1661, restoration of agriculture had been an important goal for the new dynasty.[8] They had particularly needed the "tribute grain" that selected provinces in northern and central China supplied annually to Peking (one of the few Qing taxes still paid largely in kind) in order to feed the thousands of bannermen and officials in the capital area who depended on the throne for their livelihood.

Revitalization of crop production began with relocating wandering households and encouraging settlement of empty land through tax exemptions and grants of aid—oxen, tools, seeds, or simply money. These programs, which obviously met with popular approval, gained momentum toward the end of the seventeenth century, and in the Kangxi period they were carried out in the Chengdu basin of western China, in Hunan and Hubei, and in the far southwest. Despite their concern about unruly migrants, the Yongzheng and Qianlong emperors nonetheless promoted projects to reclaim abandoned lands and settle new frontiers as the empire expanded through military conquest.

Both on the frontiers and inside China proper some new lands were opened for settlement with the aid of the New World food crops that had been introduced into China in the late sixteenth century and were simultaneously transforming the diet of people all over the world. It was in the Qing that the impact of these crops on Chinese patterns of land use became significant, largely through the actions of individual farmers. The cultivation of marginal lands expanded dramatically with the planting of maize and the white potato. The sweet potato, known as the poor man's staple, provided insurance against famine, while peanuts, a new source of nutritious oil, caused a revolution in land use on hilly land and in the sandy soils along river banks. Tobacco, another sixteenth-century discovery to which the Chinese like many others were soon addicted, competed with rice and sugarcane for the best lands and became an important cash crop.

Less dramatic and equally pragmatic changes in cropping patterns were probably even more important than the American food plants in raising agricultural production. The southward migration of northern dry-land crops such as wheat, the extension of rice cultivation to newly irrigated lands, the gradual increase in double cropping of rice in the south, and particularly the double cropping of winter wheat or barley with summer millet or rice all slowly but significantly increased output.

The construction and reconstruction of water-control projects went hand in hand with land reclamation. This kind of collective activity was so characteristic of the early phases of a dynasty that one can speak of hydraulic cycles moving in tandem with political consolidations in China. The importance of the state to water-control systems varied with agricultural and topographical conditions. In south and central China, where rice was the dominant staple crop, irrigation was essential to the agrarian economy; in consequence, elaborate systems had been devised by local communities to provide water to interconnected fields at appropriate points in the growing season. In north China, by contrast, control of the heavily silted Yellow River, which frequently flooded the eastern portion of the North China plain, required large-scale state management and coordination with the related water level of the Grand Canal, the major waterway supplying Peking.

The new dynasty restored water-control systems with great vigor, demonstrating the effectiveness of imperial action in this sphere. To the Yellow River, whose control was vital to their political survival, the Qing devoted some 10 percent of their total revenues. During the late seventeenth century, the Yellow River Administration, which was made an independent agency by the Qing, had constructed the Qing River (1686) and had dredged the mouth of the Yellow River (1688) and strengthened its embankments (1699). These projects particularly benefited the vulnerable low-lying Huaibei region (on the periphery between the North China and Lower Yangtze macroregions), whose damaged economy was successfully rehabilitated in the late seventeenth century. Elsewhere, and particularly in south and central China, government encouraged private initiative and management. In these regions, it was peace and land reclamation that stimulated reinvestment in irrigation in the early Qing. Although the Qing record in construction of new water-control systems does not compare in number (except in Gansu and Shaanxi) with the peak of Ming activity in the sixteenth century, the scale of Qing projects may have been larger; certainly the repair of older works in developed regions took place continually throughout the eighteenth century.

Because of the importance of water transport to the economy, rehabilitation of water systems was beneficial for commerce as well as agriculture. Dredging to remove silt was essential if the river ports on the Yangtze, China's major navigable waterway, were to be kept open to junks and so permit the flow of commodities required to sustain a population in the delta approaching a density of more than one thousand per square mile. These efforts were managed by local elites during the early Qing, while the government assumed more responsibility in the area around Peking. The Grand Canal was the key to grain transport to the capital, regarded by Kangxi as one of the three greatest problems of his early reign. Repairs to the canal, especially the critical junctures with the Yellow and Huai rivers, involved officials, merchants, and local elites, and were characterized by a mixture of public and private efforts. Imperial sponsorship of a large-scale effort to dig wells for irrigation in Shaanxi province in the 1730s, for example, was supplemented by private investment in well construction in the middle and lower reaches of the Yellow River drainage area.

This restoration of the economy in the early Qing, partially directed, partially spontaneous, laid the foundations for an enormous expansion not only of land under cultivation but also of population. One of the most important events of the Qing period was thus an unintended (but not unwanted) consequence of prosperity. From the mid-seventeenth to the mid-nineteenth centuries, China's population tripled, from between one hundred and one hundred and fifty million to four hundred million, while its cultivated land doubled, from six hundred to twelve hundred million *mu*.[9]

Once the economy had been restored to working order, the Qing state attempted to keep it running smoothly. Following traditional practices of demonstrated effectiveness, early emperors acted vigorously to prevent the worst consequences of famine by setting up and actually maintaining a reserve granary system. Every province was supposed to purchase or retain reserve stocks in the "ever-normal granaries" located in each county, so named because they were meant to stabilize the supply and price of grain. During the eighteenth century, the granaries generally worked with remarkable efficiency. In the famine south of Peking in 1743–1744, for example, the government announced tax remissions, surveyed affected households, classified famine victims, set up settlement camps and gruel kitchens, and distributed relief to an estimated 1.6 million people. The court was able to bring additional grain into the famine area and devise long-term measures for agricultural reconstruction in rural areas. Such efficiency was, of course, dependent not just on available reserves and good transportation but on the quality of the government's information network as well. During the eighteenth century, reports on local grain prices became a regular feature of county, prefecture, and provincial reports. Massive famine-relief operations in subsequent periods, reflecting continuing monetization of the economy, seem to have distributed cash for grain purchases rather than direct grants of grain.

Government efforts to ameliorate the disruptive consequences of famine did not, however, reflect a uniformly interventionist attitude toward the market. While emperors kept a wary eye on grain prices in cities, particularly those in key regions like the Yangtze delta, they and their advisers were very cautious about state intervention in general. One study of the debates over state grain policy in 1748 notes the Qianlong emperor's

TABLE 1: China's Population and Land Acreage, 1600–1850

Year	Population (millions)	Cultivated land (mill. shimu)
1600	120–200	670
1650	100–150	600
1685	———	470
1750	200–250	900
1770	270	950
1850	410	1,210

Source: Yeh-chien Wang, *Land Taxation in Imperial China, 1750–1911* (Cambridge: Harvard University Press, 1973), table 1.1, p. 7.

perspective: "With the affairs of the market-place, for the most part one should let the people carry out the circulation for themselves. If once the government begins to manage it, what was originally intended to be beneficial to the people will, with unsatisfactory implementation, turn out full of hindrances."[10] The faith expressed here in the responsiveness of market forces to supply and demand reveals a considerable change in the traditional attitudes of the state toward the economy. But even as the Qing state retreated from direct economic management, it continued, not surprisingly, to be ready to act in politically sensitive situations—especially those likely to destabilize markets or cause unemployment or popular unrest.

The Qing government thus played a relatively minor role in the commercial economy. Important state monopolies were created: some followed traditional models and involved foreign trade and important bulk goods such as salt and precious metals. Others were in luxury goods such as ginseng and pearls, commodities long controlled by the ruling Aisin Gioro lineage (descendants of Nurgaci). The long-range trend, however, was toward fewer monopolies and a continuously widening sphere of private production and distribution of goods. But because these monopolies involved interregional trade and were generally very profitable, merchants associated with them came to be rich, powerful, and important actors in Qing society.

The major Qing monopoly was in the production and marketing of salt, demand for which grew with population. In 1753 the state derived almost 12 percent of its total revenues from this source. The country was divided into eleven zones, and (except in Yunnan) actual production, transport, and sale of salt was handled by monopoly merchants, who in return paid a tax to the state. The salt merchants in the city of Yangzhou, who were prominent in the largest salt-marketing zone, the Liang-Huai zone in east-central China, were among the wealthiest merchants in Qing China. Despite illegal salt production and smuggling, these transport merchants supplied about a quarter of the empire's population with approximately six hundred million catties (four hundred thousand tons) of salt a year in the eighteenth century, reaping in return an aggregate profit of approximately five million taels.

The Qing state played a fairly passive role in the expansion of domestic trade. It probably affected the commercial economy most directly through the transfer and distribution of the tribute grain it commandeered (very successfully) in tax payments. Both the state and the long-distance merchants were major actors in the substantial interregional trade in rice along the Yangtze and along the coast. But the state barely began to tap the tax potential of the growing commerce, as it failed to tax the expanding agricultural base. When the state intervened in trade, moreover, it did so primarily to safeguard the stability of local economies. Such was the motive for the imperial ban on exports of raw silk from 1759 to 1762, when the emperor agreed with the Commissioner of the Imperial Silk Manufactory at Suzhou that foreign sales pushed up local prices and threw weavers out of work. Even after 1762 concern about unemployment brought restrictions on the type and amount of silk that could be exported and put a ceiling on raw-silk exports for the rest of the century.

Eighteenth-century urbanization also proceeded independent of government interference. A minimalist urban policy sought to dampen causes for unrest by ensuring stable grain markets through a system of reserves. Although the northern section of Peking (where most of the residents were bannermen) was an exception, the government generally stayed out of direct management and provision of urban services.

Nevertheless, the state's role was essential, if not sufficient, for the economic advance that characterized the eighteenth century. As we shall see further in chapter 4, the Qing had established the preconditions for prosperity by imposing law and order, encouraging new settlement and agricultural rehabilitation, and opening up frontier regions. Moreover, the government was extremely attentive to the larger social effects of economic activity. The state sought to assure full employment where possible, but was concerned above all with social stability. Although economic growth was only a by-product of Qing policy, a by-product that brought problems as well as benefits, by the end of the century growth had come to be taken for granted. The jolt given by the depression of the 1830s and 1840s was thus all the more surprising and difficult to deal with.

FOREIGN RELATIONS

It was Qing success in managing relations with China's neighbors that made possible a century-and-a-half of peace. To organize these relations, the Manchus perpetuated the tributary model inherited from previous dynasties. This model presumed the Middle Kingdom's moral, material, and cultural superiority over other nations, and it required that those who wished to deal or trade with China had to come as supplicants to the emperor, Son of Heaven, ruler of "All Under Heaven." This image—in part an illusion—of centrality, superiority, and self-sufficiency veiled considerable realpolitik in Qing behavior toward other countries.

We can see the tributary system in its fullest form in Qing relations with its model tributary, Korea. From the mid-seventeenth century to the late nineteenth, the Korean court sent an average of three embassies a year to Peking to present tribute, proffer thanks for the imperial grace, congratulate the emperor on his birthday, offer incense on his death, and consult on the conduct of foreign relations. Korea's inferior status in this relationship was symbolized in various ways. When the Korean envoy was received by the Qing emperor, he performed the kowtow (complete prostration and knocking of the head on the ground) and addressed the emperor in terms appropriate for someone of lesser status. The Korean court employed the Chinese calendar, and Qing emperors confirmed the authority of Korean kings and bestowed noble rank on them. In fact, Qing approval was sought for the appointment of Korean royal consorts, the selection of an heir, and the creation of posthumous honors for rulers. As an act of Qing generosity, gifts were exchanged in the course of the tributary mission, while envoys were usually permitted to bring along goods to sell privately.

For its part, the Qing court accepted certain responsibilities to nurture and protect its tributaries. The implications of this role were clearly spelled out in the case of the northern Vietnamese kingdom of Annam, where the Qing intervened with force in 1788 to put down a local rebellion and restore the king to the throne. Although their protégé was later ousted, the next ruler reestablished the tributary relationship, accepted investiture by the Qianlong emperor, and even attended his eightieth-birthday celebrations.

The kingdoms along China's eastern and southern borders had rarely posed important military threats to China and were, moreover, sedentary agrarian societies that had long displayed a flattering readiness to adopt Chinese ideas and institutions. The elites of Korea, Japan, and Annam studied classical Chinese and considered themselves part of China's cultural system. Relations with these countries, administered through the Board of Rites, were much more likely to fit into the tributary model. Because the Qing court also tended to view maritime trade and traders as peripheral to its strategic and economic interests and as part of this manageable sphere, the European nations who came to trade at China's ports were handled within this same tributary framework.

Central Asia was another matter. Most military challenges had traditionally come from these Inner Asian frontiers, and the Manchus, who had followed this route to power, were acutely aware of the need for military supremacy in this region. Inner Asian matters were therefore handled, deftly and with careful attention, by a new and separate agency, the Court of Colonial Affairs, established even before the Manchus had entered China proper.

In the eighteenth century, the Qing attempted to secure control of its long Central Asian frontier by diplomacy as well as force. From Nurgaci's time, there had been close ties between the Aisin Gioro and the chieftains of the eastern Mongol tribes, cemented by marriage exchanges that continued throughout the dynasty. The princes of the Mongol tribes in what is now Inner Mongolia had joined Hongtaiji when he proclaimed the Qing dynasty in 1636; in 1691 the khans or rulers of the Khalkha tribes in present-day Outer Mongolia submitted to Manchu overlordship. There was an intermittent state of war between the western Mongol tribes in Zungharia and the Qing that did not end until 1755, when the Chinese armies aided by their Mongol allies finally exterminated these rivals. But during this long period of hostilities, both trade and tribute from Central Asia continued. In the process of eliminating the Zunghars, the Qing also extended indirect control over distant Tibet, seized the Ili valley, some three thousand kilometers west of Peking, and in 1758–1759 conquered the oases in the Tarim Basin, incorporating this region into the empire as Xinjiang (New Dominions).

If force was an important component of relations with Central Asia, it was nonetheless tempered by other tactics and directed toward the expansion of the Qing empire. The Manchus, who like the Mongols had converted to Tibetan Buddhism, patronized and tried to control the Tibetan church. They invited the Dalai Lama and Panchen Lama to Peking and sponsored the printing and translation of Buddhist works in Tibetan and Mongolian. A set of temples, including a replica of the Potala complex (the residence of the Dalai Lama in Lhasa) and a wooden statue of Guanyin more than thirty meters high, was built at the imperial summer retreat in Rehe (Jehol) in northeast China to impress visiting Central Asians. (See plate 1.) Qing emperors portrayed themselves in the nomadic world as bodhisattva-rulers, reincarnations of Manjusri, the bodhisattva of wisdom, thus blending the Tibetan theory of the ruler as a living incarnation of a god and the Chinese Buddhist Manjusri cult identified with the sacred site of Mount Wutai in Shanxi. The Kangxi and Qianlong emperors both visited this mountain many times and encouraged pilgrimages by Mongols with publication of guidebooks in their language.

In their relations with Central Asia, the Qing showed a readiness to pursue flexible policies that were sometimes quite inconsistent with the tributary ideal. Relations with Russia differed from those with other

PLATE 1. Following the precedent set by Kangxi, Qianlong's sixtieth birthday in 1770 was the occasion for a grand celebration at the summer palace in Rehe attended by Mongol princes and other tribal leaders from Central Asia. To celebrate, a copy was built of the Potala Palace, residence of the Dalai Lama in Lhasa; this edifice was designed to impress the visiting dignitaries (believers in Lamaist Buddhism) with Qianlong's piety and power.

Western countries precisely because of Russia's strategic position in north Asia. The seventeenth and early eighteenth centuries saw Qing rulers attempt to check Russian advance into this region and to use the Russians as a buffer against the Mongols. Treaties in 1689 and 1727 fixed common borders and opened two markets for Sino-Russian trade. The Russians were permitted to open a small ecclesiastical mission in Peking and began to send a "tributary" mission to the capital once every three years (which they continued to do until 1755). When circumstances led the Chinese to put great importance on Russian agreement (for example, in their request that the czars remain neutral in the Chinese campaigns against the Zunghars), Qing ambassadors had been willing to perform the kowtow in Moscow (in 1731) and St. Petersburg (in 1732).

In short, the now legendary rigidity with which the Qing court seems to have responded to Western pressures for diplomatic relations on a basis of equality in the nineteenth century was not evident in the dynasty's position vis-à-vis countries along its sensitive Inner Asian frontier. Foreign trade was similarly not as restricted to formal ruler-to-ruler relations as might be implied by the tributary ideal, born centuries earlier in a less commercial era. Tribute missions were certainly occasions for trade, but extensive exchange was also permitted in markets on China's frontiers: on the border with Korea, on the Russo-Mongolian border at Kiakhta, and at selected ports along the coast.

Nor was trade always a matter of as much indifference to the Chinese as the rhetoric of the tributary model suggested: the trade between Chinese and Russians at Kiakhta, for example, allowed the Chinese to obtain the superior horses of the nomadic world in exchange for tea, textiles, and other products. Despite the inflammatory declaration by the ruling Tokugawa lords in Japan that the Qing was an illegitimate ruling house that did not have the Mandate of Heaven, a pressing need for copper motivated the Manchu court to send Imperial Household merchants to the southern Japanese port of Nagasaki during 1699–1715. Japanese insistence on trade permits after 1715 only temporarily halted the eager Chinese purchases.

In general, the importance of foreign commerce to the Qing state and economy before the nineteenth century has probably been considerably underestimated. Seaborne foreign trade, recovering from the seventeenth-century contractions, expanded to unprecedented volumes in the course of the eighteenth and early nineteenth centuries, as both Chinese and European merchants responded in ever more organized fashion to economic growth at home and the creation of worldwide trade networks. While the Qing state did not actively promote this trade, it was happy to benefit from a balance of trade that was consistently in China's favor. As a result, Chinese were drawn increasingly into the world market; coastal merchants dealt more frequently with foreigners, and Chinese producers tailored their goods for foreign sale.

The success of Qing foreign relations (measured by most standards) could be judged by the expansion of empire and enlarged participation in world trade. But although these developments promoted diversity, they also enhanced China's pride in her own culture and sense of invulnerability. These attitudes of complacency and self-confidence, characteristic of Chinese society in the eighteenth century, were a mixed legacy for the future.

Our survey of early Qing government policies to reestablish and maintain order underlines the importance of the state to social and economic developments in the early Qing. Although Chinese historians in their almost obsessive concern with the state may have exaggerated its power, Qing policies and programs did play crucial roles in securing the frontiers, rehabilitating the war-damaged economy, restoring the traditional status system, and reinvigorating the bureaucracy. Our assessment of the limitations of imperial and bureaucratic power does not contradict the undeniable role of the state in eighteenth-century history.

In our next chapters, we shall consider how social and economic institutions, systems of belief, and modes of action, not only directed by the throne but also inherited from the past, responded to the new order established by the Qing rulers and to the long-term economic growth that had begun in the late Ming. Later, when we shift from a national to a regional perspective, we shall see how government policies affected different areas very differently.

2

Social Relations

From very early times, the orderly management of human relationships has been a central concern of Chinese thought. Since at least the time of Confucius (who lived in the fifth century B.C.) hierarchical relations between individuals have been upheld as the source of social order, and the family has been a primary social institution. These ideals persisted even as social realities became far more complicated. A look at the Qing period will illustrate this complexity and will show how social relations beyond those created by family or state came to be extremely important.

Admirers of Chinese society have praised its ethics and family values, supportive kinship networks, and appreciation of the lubricating effects of etiquette and good manners. Critics have emphasized its social fragmentation, pervasive particularism and localism of social relations, lack of developed class consciousness, state intolerance of competing networks, and the excessive importance attached to kinship ties. Without denying the general validity of these views, we would prefer to emphasize here the basic *versatility* of the Chinese repertory of social relationships.

This entire book is about Chinese society, but we shall begin with a look at the most important grounds for association and community in the eighteenth century. Future chapters will show in more detail not only how social relations responded to the events of this period but how they varied in different parts of China.

KINSHIP

The basic unit of production and consumption in Chinese society was the *jia*, the unit consisting of kin related by blood, marriage, or adoption, that had a common budget and common property. Daughters married out of the patrilineal group, while sons (and their wives) shared the residence of their fathers. Popularly translated as "family," the *jia* was upheld in traditional China as a metaphor for the state and the foundation of correct—and hierarchical—relationships. Because the normative ideal admitted no room for historical change, Chinese commitment to it has tended to hide from the historian developments in familial structure over time and differentiation according to class.

The pooling of resources and energies into a corporate economy at the household level and the concerted effort to maintain the patriline were characteristic of families at every level of society in the Qing. For a significant portion of the population, however, merely sustaining the *jia* resources and the patriline from one generation to the next was a terrible struggle. Small fragmented families were especially common among the poor, where family cycles were short and relationships simple.

Among the wealthy and in certain types of farm economy, families were larger and more complex. A rich man could afford to marry young, remarry if his wife died, and take secondary wives even as an old man; consequently, the wealthy fathered more surviving children. The Chinese ideal was just such a family of multiple conjugal units of many generations. Including servants, the size of a rich household could total several hundred persons. These joint families had characteristically complex internal dynamics. Family affairs were typically controlled by the patriarch, head of the *jia*, who had extensive powers backed by law over members. The patriarch divided up the budget among the constituent conjugal units, assigned his sons to different careers, arranged his children's marriages, and punished them at will. With each member working for a common goal, the *jia* at its best was a powerful institution for achieving and perpetuating wealth and status.

Judging from developments in fiction, where the household becomes an enveloping world in itself, domestic life among the wealthy appears to have become more absorbing and more important to personal development. Indeed, one of the best introductions to life among the Chinese elite in the eighteenth century is the long novel *Dream of Red Mansions* (also translated as *The Story of the Stone*), which describes in remarkable detail the enormous household of a wealthy family in slow decline. Family life was a microcosm of the larger society, with deep ties of affection constantly threatened by sibling rivalry, inappropriate sexual attraction, bickering among concubines and wife, and skirmishes between mother-in-law and daughter-in-law. The social gap between first and secondary wives—the latter were usually purchased and came from a lower social stratum—was paralleled by the different regional and social origins of the domestic servants.

Despite these undercurrents of potential conflict, the overriding contrast lay between the secure domestic milieu and the outside world of men, where the family's fortunes had to be made and defended. The pampered upbringing given to sons of elite households was frequently antithetical to the self-discipline and personal exertion required to move ahead in the larger society. The immense popularity of *Dream of Red Mansions* suggests that the great reluctance felt by its teenage hero to leave his sheltered life in Prospect Garden and go out into the world of adult men was shared by the book's elite male readers. The sympathetic portrayal of women in this novel, and the dozens of popular plays of the scholar-beauty genre, in which the stranger with whom one falls in love turns out to be an eminently suitable marriage partner, suggest a tension between individual preference and family interests that was not so easily resolved in real life, where arranged marriages and submission to parental authority was the accepted norm.

Economic trends also threatened solidarity. Most households, especially in the more commercially prosperous parts of China, diversified the occupations of their members. Although cash crops and the spread of markets allowed individuals to develop their own (sometimes seasonal) contributions to *jia* income, successful pursuit of family strategies demanded the cohesiveness and solidarity of the family unit. Geographical mobility, especially sojourning by males (which was so common in this period) rested firmly on *jia* and lineage solidarity. But unless shored up, the entrepreneurship encouraged by mobility and opportunity could work against the expected domination of both women and younger men by their elders and by collective interests.

The family was the central, all-encompassing institution for the women and children who made up fully 65 percent of this society. Social organizations beyond the family were run by and for men. This male world began with the extended family. Households were organized and property inherited through the patriline, and agnatic descent was a venerable and orthodox basis for public action. Lineage organizations based on descent from a common ancestor were the natural extension of the *jia* and, in the Qing, developed a range of activities in response to local conditions and needs.

The repertory of collective actions engaged in by agnates (males related to one another through the male line) in this period followed enduring patterns. Shared graveyards and rituals, ancestral tablets and halls, written genealogies, and corporate income-producing property used to support education, charity, and rites were hallmarks of family organization at least as early as the Song (960–1279). They also characterize the lineages created in the late seventeenth century, when the end of the conquest phase stimulated an increase—as documented in the number of genealogies and in the acquisition of corporate property by kin groups—of this form of family organization. Different forms and degrees of cooperation were to be found in different parts of China among different social classes, but in general terms, it was shared property that enabled a descent group to act as a corporate organization.

The Chinese patriline emphasized continuity between the living and the dead over the generations and created this community through regular religious rituals known in English by the misnomer *ancestor worship*. (Because ancestors could help their descendants, offerings and prayers were made to them, but they were not worshiped as gods.) Annual ancestral rituals and common gravesites were the cheapest and probably most ordinary form of agnatic cooperation; they were found throughout China among all but the very poor. Responsibility for such rituals was inherited by the eldest (often the only) son. It was more difficult for most people to gather enough money to purchase land whose income could be used to finance the rituals; but ownership of ritual land was an ideal, and it was the most common form of corporate property. Literacy and wealth were required for the compilation of genealogies, which can be seen as social charters for these kin groups. Even more money was necessary to endow and build ancestral halls, so the appearance of these magnificent edifices was a public declaration of wealth and local power.

The forms of lineage organization were differentiated by region and to some degree by class. The dominant lineage type, which owned large corporate properties, exercised extensive control over its constituent *jia*, and subordinated lesser surnames, was rare in North China and the Northwest and common in Lingnan and the Southeast Coast. Such lineages, typically found in rural areas, maximized their local dominance through the collective action of rich and poor relatives. Although they presented a united front to the outside world, they were at the same time highly stratified internally and rife with competition among branches and subbranches. Periodic endowments to support separate branch ancestral halls reflected (and contributed to) the continuous process of internal segmentation and the growth of some branches at the expense of others.

The more open, inclusive, prestige-oriented lineages of Tongcheng county in Anhui studied by Hilary Beattie appear to be typical of areas (like the Lower Yangtze) that had better opportunities for entry into elite circles beyond the rural village. By contrast, the boundary-conscious, defensive, exclusionist, and highly corporate nature of twentieth-century Guangdong lineages may reflect, in addition to their local orientation, the intense competition for resources characteristic of the economic down-swing this region had experienced since the early nineteenth century. The Tongcheng lineage was composed of only the most successful lines (in terms of holding office) within the descent group. This type of lineage owned relatively little corporate property (when measured against the holdings of individual households), exercised weak authority over mem-bers, and directed strategies toward national rather than local promi-nence. Oriented toward degree-holders who were part of the Qing national elite, they competed (and intermarried) not with their neighbors but with these other more distant prominent families. Such an organization enabled elites to tap a very large and dispersed network of agnates: the Hengyang (Hunan) Wei lineage studied by Liu Ts'ui-jung, for example, had five branches that had spread throughout this Middle Yangtze region and extended into the Upper Yangtze, the Southwest, Lingnan, and even Northwest China.

Outside parts of central and south China, lineage organization tended to be even more attenuated and rudimentary. Many North China descent groups, even those boasting degree-holders and officials, pos-sessed only miniscule parcels of corporate land. Few compiled printed genealogies, and the primary purpose of the lineage seemed to be to make good marriages and so create useful networks of affines (relatives through marriage).

Public forms of lineage collective action appear to have been affected also by the varying types of status competition found in different localities. In places where lineages were strong and visible, higher-order lineages united component lineages to attempt to dominate marketing areas or even a whole county, encouraging the formation of competing same-surname organizations based on fictive kinship. In places where genealogies were commonplace among the elite, no respectable descent group could be without one; where ancestral halls were public symbols of a lineage's longevity and prosperity, any rising group needed one. When some elite families demonstrated their public spirit by building orphanages, schools, roads, bridges, or granaries, other families did likewise. Some activities served best to enhance the status of a group as it grew and acquired prestige, others served to protect its resources in hard times. But many elite families found that the lineage did not fill their need to create broad alliances with other powerful elites or to narrow their obligations to poor kinsmen. Such households found their strongest allies among affines rather than agnates.

Marriage, as Maurice Freedman has noted, was "by far the most important contractual relationship in Chinese society."[1] It took place through a variety of arrangements that displayed considerable flexibility in constructing predictable relationships between families. At all levels, moreover, ties between affines—although not part of the patrilineal model—were important grounds for cooperation through other corporate and voluntary institutions.

Because access to women was unequal in this society and males outnumbered females, marriage patterns varied with class as well as with conditions in the society at large. In general, the Chinese preferred to select brides from families that were slightly lower in social status than their own; this custom helped promote docility in brides (and thus a peaceful household). People of higher social position, however, found their marriage partners from among a more exclusive set of families spread over a wider geographic range; they had a preference for what Arthur Wolf calls the "major" form of marriage, in which the wife came as an adult to join her husband's household. Wealthy households were able to provide secondary wives for their men and preferred to keep widows of deceased male members from remarrying, as symbols of fidelity and chastity. Sustained intermarriage between certain surnames supported a corresponding intensification of relations with affines among literati and merchants of the eighteenth century, as among earlier elites. The noted scholars Zhang Xuecheng (1738–1801) and Liu Fenglu (1776–1829) were among many men of the period whose ties with their maternal relatives were strong and decisive in their careers. Naturally the bride, protected by prominent parents and brothers, was able to hold a position of considerable authority and respect in her husband's household. As a first wife (she would never have been given as a secondary wife), she would eventually become the matriarch of the *jia*, with control of the household. She would receive ritual homage from any secondary wife chosen by her husband and be ritually acknowledged as mother by all offspring, not just her own. She brought in a considerable dowry if she came from a well-to-do family, and at least a portion of that dowry was her own, to dispose of as she pleased. Occasionally, the sums over which women exercised control were extremely large: it was not just in novels that women lent out money at high rates of interest or invested in commercial ventures.

Among the poor and in areas and times of economic contraction, a reverse pattern existed. Men, if they married at all (they had to be able to pay the brideprice), had fewer wives and were more likely to remain widowers; widows, on the other hand, were in great demand as wives, and their kin were eager to be paid to see them gone. Wives of humble households came from nearby communities, and the less prestigious but economically advantageous forms of marriage in which brides were acquired as children or men married into a woman's family were much more common. Finally, even when poor men married, their poverty hindered their chances of perpetuating their line. Only the wealthy could afford to buy an infant son as heir, and a man with no estate could not hope to find an adult male to take on the role of heir and make offerings to his dead spirit. Without sufficient means, a man with a daughter and no sons could not expect to attract a husband-by-adoption into the family and thereby perpetuate the descent line. Enforced celibacy among poor men and the misfortune of having no heirs worked to ensure that the poorest strata in society did not reproduce themselves; polygyny (the custom of a man having multiple wives at one time) and partible inheritance resulted in a process of downward rather than upward mobility for Chinese society as a whole.

Like its predecessors, the Qing government viewed all forms of social organization beyond the family with suspicion, even those based on agnatic descent. Although the existence of some exceptional kin groups among the elite (like the ruling Aisin Gioro lineage) clearly demonstrates the potential for powerful patrilineal organization, dominant lineages were, as we shall see, often criticized and survived best in localities that were out of the reach of the state. Also, the number and extent of the hereditary fiefdoms in the Qing, as compared with other eras, were small and getting smaller.

Kinship organization had other limitations as well. For men who were working away from home—an increasingly common phenomenon in the eighteenth century—ties with one's immediate relatives were of limited use and grew fragile with time and distance. Lineages took time to develop strength and were not always effective organizations for uprooted individuals in cities or on the frontiers. In the fluid society of the eighteenth century, both for those with and without large kinship networks, patrilineal descent came to be supplemented regularly by other forms of voluntary association.

RESIDENCE AND COMMUNITY

The most common grounds for association among people who were not related was proximity of residence. The primary residential unit appears to have been the neighborhood, whether village hamlet or urban ward. Although we have few detailed accounts of such neighborhoods, we can perhaps infer their centrality to the daily activities of peasants from modern studies on the importance of small voluntary mutual-aid teams in agriculture and of hamlet divisions (identified with competing surname groups or lineage segments) in village politics.

Anthropological studies of villages in China, Taiwan, and in the New Territories of Hong Kong indicate the great range in residential patterns. Some villages were inhabited by a single surname group (although these were a minority even in Lingnan and the Southeast Coast): here village and kinship boundaries were identical. When villages were home to several surname groups, solidarity was often weakened, and the lineages were the primary units of social action. In other cases, coalitions of competing surname groups divided and rotated collective responsibilities. In some multisurname villages, lineage identities were not strong, and inhabitants emphasized solidarity through temple associations or militias. And the same village might pass through different phases depending on the external environment: stressing village solidarity during times of disorder, surname competition during periods of prosperity.

The specificity of the social scene in late imperial cities, which had highly differentiated clusters of elite, business, and poor neighborhoods, may also have tended to make urban wards an important unit of human interaction and may have influenced intercourse among wards within a city. Temples served as foci for neighborhood solidarity in cities as well: natives of Suzhou, for example, identified themselves not with a residential address but with a particular earth god, and in Quanzhou, Fujian, factional conflict was heightened during the festivals of the competing earth gods who reigned over the east and west portions of the city. For the most part, however, we are ignorant about these small residential communities. We must turn instead to the larger unit, the village or town.

Although we also know too little about Chinese villages in this period, it appears that, unlike villages in some peasant societies, they were not self-sufficient, closed, corporate worlds. The development of market networks that had paralleled the growth of a commercial economy in China had been accompanied by the emergence of marketing communities as active foci for peasant social life. As the work of G. W. Skinner has suggested, periodic markets, held on regular interlocking schedules, drew villagers into sustained trade and social interaction with those in the same standard marketing area. These market areas tended to be linguistically homogeneous, set the regional boundaries within which non-elite marriage alliances were formed, and defined the recreational, religious, and social community of the peasant.

Unlike the Ming, the early Qing state had not been willing to empower natural village leaders with delegated responsibilities for tasks like tax collection; even the successful eighteenth-century efforts to establish the constable as a government agent in villages and cities did not strengthen indigenous organizations. The village as such was probably most organized where it overlapped with other, more powerful forms of affiliation. Single-surname villages in the Canton delta, Ningbo, and Huizhou gained their solidarity from kinship structures, and Hakka villages from subethnic homogeneity (the Hakka being among the most sharply differentiated minorities in the Han Chinese population). On the undeveloped peripheries of the empire, however, where new institutions were created with difficulty, the village unit had some useful organizing potential even among heterogeneous groups. The militarization, economic hardships, and elite encroachment on government functions that began at the end of the eighteenth century thus accompanied and stimulated the later emergence of villages that were armed and walled. Within a hundred years, a major transformation of the countryside would produce fortified and much more solidary villages across much of China.

Given the relative weakness of the village (and of the urban ward, which was likewise rarely empowered by the state), a common focus for community organization beyond the kin group was the temple. A 1667 census (surely incomplete) listed nearly eighty thousand temples and monasteries (for a population of perhaps a hundred and fifty million), and by the eighteenth century, cities and countryside were dotted with places for worship of an array of deities. Represented variously by slips of paper, prints, or statues, Chinese gods were housed on altars in homes, small shrines, and temple buildings of all sizes. A great many spirits were unknown beyond a single locality, some had demonstrated their powers within a larger region, and a few were worshiped throughout the empire. Loosely related to one another through a celestial bureaucracy that mirrored the imperial government, these deities were somewhat interchangeable in behavior and function; commitment to one god rather than another was usually a matter of perceived differences in efficacy and convenience, not doctrine. (Government policy, expressing an entrenched fear of organized religion, encouraged such fragmentation.)

In fact, household, neighborhood, village, and city were all communities within a religious hierarchy: the local earth god acted as an intermediary between the stove god found in each household and higher authorities. In cities, earth gods were under the authority of the city god, who was the celestial equivalent of the county magistrate. All births and deaths were reported to these territorial gods, while annual festivals reinforced the bonds of their communities. Beyond the hierarchy of territorial gods, however, was the vast array of other deities who united other groups of believers.

At one level, temples could be used for any public purpose. They doubled as inns, community schools, soup kitchens, and public parks. Temples were the sites for annual festivals and fairs, even the locus for confrontations between citizenry and officials. To this extent, they belonged to everyone.

Nevertheless, temples were actually the collective property of the communities that periodically invested in them. The construction, renovation, and maintenance of a local temple, as well as its regular festivals, required organization and money. Fund drives were used to solicit contributions from those who lived nearby; ideally, an endowment would be set up so that a regular income could be used for rituals and maintenance. Not everyone had to participate equally, however, and it was usually the wealthy and prominent members of the community who took the lead in giving money and land. They were the majority shareholders, we might say, and leadership posts rotated among them. Although many temples had a religious professional in residence (usually a Buddhist monk), these men (in contrast to the European parish priest) were not essential to community worship or important in temple management. They existed at the sufferance of temple managers, objects of public charity who were easily replaced.

The principles behind these temple organizations (called by a variety of local names) were similar to those at work in many other social organizations in Qing China. Like well-established lineages, temples shared property and collective rituals, were concentrated in a loosely defined territory, and although dominated by local elites were multiclass in their constituencies.

These highly personal and somewhat ad hoc organizations functioned best for small communities where decisions could be made by consensus among a few leaders. Most temple communities were relatively small in size and territory. Moreover, each was a separate, independent unit; there was little relationship between temples, even those of the same deity. (It is not clear if the idea that we see in Taiwan of newer temples being the offspring of older temples from which their incense had come was commonplace elsewhere.) Temple organization thus provided no framework for linking large numbers of people and worked poorly when the community was not a homogeneous one.

Temples could, nevertheless, be important to community formation, as in resettled areas on frontiers and among urban immigrants, since they provided a manageable structure for incorporating newcomers and carried with them the promise of supernatural assistance. But because their management reflected existing structures of power, temples could also become the foci for community rivalries. Harmless competitions of display between neighbors during festivals could turn violent when other tensions were at work. In the fragmented world of the Southeast Coast, subethnic rivalries were frequently manifested in this manner. Houses of worship for other religions (Islamic mosques, Lamaist monasteries, White Lotus sutra halls, and Catholic churches) similarly generated solidarity and hostility in equal measure.

In the Qing, both state intervention and the circulation of people throughout China contributed to a growing standardization in the physical structure, iconography, and organizational mechanisms of temples. Although government measures to register all temples and religious personnel were finally abandoned in the 1770s, the elevation of certain regional cults to national prominence and the stipulation that local officials throughout the empire would perform a fixed set of rituals of worship for official cults did encourage some uniformity. In some cases (e.g., at city-god temples and Confucian shrines) officials were actually part of the temple communities, contributing public funds and taking a corresponding lead in collective decisions and annual rites. Pilgrimage sites attracted groups who traveled to temples famous for their crowds, scenery, and historic monuments as much as for their efficacious deities. Travel was relatively easy (route books that provided maps and tourist information were increasingly available), and emperors and common people, tribes and Han Chinese, made pilgrimages to the most famous mountain sites. (See plate 2.)

Temple organizations, however versatile, did not meet all local community needs. Irrigation in particular posed difficult problems for collective action beyond the household or village, although here too a local cult could serve to organize an entire irrigation community. The construction of dikes, canals, and polders involved cooperation by owners of adjacent properties along waterways, often over a large area, while the need for access to water frequently generated competing demands that were difficult to reconcile. Yet the model for constructing, maintaining, and renovating waterworks was similar to that of the temple association.

PLATE 2. This large porcelain figure, made in the Kangxi reign in the
factories at Jingdezhen, Jiangxi, represents the goddess Guanyin seated on a
lotus throne. A popular deity worshiped by Chinese women of all classes,
Guanyin was also a protector of seafarers. The temple complex at Putuoshan
near Ningbo off the Zhejiang coast was dedicated to her cult. Reproduced from
the Metropolitan Museum of Art, gift of Edwin C. Vogel, 1964 (64.279.9ab).

Members donated either money or labor, and a manager was designated to
take charge of the project.

As with tax collection, the early Qing had moved away from the Ming
model, which had placed responsibility for water management with local
elites, and tried to rely instead on local officials. In the first century of
Qing rule, when the agricultural infrastructure had to be rebuilt, it was
local officials who took the leading role in waterworks. They solicited
contributions, managed labor, and oversaw construction. By mid-century,
the effectiveness of their leadership was inhibited by population increase
and a divergence between public and private interests. The state, as
Morita Akira and others have argued, attempted with decreasing success

to protect the public interest, by maintaining drainage canals and reservoirs to alleviate drought and flood, against the private interests of increasingly land-hungry communities eager to turn lakes into fields. Privately run corporations that took charge of irrigation, unlike those that ran temples, neither reflected local solidarities (which they frequently superseded) nor had clear-cut collective goals. Because the private interests of members undermined these projects, disputes over waterworks were most likely to be solved by litigation or violence. Such private structures were not usually enduring, and in many places they could not replace the officially managed organizations that weakened as the government became overburdened during the middle Qing.

The need for other public services put similar demands on local communities as well as local government. Welfare activities, originally associated primarily with Buddhist institutions, had been taken over by the government in Song times and included orphanages, hospitals, dispensaries, public baths, toilets, wells, garbage disposal, and public cemeteries. In the late sixteenth century, as financially strapped magistrates gradually abandoned these tasks, many were taken over by local elites inspired with a desire to stabilize social relations within their communities. The eighteenth century saw this trend toward private philanthropy continue.

Articulation of this renewed interest in philanthropy was voiced in both Buddhist and Confucian terms. Buddhist activities flourished in the late Ming and into the early Qing, when shelter temples used the revenues from endowed lands given as donations not only to house Buddhist clergy but also to succor the elderly, the poor, and the socially isolated. The inspiration for this charity was the bodhisattva ideal of compassion and empathy with all sentient beings that had long been part of Chinese culture. Among Confucian writers, unease at the social mobility and social unrest produced by the post-sixteenth-century economic boom stimulated degree-holders who were temporarily out of office to act directly to ameliorate social problems. Charitable deeds became acts of Confucian self-cultivation, and Confucians began to organize "benevolent societies" in order to promote long-term stability and harmony in the community.

After an initial period of government leadership in the early Qing, we see the steady growth, particularly in cities, of residentially oriented philanthropic organizations funded by private groups and persons. Orphanages, for example, began to be established in major urban centers in the Yangtze delta almost as soon as the military phase of the Qing conquest was over. From the early eighteenth century, every county was supposed to support a home for the poor, disabled, and aged. As in other activities, local officials initially took the lead, cooperating with local landed and mercantile elites in raising endowments. In time, merchants and degree-holders increasingly bore the burden of responsibility and reaped the rewards of local prestige. From the more traditional schools, granaries, and public graveyards, local officials and elites went on to fund fire-fighting brigades and local militias. (Merchant associations called *huiguan*, which we shall discuss below, often played prominent roles in such public works.) A great many of these activities, like the elites who organized them, were urban based and were usually aimed at the urban public.

Emergency relief during natural disasters was usually paid for by contributions of grain, labor, or ready cash. More enduring relief organizations were funded through the ubiquitous institution of the endowment. The interest or rent from landed property (increasingly urban real estate) could be used not just to provide services but to hire a permanent manager. In contrast to the late Ming when founders of benevolent societies were high elites, Qing managers tended to be commoners without even lower-level degrees who used this activity as a means of upward mobility. As the endowment was used up and services dwindled, new donations would be sought and the organization revived. It was this expanding sphere of ad hoc public activities that took the place of formal city government.

ECONOMIC ORGANIZATIONS

As we have indicated, there seems to have been unprecedented geographic mobility in eighteenth-century China. In addition to the scholar-officials who had long been drawn out of their local communities to take examinations and pursue official careers, merchants and entrepreneurs, skilled and unskilled workers, and land-hungry peasants (usually all males) left home in search of opportunity. Sojourning, a type of sustained migration that involved explicitly temporary but often effectively permanent movement from villages to large cities within one region and from less urbanized regional systems to more urbanized ones, became commonplace. The expansion of regional economies and the emergence of a national market in bulk commodities stimulated a shift in the scale of formal economic organization, leading to the creation of larger structures that could make possible mutual trust and cooperation among unrelated individuals.

In China, as in other premodern economies, the basic business unit had been an extension of the *jia* economy through the family firm. In the late Ming, as market expansion provided opportunities for traders to increase the scale of their operations, the need for capital and coordination had stimulated use of the share partnership. Based on principles quite similar to those underlying lineage and temple endowments, the share partnership allowed persons who were not blood relatives (often affines, it seems) to pool resources to establish a business. The form of the business could shift flexibly to accommodate changing economic conditions: a recent study of a Chinese medicine store in Peking, the Wanchuantang, shows that the firm began as the family enterprise of a Ningbo (Zhejiang) merchant named Yue in the early eighteenth century and became a share partnership in the 1740s as the firm expanded. Its sister firm, the Tongrentang, went through three phases: originally owned by the Yue, it was opened up into a share partnership in the mid-eighteenth century but reverted to Yue family ownership in the early nineteenth century.

During the early Qing, economic opportunities encouraged the spread of this share partnership. It was used to finance and manage a variety of enterprises: theaters, copper and other mining ventures, coastal and overseas shipping, commercial agriculture, and money shops. The trading empires built by Anhui and Shanxi merchants in the late Ming and extended in the Qing are the most successful examples of networks of such partnerships cemented by kinship and native-place ties.

Native place was the principle most often invoked as grounds for affiliation and assistance by men who left their homes to work in an alien environment. Firms sought trustworthy and skilled managers (who often received a share of the business) from among fellow natives. The Wanchuantang hired either relatives or men who were also from Ningbo. The survival of the firm over several centuries, even after the Yue stopped managing it personally, rested on effective recruitment and incentives for employees. The key employee, the manager, while not a shareholder, was given favored treatment: six months' home leave with travel expenses once every two years and retirement at age seventy with a lump-sum gift. Store clerks and apprentices were hired employees, but their loyalties were assured by shared kinship and native place. These personal and paternalistic relationships made for firm solidarity and cut across potential class cleavages.

In the Qing, the *jiaxiang*, the place where one's family roots were and where one was born and buried, was an integral part of a man's identity. Native place could, moreover, be defined by contrast with other places at a variety of levels and could refer to a village, town, county, prefecture, or even province. The hierarchically cumulative nature of this concept gave individuals expanding levels of affiliation that were progressively useful as they moved farther from home.

Because communities often specialized in certain goods and services, common occupation usually supplemented native-place ties among sojourners and migrants. Occupational niches in cities were frequently filled exclusively by natives of specific rural communities. Both principles were expressed not only in informal association—residence, friendship, contacts—but in more formal organizations as well. Such corporate groups, usually called *huiguan* (lodges), first emerged in the Ming, spread throughout the empire in the early Qing, and reached their most spectacular numerical growth (at least a tenfold increase) in the nineteenth century. Like lineage and temple associations, *huiguan* were run by their well-to-do members who managed communal property acquired by contributions. A shrine to a patron deity was at the heart of most *huiguan* organizations, providing a structure for collective celebrations and a symbol of the community.

Some lodges were primarily intended for official and examination candidates (and were located in Peking and provincial capitals), others were for immigrants (as was common in newly colonized areas such as Sichuan and Hunan); but most were originally created and used by occupational groups. The *huiguan* provided a meeting ground, lodging, financial assistance, and storage facilities (for coffins as well as goods). For merchants and artisans, the *huiguan* also provided a mechanism for regulating trade. Regional specialization was premised on the idea of comparative advantage but became a device for a vast interlocking network of small monopolies. The *huiguan* helped maintain such monopolies by preventing competition from within the trade and by negotiating on behalf of the group with the state or other merchants.

In the course of the eighteenth century, we can see the spread of the *huiguan* institution to commercial centers throughout China. Prosperity also promoted the expansion of the activities of individual lodges, as men from a few clusters of counties in Shanxi, Anhui, and Fujian (and later Zhejiang and Guangdong) penetrated and took control of major markets in key commodities. The *huiguan* of such highly successful sojourning groups often became powerful urban property owners and civic leaders. The Huizhou (Anhui) merchants of Hankou, for example, completed a guild hall in 1694 that had cost more than ten thousand taels and ten years' labor. They gradually expanded, building a lecture hall, large temple, and dormitory rooms and dominating one busy street, wharf, and corner of the city. They invested heavily in urban property and promoted Hankou's growth in the eighteenth century. (Such extensive operations reflected the unusual multioccupational character of Huizhou sojourning, which involved both merchants and high-ranking government officials.)

In the course of the eighteenth century, two somewhat contradictory trends in the development of *huiguan* are visible. On the one hand, craft and commercial organizations became more differentiated, paralleling increased specialization in the economy as a whole. On the other hand, there was a more important trend toward deparochialization of *huiguan* through inclusiveness and a weakening of narrowly native-place ties. Their effectiveness demonstrated, *huiguan* began to be used more frequently to coordinate the activities of related trades involving larger numbers of people. At the same time, services once provided only for guild members were extended to more of the urban community. When White Lotus rebels threatened Hankou in the 1790s, for instance, the Huizhou salt merchants financed a local militia for the entire city. The creation of large trade associations did not mean the disappearance of exclusively native-place and occupational groups, for they became working subunits of guilds that were called *gongsuo*. This latter trend, which gained force in the nineteenth century, may have protected businesses in hard times and helped convert guilds into urban quasi-governments, and paralleled the shift in that century toward the nonbureaucratic handling of public business. Among overseas Chinese (whose numbers did not grow dramatically until the nineteenth century), community affairs were explicitly coordinated by the major guilds, called *kongsi* in Southeast Asia.

Despite the possibilities for associations based on common occupation, unionlike organizations of workers developed only with difficulty in imperial China. Even the large-scale industries of the eighteenth century (such as porcelain, salt, textiles, and mining, each of which may have employed more than ten thousand workers) were usually aggregations of relatively small establishments. Because each stage of production and distribution was separately organized, workers were integrated into the economy only through an enormous network of brokers and contractors. And neither merchants, middlemen, nor the state had much to gain from encouraging organizations that represented purely worker interests.

We can see elite resistance to worker organization in the difficulties encountered during the early eighteenth century by the calenderers of Suzhou, who performed the heavy pressing of cloth on large stone rollers to give it gloss. The growth of the cotton and silk textile industries in Suzhou had brought a large increase in related unskilled jobs such as calendering, and there were at least ten thousand calenderers in the city in 1720 (in some three hundred workshops). They had organized strikes in 1670, 1693, and 1701 to demand higher wages and in 1715 petitioned for the right to establish their own *huiguan*. Their employers, the contractors and cloth merchants, indignantly opposed the petition on the grounds that such permissiveness would encourage rascals to infiltrate the work force and increase labor unrest. Calenderers continued to riot into the 1720s but never won the right to organize.

The earliest and most effective worker organizations were not developed until the end of the eighteenth century and were not found initially among industrial workers. These groups were most usually called *bang* (frequently translated disparagingly as "gang"), a term that had originally referred to the fleets into which the boats that transported tribute grain along the Grand Canal were organized. By extension, *bang* had come to mean the hired laborers who manned those boats. Other eighteenth-century usages of this term appear also to indicate increasingly tighter, more self-conscious organizations among the other water-transport workers who were so crucial to long-distance trade in China. The organization of Grand Canal workers, influenced in part by the sectarian religion to which many adhered, eventually developed into the Green Gang, notorious gangsters of the twentieth century. Although by the 1820s *bang* could denote informal merchant alliances as well, other transport-worker associations also grew significantly in the nineteenth and twentieth centuries, sometimes adopting Triad structures (which we discuss in chapter 4). In general terms, however, the development of economic organizations with the power to threaten established interests did not take place until the Qing state and the traditional elite had become much weaker than they were in the eighteenth century.

PATRONAGE

The most prestigious network that led out of local communities was through the imperial examinations and bureaucracy. Well before the Qing, a national elite of educated men had been created by the experience of this common career. In theory, it was the impersonal examination and bureaucratic structure that shaped the relationships between officials. In reality, particularistic ties entered the pristine structure of examination and bureaucracy thanks to the inherent instability of official life (where promotions, demotions, and transfers were routine), the need for cooperation between officials from different areas, and the built-in competition between bureaucratic units and between officials and emperor.

Government academies and the exams themselves generated a horizontal bond between fellow students and examinees as well as a vertical bond between pupil and teacher, examinee and examiner. Such connections lasted a lifetime. In addition, men who were both scholars and bureaucrats shared a common elite culture and found friends, allies, and patrons through similar intellectual, literary, and aesthetic interests.

The cultivation of connections (*guanxi*) was essential to the ambitious man, and among literati and officials in the eighteenth century relatively superficial connections could form the basis for large commitments of mutual assistance. The enormous number of relationships described in the classic satirical novel of literati life, *The Scholars* (written in the 1740s), indicates how the most casual of acceptable connections could generate the giving and receiving of very substantial gifts and the immediate inclusion of perfect strangers into existing scholarly communities. Fortunately for aspiring literati, patronage of scholars within and beyond the formal bureaucracy became a favored form of status display in the middle Qing. Imperially sponsored projects, of which the compilation of the 3,450-volume "Complete Library of the Four Treasuries" (*Siku quanshu*) is only the best known, were imitated on a reduced scale by education officials, well-to-do scholars, and rich merchants.

Although most scholar-officials used common origin, a teacher, or kinship to find friends in distant cities, the primary purpose of these contacts was to forge the alliances and patronage networks necessary to a career. These so-called factions were as old as the bureaucracy itself, and had been denounced for nearly as long. Early Qing emperors and officials both viewed with horror the violent conflicts between rival groups in the late Ming. Kangxi and Yongzheng (in 1661 and 1724, respectively) went on record against cliques, characterizing them as expressions of private rather than public interests. (See p. 13 above for some of Yongzheng's views.) Eighteenth-century literati were themselves quick to criticize factions in theory and to denounce the networks of their rivals.

Qing emperors continually attempted to tighten the system so as to discourage personal ties within the bureaucracy and to keep politics out of scholarship. At best, however, they were merely able to keep the forces of *guanxi* at bay. Not only were they endemic to the system, they were crucial to emperors as well as officials. The largest and most powerful networks of the eighteenth century were those built around men who had become friends and confidants to rulers. Even Yongzheng, despite his mechanical vision of government and denunciation of factions, leaned heavily on a few men with whom his relations were intensely personal.

Our understanding of factionalism in Chinese history and culture is at best preliminary, for most accounts focus on individuals (painted in black-and-white language) rather than on basic principles and dynamics. Nevertheless, we can hypothesize about how the system worked in the Qing and analyze in terms of three phases those patronage systems that extended to the emperor and the changing arenas within which they operated.

In the first phase, ending in the 1730s, imperial princes and Manchu institutions were central. For the first century of Qing rule, there were two competing arenas for upper-level politics: the bureaucracy, recreated on the Ming model, and the Manchu banners, headed by imperial princes. Politics was characterized by a series of shifting alliances between Manchus and at first Liaodong Chinese (bannermen), then northern Chinese who dominated the exams in the Shunzhi reign, and finally (after the Rebellion of the Three Feudatories) Lower Yangtze elites. Connections with bannermen, especially the princes or the emperor himself, were crucial to career success, and the violence of repeated struggles over the succession and between regents continually spilled over into bureaucratic politics. This phase was effectively terminated by a series of measures in the Yongzheng and early Qianlong reigns: the banners were finally bureaucratized and the princes' power base eliminated; the Hanlin Academy was restored as a central channel for official careers; and the Grand Council became the locus for decisions at the highest level.

In the second phase, lasting into the 1820s, the examinations at one level and the Grand Council at another had become the main nodes for political connections. More extensive factions were created, and imperial favor continued to be crucial in generating these networks, but the primary access route to power for both Manchus and Chinese was now the examination system. Despite the quotas, the elites from the Lower Yangtze still dominated the bureaucracy. Creation of a national system of feeder academies for the exams (after 1733) and the simultaneous spread of evidential scholarship (which favored philological research) kept intellectual commitments generally divorced from policy debates. The bureaucracy, like the economy, was more commercialized, and profiteering by officials became easier. This phase is best known for Heshen, the favorite of the Qianlong emperor who built a clientage network of considerable size at court and within the bureaucracy in the last two decades of the century.

The third phase lasted from the 1820s through the end of the dynasty and witnessed the dominance once more of extrabureaucratic networks, the increased importance of provincial posts, and a resurgence of Manchu control at the very top. This stage developed in response to the crisis conditions of the early nineteenth century. Private academies devoted to classical and practical education such as the Xuehaitang (founded in Canton in 1820) encouraged the reunion of intellectual and political networks. Extrabureaucratic avenues into office were promoted by both emperors and officials, and in the middle of the century there was a dramatic and irrevocable shift in the political center of gravity from the court to the provinces. The power of Lower Yangtze literati, already challenged by Cantonese and Hunanese, was drastically undercut by the damages of the Taiping rebellion in the 1850s and 1860s. At court, a series of young or short-lived emperors brought about a revival of joint rule by Manchu regents and their favorites as well as the seizure of ultimate power by a woman, Empress Dowager Cixi.

Because it is the second period (ca. 1730–1820) that is most characteristic of the eighteenth century as a whole, we might look at it in more detail. Its crucial actors were metropolitan officials and holders of the highest examination degree, especially those who made it into the Hanlin Academy. From the Hanlin, called a "Taoist paradise" by the poet and official Yuan Mei, came not only officials but also examiners, the natural magnets for clientage networks. Like examiners, education commissioners were crucial to the careers of aspiring officials; they affected who entered the local academy and who was eligible to sit for exams, and they mediated disputes and legal cases involving degree-holders. Because of the income and leisure that this post could afford, education officials also became important patrons of scholarship in the eighteenth century. Even for men whose goals were not to join the immortals in Peking, these local patronage networks set up through the exams and schools were crucial to a career.

Money, usually in the form of gifts exchanged between patrons and clients, was an essential element in most networks. It became as important as the ascriptive ties that were the excuse for the relationships. Some of the money that flowed through these patronage networks came from the private incomes of individual members of the elite, who had their own agricultural, commercial, and investment income. The rest came from "engorgement at the middle"—the shunting off by officials of revenues theoretically owed to the central government. (Sometimes officials handed Peking less than was due; sometimes they collected more than was owed.) The failure to control the growth of tax surcharges may not have harmed local communities in prosperous times and places, for everyone recognized the benefits of having good relations with local officials, but in bad times, the effects were more serious.

Taking the throne in 1736 at age twenty-five, the Qianlong emperor dominated the rest of the century. Like his predecessors, he had his personal favorites, Chinese and Manchu, who were likely to be well known to him through the private memorial system initiated by his grandfather. In the last two decades of his reign, Qianlong showered a handsome young Manchu named Heshen with extraordinary favor. Heshen, himself twenty-five years old when he first attracted the aging ruler's attention, was according to his jealous contemporaries a man of little culture or learning but vast ambition and greed. Within five years of his access to imperial favor, this man with no high degrees was catapulted into the presidency of the Board of Revenue. He was given noble titles, later married his son to the emperor's favorite daughter, and in the period 1797–1798 at the end of Qianlong's life exercised de facto control over three central-government ministries. Although Heshen's personal power was resented by some, others built extensive factional alliances around him and few dared to sound partisan or to question the emperor's judgment by speaking out against him. Not until Qianlong's death in 1799 removed his patron was Heshen arrested and his vast estates confiscated. (The vilification of Heshen by his rivals and their successors in the Jiaqing period remains a major impediment to our understanding of him.)

Kinship, common residence, and common occupation were the most widespread bases for bonds between men in Qing society, but they were used in a variety of combinations to secure employment, promote collective action, and provide assistance for those far from home. Many used an endowed fund as the basis for corporate activity and relied on such wealth to perpetuate the association over many generations. In the eighteenth century, the existence of lineages, temple organizations, large-scale businesses, and factional networks became commonplace. Although the state discouraged all forms of association beyond the family as a matter of policy, it in fact depended on a great many elite-dominated organizations to carry out the tasks of government. But, as we shall see in more detail in chapter 4, social and geographical mobility in the eighteenth century also helped create other, less manageable, forms of social organization.

3

Cultural Life

In preceding chapters we introduced some of the fundamental economic and social structures of Qing society. In this chapter we turn to the cultural life of eighteenth-century China, urban and rural, elite and popular. Our definition of culture is a broad one that includes values and beliefs, rituals and festivals, and the material culture of daily life. These aspects of society are difficult for historians to recapture, partly because we lack the kinds of materials that anthropologists have at their disposal but also because few historians have ventured far into these waters. Even a cursory survey of the major topics, however, should convince readers of their fascination and, we hope, prompt others to enter this field.

CITY LIFE

We begin with urban culture, not because we do not appreciate the importance of the countryside but because we believe that by late imperial times, all Chinese culture was influenced by what was happening in China's towns and cities. The efflorescence of urban culture in the eighteenth century was based on the resumption of the cycle of urban growth that had begun in the sixteenth century and been temporarily disrupted by the dynastic transition. Although there was no significant increase in the general rate of urbanization in the Qing, a hierarchy of central places ("cities, towns, and other nucleated settlements with central service functions")[1] was created in less developed regions and fleshed out in advanced areas. Administrative centers grew with official encouragement, while commercial towns flourished on their own. The population in

China's macroregions was spread along a spectrum from (in G. W. Skinner's terms) the more remote and empty periphery to the densely populated commercialized cores. The result was a more fully integrated system of central places, reinforced by the close relationship between village and market town and by regular urban migration and sojourning on the part of both rich and poor.

Nanjing, a national cultural center in the late Ming, had been eclipsed by Yangzhou, Suzhou, and Peking in the early Qing. These cities attracted educated men of both landed and mercantile backgrounds, many without degrees, who formed literary coteries, patronized the arts, and consumed on a lavish scale. They set an example for smaller cities and towns and were models for regional metropolises such as Chengdu, Xi'an, and Fuzhou, as well as for the rising cities of the next century—Hankou, Canton, and Shanghai. The growth of urban places facilitated what James T. C. Liu has called the "radiating diffusion" of urban culture.[2] It seems fair to say that in the eighteenth century we can speak of the culture shared by urban residents who came not only from different social strata but also from major cities throughout the empire. State patronage, merchant networks, and geographic mobility were the major ingredients in the process by which this culture was blended and diffused.

The sixteenth-century boom had tied rural markets more closely to cities through marketing networks and merchant associations. Rural elites were also drawn into town. Zhao Jishi, a Huizhou native of the seventeenth century, noted that his father used to say that persons living before the last quarter of the sixteenth century could spend their entire lives without entering the city walls, but that now "people laugh at those who close their doors and don't go out, they consider them unsophisticated."[3] The money economy and its impersonal values penetrated even into remote regions. Commercial expansion was paralleled by increased written and oral communication within the empire: books written for varied audiences were printed and sold widely, popular drama flourished, and more men worked far from home. Sojourners disseminated culture from the countryside to the city and back again. The centralizing influence of the Chinese state, whose administrative centers were overwhelmingly in cities, also affected public behavior, family life, and personal morality. In short, urban culture was important not just for the 5 percent or so of the population that actually resided in central places but for virtually all Chinese.

Chinese society in the developed macroregional cores had its distinctive qualities. The Qing elite had long been concentrated in the densely populated commercialized lowlands and were increasingly attracted to cities and towns. In sharp contrast to the peripheries, where there were few established elites, the cores were only too full of powerful individuals and families jockeying for position. Although competing with one another for wealth and prestige, these elites were quick to unite against threats to their common interests.

Tensions among the degree-holding elite derived both from their attempts to perpetuate their descendants in this status and from conflicts with imperial authority. The dimming of prospects for government careers in the late eighteenth century was felt most strongly in wealthy urban areas. In the cities, upwardly mobile and wealthy merchants imitated literati life-styles even when they did not have official careers and consequently were a ready market for guides to correct behavior written by scholars. Partible inheritance made downward mobility more likely among large elite families, and most household heads were grimly aware of the prospects for family decline. The attitudes of the urban degree-holding elites toward the social mobility so apparent around them were thus profoundly ambivalent.

Literati, generally atomized in their stance toward imperial control, both acted and were acted upon in the struggles for national political power that were waged in prefectural and provincial capitals. Violent resistance was rare, but it did occur during occasional protests against examination corruption. When the list of successful candidates for the *juren* degree in Yangzhou in 1711 included many sons from salt-merchant families, the students who had failed accused the governor-general and the deputy examiner of accepting bribes. More than a thousand candidates paraded through the streets of the city, broke into the prefectural school, and held its director captive. The investigation, which lasted for nine months and became entangled in bureaucratic rivalries and Manchu-Chinese tensions, eventually found the chief examiner, his associates, and some of the successful candidates guilty and condemned them to death.

Such overt protest was unusual, and resistance generally took subtler forms. Local elites in the wealthy Yangtze delta managed, as we have noted, to resist early Qing attempts to carry out new land surveys, and many families not only influenced local affairs from behind the scenes but eventually began to organize and encroach on government authority. The relationship between the government and merchants was likewise an ambivalent one. Officials might informally cede municipal authority to merchant organizations in cities that were not seats of government, but such open concessions were slower to come in administrative centers. In the course of the century, however, merchant groups became the most dynamic community leaders and the source of numerous welfare and municipal services. By the nineteenth century, this process of literati and merchant usurpation of government functions in cities was well advanced.

Traditional urban landmarks were the city wall and moat, drum and bell tower, Confucian and city-god temples, magistrate's office, military barracks, and examination hall. Eighteenth-century cities and towns were also dotted with restaurants, theaters, merchant *huiguan*, and the mansions and villas of the elite. The value of urban real estate was climbing, and (despite high mortality rates) construction to keep up with business expansion and the tripling of population was probably continuous during the eighteenth century. Commercial activities within cities were also being intensified (the number of pawnshops may have tripled) and had long since spilled over beyond the walls along the roads and rivers. As we have suggested, city services such as relief, security, fire fighting, and road maintenance were gradually being performed by associations of sojourning merchants.

Excitement and entertainment was provided for city residents at public events such as the arrival and departure of officials, executions and funerals, temple celebrations and seasonal holidays. Monumental imperial constructions provided space for ceremonies in which community leaders participated (such as the rites celebrating Confucius' birthday), while public spaces for elite activities (like Tiger Hill in Suzhou or West Lake in Hangzhou) became more numerous as one moved from a market town up to a county seat and thence to a metropolis. Most temples had a courtyard in which members of the community could gather, and open space for markets provided meeting places in cities of all sizes for the populace at large.

One component of urban culture was literacy, stimulated by commercialization and urbanization. Of course, education was not restricted to cities: most elementary instruction was privately financed and took place within well-to-do households and in village and lineage schools. The narrowing of hereditary privilege and more open access to the examination system of the early Qing were important incentives for education, but there were also other rewards for literacy. Qing society relied increasingly on written records and signed contracts in the management of business, voluntary associations, lineages, and local affairs. The urban milieu particularly enhanced and encouraged literacy, even if one's sole motivation was to avoid being cheated. Cities had an abundance of posted regulations, shop signs, placards, advertisements, and other materials to read for profit and amusement. Literacy for women was also more likely in cities where there would be private tutors for the daughters of the elite and brothels specializing in educated courtesans for an elegant clientele.

The creation of Qing urban culture was stimulated in addition by some unintended consequences of educational expansion. Of course, there was a general correlation between urban prosperity and examination success; indeed, there are indications that in the eighteenth century even provincial degree-holders in the highly urbanized Yangtze delta came more and more often from cities. But in the most densely populated and prosperous regions, a sharpening of examination competition turned many intellectuals away from orthodox careers to activities in the cultural realm.

Book publishing took place across a highly differentiated spectrum in the Qing. While imperial patronage led to huge publication projects ranging from encyclopedias and histories to poetry and sutras, commercial firms from the Lower and Middle Yangtze produced primers, fiction, morality books, and plays. These in turn were imitated in cheaper form by printers in other regions and smaller towns. Ming novels that attained wide circulation in the Qing included *Romance of the Three Kingdoms*, a fictionalized account of the breakdown of central-government authority in the second century that immortalized the sworn brotherhood of Liu Bei, Zhang Fei, and Guan Yu (who later became the god Guandi), as well as Liu Bei's wily adviser, Zhuge Liang. *Water Margin*, "traditional China's best-loved novel," described a righteous brotherhood of outlaws who protected the humble and oppressed. *Journey to the West*, China's first allegorical novel about the seventh-century pilgrimage of the monk Xuanzang to India in search of Buddhist scriptures, presented unforgettable characters in the timid monk's companions, Monkey, the irrepressible hero, and Zhu Bajie, the greedy pig. These novels were extremely popular in the Qing; episodes appeared in drama and other forms of oral performance, in temple decorations, posters, and proverbs, so that even illiterate peasants knew the plots and major characters.

Urban elites had their own more exclusive urban culture. Rural residence could not match the lures of the large city, with its well-stocked booksellers, luxury goods, excellent food and drink, and above all the company of kindred spirits. Elite entertainment ranged from parties and outings to writing poetry, raising flowers, attending the theater, and traveling to visit friends and famous sites. The wealthy and cultured collected rare objects: books, paintings, calligraphy, seals, bronzes, curios, and rubbings. The rich did so on a grand scale; the others imitated as best they could. Unlike the fine individualist painters of the seventeenth century, many amateurs were willing and—because of eager merchant patronage—able to paint for a living. Jin Nong (1687–1773), an artist whose calligraphy imitated the archaic inscriptions on bronzes then being collected and analyzed by scholars, took advantage of this public demand for his works, as did the other so-called Eight Eccentrics of Yangzhou. Even more painters became professional academicians at court and enjoyed imperial patronage in Peking.

Sojourning merchants, who had come to regard their business residences as their homes, did not merely ape the literati life-style but were leaders in it. Huizhou merchants, simply to take the most prominent example, made up many of the eighteenth century's preeminent book collectors and patrons of evidential scholarship, and they carried these activities to regions where they sojourned. The list of important eighteenth-century intellectuals and officials from the area is a long one. The Anhui style of painting, exemplified by the spare, geometrical work of Hongren (1610–1663) grew directly out of the woodblock printing and illustrating traditions of Huizhou itself (long a center for book and ink-cake production). The local dramatic style, moreover, was actively promoted and diffused by private merchant companies; toward the end of the eighteenth century, the popularity of the Anhui acrobatic style made it a major ingredient in the development of Peking opera. These Huizhou merchants had also written and published the earliest guidebooks to domestic trade routes, promoted cultivation of the peanut, and set standards for *huiguan* organization and public mindedness. Their innovative activities were paralleled by those of other merchant groups who also operated on a wide scale—especially those from Shanxi, Guangdong, Fujian, and Jiangxi. These national merchants, as we may call them, took their foods, entertainment, and even their gods with them (it was surely no accident that imperially sponsored deities such as Guandi and Tianhou were the patrons of two of these groups); they were key actors in urban life in this period.

Drama ("Chinese opera") was a vital part of Qing culture. The eighteenth century saw both an explosion of dramatic styles (Colin Mackerras has called it "the golden age of regional drama")[4] and the emergence of public theaters and enthusiastic urban audiences. Ming dramas written by and for literati had emphasized scripts and melody, but mid-Qing audiences were just as interested in performance and acting. Opera troupes no longer played just for religious festivals and in the homes of the elite but now moved from one permanent theater to another. Out of the play emporium located in the *huiguan* grew the theater that was a separate building open to the public. Actors had their own guild in Peking by at least 1732, the Imperial Household set up its large private troupe in 1740, and by 1816 there were twenty-one public theaters in the capital.

Imperial and merchant patronage both played key roles in the circulation of dramatic forms as well as in the growth of theatrical institutions. Merchants carried their own troupes and regional dramatic styles with them, while the emperor and metropolitan officials eagerly imported famous actors to the capital. By the end of the century, patrons in Peking were determining fashions for the cities throughout China from which aspiring actors and patrons came.

In the late Ming, the elegant and melodic Kunqu style that had originated in Jiangsu had attracted the energies of literati playwrights and the admiration of Lower Yangtze elites. Kunqu's popularity continued in the early Qing, enhanced by Kangxi's attentions on his southern tours and by the successful plays of Hong Shen (*The Palace of Eternal Youth*, 1684) and Kong Shangren (*The Peach-Blossom Fan*, 1699). Literati and official devotees kept the tradition alive in the eighteenth century, even though it yielded center stage to more upstart styles from other regions. Competition was offered mainly by the Yiyang style from Jiangxi and its numerous Lower Yangtze variants that emphasized noisy, faster music and colloquial prose sections popular with less refined audiences; it was carried by merchant patrons to Peking and beyond in the early Qing. Similarly, the Qinqiang of the Northwest was transported by the ubiquitous Shanxi and Shaanxi merchants. This dramatic style used very colloquial language and lewd innuendoes and was known for its reliance on seductive female impersonators in starring roles. It became immensely popular in the 1770s and 1780s when there were dozens of Qinqiang companies in many major cities, playing in public theaters to enraptured male audiences. Wei Changsheng, a Sichuanese female impersonator with a bewitching manner, was the most famous Qinqiang actor of his day, lionized after his 1779–1780 performances in Peking, probably on the occasion of the Qianlong emperor's seventieth birthday.

The explicit sexuality of such performances offended conservatives in the capital, and in 1785 this Qin style was formally banned in Peking, making way for other regional styles. The "clapper opera" of the Northwest, with its reliance on loud instruments, and the acrobatic troupes of Anhui developed a wide following and reflected the new popularity of more martial subjects. By the 1830s, the ingredients of Peking opera were in place, and it became the dominant theatrical form in the capital in the late nineteenth century.

Official denunciations of drama as a corrupting influence on public morals were belied by imperial enthusiasm and eager patronage even by members of the Hanlin Academy, but attempts to keep political topics off the stage were a good deal more successful. Subjects for drama that had flourished in the Kangxi period such as examination corruption, Manchu-Chinese relations, and late Ming history disappeared in the Qianlong reign. An immense repertory of scripts was nevertheless developed (more than one thousand were listed in a 1780 survey), and scholar-beauty romantic comedies and historical dramas became part of the common culture of urban audiences everywhere.

Drama of a popular sort lived side by side with the performances sponsored by the elite; indeed, the popular drama of the commercial urban theater had first grown out of and then in turn reinvigorated the local opera troupes that worked without fixed scripts or theaters. These troupes in their turn were intimately connected with street entertainers who featured story telling, puppet shows, instrumental performance, and ballad singing. Not only were there interlocking influences in terms of instruments and stage styles but also strong continuities in terms of the stories themselves. Tales from the *Journey to the West* and *Three Kingdoms* story-cycles were the basis of countless variations and levels of performance. Because some troupes went regularly into the countryside to perform at temple festivals (where such performances were essential) there was also a continuous transmission of urban drama into the countryside. More than any other activity, drama in the Qing period contributed to cultural integration and to the vitality of a Chinese culture in which all could share.

Drama was not the sole form of Qing urban culture that came under censure. Gambling—in the form of dice, cards, and betting on cock, quail, and cricket fights—was commonplace among all social classes, despite repeated official assertions that it was associated with crime and violence. Less troublesome but still distressing to some, the sexuality of the opera stage was reflected in the real world as well. Prostitutes and actors, overlapping categories and both supposedly degraded statuses, behaved as the social equals and the bedfellows of the elite. Male and female prostitution were booming businesses, flourishing at all urban levels from Peking down to the remotest mining camp in the southwest. There was a national traffic in beautiful concubines and elegant male servants, in "jade cocoons" (young girls) and "little hands" (young boys).

The popularity of female impersonators in the Qianlong reign brought a new stylishness to homosexual relationships. Bi Yun (1730–1797), a respected scholar-official, had publicly installed a young male actor as a kind of wife, a relationship parodied in the salacious early nineteenth-century play, *Precious Mirror for Gazing at "Flowers."* The fondness of the aging Qianlong emperor for Heshen and the latter's patronage of handsome actors gave an unspoken encouragement to such relationships.

"Decadence" and "extravagance" were already the objects of criticism by conservative officials such as Zhang Ying, who at the end of the seventeenth century had warned his descendants against the evils of urban residence. In 1781, Liu Tiancheng (probably a censor) memorialized about the social problems of the Qianlong reign. He criticized the wasteful expenditures that took place in inns, teahouses, and wine shops, where men were reckless with their money and indulged in drunken sprees, spending in a day what could suffice for several. The emperor replied by pointing to the peace and prosperity of the empire, noting that this admitted shift from frugality to extravagance could not be easily controlled by fiat. Nor would curbing wastefulness lead necessarily to the betterment of the populace. "I labor night and day; it is not that I do not desire that the people's mores become simple and pure. . . . But customs daily become more extravagant and the situation cannot be altered by law; just as the waters of the rivers flow east, who can block them and turn them westward? . . . Liu Tiancheng's memorial is acceptable as good counsel, but it is not a good method for ruling in today's world."[5] Qianlong realistically recognized that this style of life was imbedded in the conditions of the times.

But mobility and change—as well as prosperity—were reflected in the urban life of the eighteenth century, and mobility also meant insecurity. The highly commercialized ethos undermined traditional relationships and produced a stratified society rife with both opportunity and anxiety. The repercussions of market participation touched virtually every sphere of life: as peddlers, peasants, landlords, and others came together in periodic markets, the horizons of the peasant's vision were gradually broadened. Exposure to market forces tied household welfare to forces operating outside the village and raised the value of knowledge about the larger world. Money became the measure not only of exchange but of accomplishment as well.

While many sought upward mobility, others feared the loss of their wealth and status. Members of the old degree-holding elite looked with alarm on the nouveaux riches who challenged their position as cultural and social arbiters. The anxiety of elite families as they contemplated strategies for maintaining their status struck a responsive note in more ambitious villagers too. Those who produced cash crops were exposed to price fluctuations beyond their control, and the risks and benefits of market participation must surely have sharpened the competitive environment in which villagers lived. Intergenerational mobility was probably enhanced: peasant households moved up and down the socioeconomic scale in their villages in response to market as well as domestic cycles. The impact of market participation on peasant mentality lies behind Elvin's observation that "society became restless, fragmented and fiercely competitive."[6] The system of spiritual credits expressed in late Ming morality books such as *The Ledger of Merits and Demerits*, widely reprinted, can be interpreted as an attempt to link charity and moral action to material reward and provide reassurance in a world that had grown more fluid and unstable. But the social problems created by a more complex competitive milieu continued to feed feelings of insecurity and anxiety.

Economic conflict and competition were endemic, particularly in expanding sectors such as the rice or soybean trades. Incidents that some see as class conflict were commonplace. Rice riots pitted consumers against merchants and potentially against landlords, who often stored grain in cities. Labor unrest was frequent in places like Suzhou, where, as we have seen, the expansion of the textile industry in the late seventeenth century brought a large and potentially menacing group of unskilled workers into the city. Such incidents, even if few in number, point to the problems of controlling a work force under conditions of rapid growth in China's large cities.

LITERATI CULTURE

Although the literati acted as natural informal leaders in cities and towns and, together with merchants, played important roles in the creation of a distinctive urban culture, they also tried to maintain more refined traditions in scholarship, art, and entertainment—traditions nurtured at home in rural villas and academies, traditions that would distinguish the well bred and well educated from the merely rich. The realm of literati culture was both urban and rural. It was dominated by the households whose males prepared for and won degrees but in the Qing it was invaded more and more by the monied and leisured.

In the 1680s to 1710s, after completion of the conquest, the Qing rulers had succeeded in bridging the gulf between their new regime and the Chinese scholarly community by relying on intermediaries like the three Xu brothers of Kunshan, Jiangsu, who won degrees under the Qing and then served as directors of the *Ming History* project, attracting and employing others who would never have served directly under the new dynasty. Many intellectuals found solace in comparing Manchu to Mongol rule, concluding that Chinese culture could not merely survive but indeed flourish under a foreign dynasty. The goal of preserving the culture under such conditions presented some with the rationale for serving the Manchus. Semiofficial patronage brought the government and the intellectual community together and was "crucial to the legitimation of Qing rule."[7]

Evidential (*kaozheng*) scholarship, the major intellectual movement of the early Qing, flourished in the Yangtze-delta cities where official and private patrons were located. Reacting sharply against Confucian developments of the preceding seven hundred years, scholars blamed the downfall of the Ming dynasty on literati pursuit of sagehood and involvement in factional disputes. Instead, early Qing literati sought to reconstruct the ideal Confucian order through philological attention to ancient texts. They searched for the Confucianism of an earlier age, before it had been sullied with Buddhist and Taoist notions. Rejecting Zhu Xi's method of interpreting the classics broadly, evidential scholars focused on close study of the texts themselves, subjecting the classics to rigorous philological tests. In the process, men such as Yan Ruoju (1636–1704) began to raise serious questions about the very authenticity of classics that had long been accepted as the source of enduring absolutes, although these doubts remained submerged in stronger currents of confidence in the heritage of the past. Similarly, although the methods of these evidential scholars were influenced by their knowledge of European mathematics and astronomy, and their academies included mathematics, astronomy, and geography in the curriculum, it would not be until the nineteenth century when the adequacy of the Chinese tradition was seriously challenged.

Philological studies went hand in hand with extensive printing and library building on the part of such men as Huang Peilie (1763–1825) in Suzhou and Bao Tingbo (1728–1814) and his fellow bibliophiles in Hangzhou. In the Yangtze delta, these scholars formed what Benjamin Elman has called a unified academic community with a distinctly professional outlook. The men who were the leaders in evidential study were overwhelmingly degree-holders from the Lower Yangtze core: one study of 180 important works of evidential scholarship shows that almost 90 percent of the writers were from Jiangnan, 92 percent held degrees, and more than half (53 percent) were *jinshi*.

The introversion of this specialized community, seen in its rejection of Socratic modes of discourse or any kind of lectures (to the public or one another), was in deliberate contrast to those Ming Neo-Confucian schools inspired by the sixteenth-century philosopher Wang Yangming that had been innovative in precisely these directions. Evidential scholars relied on the patronage of leading officials, but they generally did not become bureaucrats themselves; those who aspired to enter the civil service were still better off studying in the Zhu Xi tradition. Evidential scholarship still had a concern with government, however, and an interest in practical affairs that was developed in statecraft writings on hydraulics, cartography, and governance.

Compilation projects flourished in this intellectual milieu: local histories were compiled and published on a scale previously unknown. The government-sponsored *Complete Library of the Four Treasuries* project (1772–1782) was the most important and politically the most sensitive compilation effort of all. An imperial commission undertook to collect for reprinting the best editions of the most important books and manuscripts hitherto produced in China and arranged them in the four categories of classics, history, philosophy, and belles lettres. Several hundred literati participated in looking for and inspecting books from private libraries and the imperial collection. As R. Kent Guy has pointed out, under the direction of distinguished scholars like Dai Zhen (1724–1777), evidential methods of evaluating texts, collating variant editions, and revising or verifying errors were used in this effort, and the compilation may be seen as a cardinal achievement of the evidential school. Eventually seven sets of thirty-six thousand volumes each were reproduced, along with an extremely valuable annotated catalogue of the more than ten thousand works inspected by the compilers.

The darker side of the project, the ferreting out and destruction of some two thousand works deemed subversive by the throne, many of them dating from the late Ming, has prompted some scholars to call this project a "literary inquisition." As Guy shows, however, a detailed study of this inquisition reveals the complicity of Chinese in it. Success in obtaining the best editions rested on the cash paid out for these tomes by salt merchants as well as provincial treasuries; moreover, the campaign to collect seditious materials had faltered until responsibility was turned over to expectant educational officials, who were to be rewarded with appointments for their diligence. Since such posts were very difficult to get, ambitious *juren* flooded provincial-government offices with books, only then permitting the inquisition to attain its full destructive potential.

Evidential scholarship and government projects were for the cream of the elite. Other important eighteenth-century literati activities had a broader spatial and social base, encompassing unsuccessful scholars and holders of lower academic degrees scattered across the country. These men defined themselves as much by contrast with the commoner populace as with the capital elite. They regarded the masses in highly ambivalent terms, seeing them both as the proper objects of elite and state paternalism, children who needed constant guidance and instruction, and as dangerous mobs, capable of spontaneous and unrestrained violence. In consequence, like their late Ming predecessors, these elites not only provided concrete assistance to the needy through philanthropy but also wrote and distributed morality books and manuals to indoctrinate and shape behavior.

The fluidity of social statuses and the acceptance of political censorship may have played an indirect role in provoking a pessimism about the ability to achieve sagehood that hounded intellectuals of this age. Pei-yi Wu has described this mood as "a deep awareness of the human proclivity to evil, an urgent need to counter this proclivity, a readiness for self-disclosure, and a deep anguish over one's own wrongdoings"—an attitude revealed in unprecedented public confessions by Confucians of their sin and unworthiness that represent "a new development in the history of Chinese moral culture,"[8] one that may be linked to the new emphasis on internalization of values and self-judgment seen in the morality-book literature of the time.

Alienation is an important theme in the eighteenth century, continuing into the late Qing. The increased dissonance between the difficulty in achieving the educational and moral qualifications theoretically necessary for high status and political leadership and the ease with which money could now buy these privileges aggravated the frustrations of some failed scholars. They viewed official society with an increasingly critical and cynical eye. Wu Jingzi, author of *The Scholars*, is a case in point: a licentiate from a prominent literati family in Anhui, he could not win a higher degree and eventually squandered his family's wealth. The novel Wu wrote in the 1730s and 1740s attacked an officialdom rotted by toadying and corruption and an examination system that rewarded mindlessness and incompetence. Only a few decent individuals escaped his mockery. Wu's relatively sympathetic portrayal of women—who were barred from the professional world of men and were thus in some sense untainted by it—was later surpassed in Li Ruzhen's novel, *Flowers in the Mirror* (published 1828), a fantasy in which women are shown as capable bureaucrats and officials. In fact, the vernacular novel attained new stature in China in the eighteenth century as a respectable intellectual endeavor and a vehicle for the expression both of political criticism and orthodox values. The middle Qing witnessed the production of two other major works of prose fiction: the 445 short stories of Pu Songling in *Strange Stories from an Eccentric's Studio* (written 1669–1679, published 1766) and Cao Xueqin's *Dream of Red Mansions* (written 1754–1763, printed 1792).

For the authors of these and other, lesser-known works, literature itself was very nearly their career. Wu Jingzi subsisted in Nanjing on his writing, supplemented with gifts from friends and relatives. The successful poet and official Yuan Mei (1716–1798), like many literati, contributed to the growing corpus of short-story literature that included ghost, detective, historical, and romantic tales written and read by urban elites. But even Yuan, who was relatively successful at making money from his writings (which he published himself), had to rely on private commissions for a large part of his income. Not until the very end of the dynasty would it be possible for intellectuals to support themselves by writing for a mass audience.

In painting, the eighteenth century saw a reintegration of the court-sponsored style and literati painting that had followed separate lines of development in the Ming dynasty. Literati painters such as Wang Hui (1632–1717) and Wang Yuanqi (1642–1715) were invited to the Kangxi court and accepted imperial patronage. There, versatility, mastery of technique, and a willingness to work on a grand scale were preferred to the individualism of masters of the seventeenth century like Daoji and Zhu Da. Instead, the theories of the Ming painter Dong Qichang were enshrined as the new orthodoxy. The Qianlong emperor carried on the cultural and literary style of the Kangxi reign. He became the greatest imperial art collector since the Song, acquiring the masterworks of past eras, compiling catalogues, and—in this field as in many others—dictating taste from Peking, where literary and artistic talent gathered. Artists, even European Jesuits such as Guiseppe Castiglione (who painted under the Chinese name Lang Shining), were used to record the rituals at court and commemorate victories on the battlefield.

Art connoisseurs and historians may deprecate Qianlong's own poetic and artistic abilities, but no one can deny the impact of his taste on his age. His preference for the monumental and the didactic, for art that was decorative, exotic, ornate, and extravagant, had an overwhelming influence. In addition, the objects gathered in imperial collections, although as various as the complex empire that Qianlong ruled, were limited by the safe confines of orthodox practice and further tamed by the stamp of the imperial seal or brush. Diversity there was, but diversity contained and homogenized.

Imperial patronage made possible greater access to the inspirational works of the past and encouraged a creative exchange of artists between the capital and the Lower Yangtze. There art collections were also a sign of culture, and paintings were in high demand among men of wealth and uncertain status. The intimacy and spontaneity of the centuries-old literati painting tradition were imperiled by these eager attentions, and, as we have noted, artists able to resist the lure of the court found their amateur status threatened by the temptations of professionalism at home. The gentleman invited to paint for a rich patron preferred not to be reminded that he was also being paid to do so. These uneasy distinctions were expressed not only in social relations but also in the subjects painted. Refined amateurs clung to landscape painting, following a long stylistic tradition of *fang*, or imitation of the ancients. The constant stylistic allusion to earlier paintings fed an intellectualized perspective characteristic of this whole period: style became subject, deliberately selected to express the artist's position.

Merchant patrons, by contrast, wanted more accessible subject matter. They preferred portraits, intimate scenes of city life, or decorative pictures of birds and flowers. Many painters therefore practiced a kind of calculated amateurism, one that imitated only the forms of the past; others were unabashedly professional, selling seasonal pictures or paintings of a preferred style in city shops. Even the so-called eccentrics of Yangzhou were only able to present themselves as the heirs of past individualism by departing from the expected forms in accessible ways. Nevertheless, Luo Ping's casual portraits of himself and his acquaintances presumed an intimacy and informality that would have been inappropriate at court and shocking to dignified literati of earlier eras. Even refined patrons, such as the Ma brothers (Yangzhou salt merchants), liked a straightforward and unpretentious style. Fang Shishu's 1743 painting commemorating the visit of the scholar Quan Zuwang was actually no more than a kind of souvenir photograph of the occasion. That scholars, merchants, retired officials, and quasi-professional painters could meet as members of a poetry club, in a villa purchased with mercantile profits, is characteristic of elite life in this period.

PLATE 3. The poet Fang Shishu and the Suzhou portraitist Ye Fanglin collaborated to produce this memento of the double-ninth celebration in 1743 at the Yangzhou villa of the wealthy Ma brothers, Huizhou salt merchants who were patrons of the arts. Each guest wrote on the painting, and an essay describing the event was appended to the handscroll, which captures the mix of old and new money and the activities typical of the eighteenth-century elite. This detail from the painting depicts guests (including retired officials, poets, and painters) examining a scroll and listening to the zither in the garden. A colophon by the poet Li E captures their mood: "We are lucky in being born during a reign of peace, in a place of beauty, and in the company of friends who are cultured and understanding. How rare indeed are such gatherings in this world!" (cited in Ju-hsi Chou and Claudia Brown, eds., *The Elegant Brush: Chinese Painting under the Qianlong Emperor, 1735–1795* (Phoenix: Phoenix Art Museum, 1985), p. 137. Reproduced from the Cleveland Museum of Art, the Severance and Greta Millikin Purchase Fund.

Would-be artists without connections could not study the great masterworks of the past, for there were no museums of public collections, but the vigorous Qing book industry popularized art as well as literature and philosophy. The *Mustard Seed Garden Manual of Painting*, first published in Nanjing in 1679, expanded in 1701, and thereafter republished many times, was intended to teach the fundamentals to anyone. Styles of the past were illustrated (not always correctly), and the method of painting different kinds of rocks, trees, animals, and so forth was shown step by step.

Even in poetry the privileged world of the scholar was opened up to a wider public. Of course poetry continued to be one of the hallmarks of high literati culture. The ability to compose and write elegant poems was considered essential to any young man's education—and indeed to many young women's. The literary man had to master a variety of complex rhyme schemes and verse forms, compose quickly in public, write elegantly in fine calligraphy, and sound original while alluding to a poetic tradition stretching back more than a thousand years. Those able to publish their verse did so, and in large numbers. A popular genre of this period was a kind of anthology of poetry (or sometimes an album of sketches or a combination of the two) that a man put together by inviting contributions from as many influential people as he could, usually on the pretext of honoring a teacher or friend, in order to display his connections and good taste.

For outsiders seeking acceptance and status in this society (Manchus, men from culturally deprived regions, upwardly mobile merchants), skill at poetry could be proof of social acceptability. In *The Scholars* a young man whose family's shop sold incense and candles admitted, "Tradesmen like us can't dream of passing the examinations. All I want is to read a few poems to acquire a little refinement." When asked if he could understand these poems, he confessed, "Very few of them. But when I can understand one or two lines, that makes me very happy."[9]

Although some dour scholars and bureaucrats saw the writing of poetry as an expression of the frivolity of the young, Qing examinations in fact tested this skill; in 1757 poetry was made a still more important part of the exam curriculum. Poetry clubs provided occasions for drinking and conviviality among friends, but, because they were also one of the few acceptable informal associations among the elite, they also provided networks for more serious endeavors—preparation for exams, literary and scholarly discussion, or simply social and political advancement. In the early nineteenth century, the Xuannan Poetry Club in Peking served even more ambitious political purposes among its reform-minded members.

In poetry, as in painting, there were occasional eighteenth-century individualist poets like Yuan Mei, a number of important scholarly theorists and critics, and a great many of the ponderously erudite. (Qianlong was a model for the latter.) Those in the Changzhou (Jiangsu) school who were concerned with the poetic form known as the *ci*, for example, tried to analyze and shape this tradition by charting a course (as painters were also trying to do) between the accessible and vulgar, on the one hand, and the elegant and incomprehensible on the other. It is indicative of the increasing politicization of scholarship at the turn of the century that Zhang Huiyan (1761–1802) and others tried to claim that the best use of the *ci* was actually for allegory.

The eighteenth century, like the seventeenth, was a great age of travel, and through travelers both urban and more narrowly literati culture were diffused throughout the empire. Not only did men of all social classes sojourn in search of employment, but many of the wealthy traveled simply for pleasure. Literary men visited friends, sought patrons, or undertook employment; officials were shifted from post to post; merchants inspected branch businesses and new opportunities. The explosion of local history projects under the patronage of Qing provincial officials sent scholars out to find stone stelae, abandoned monasteries, and famous pagodas. Others went in search of the sites of famous events, graves of historical figures, mountains painted by earlier artists, vistas commemorated in well-known poems, caverns and grottos noted for their mystery and beauty. The "jottings" literature of the period that circulated in manuscript and in print included accounts of these travels, generally making members of the educated class (and those who aspired to that status) better informed about the large and diverse empire in which they lived.

We have tried to indicate in this section the ways in which the fashions and activities associated with China's degree-holding elite were opened up to the socially ambitious. In the process, attenuated literati arts and their defenders were nearly swamped in the sea of eighteenth-century urban culture, diluted but perhaps also reinvigorated in more popular and vulgar styles.

The literati and their imitators were the pacesetters for China's urban culture, and they were certainly far removed from the culture of peasants in their commitment to the arts and letters. At the same time, it would be a mistake to think of the cultural gap between China's highest social strata and the peasantry as a deep chasm. We have already pointed out that drama and storytelling gave literatus and peasant a shared knowledge of China's past and helped create common values and ideals. When we turn to material culture and to life-cycle rituals, we see additional confirmation of the broadly based cultural practices that Han Chinese shared during Qing times.

MATERIAL CULTURE

The objects of daily life, from food and clothing to dwelling places, were yet further expressions of late imperial culture that reflected both the elaborate differentiation among social strata and their integration through a common core of symbolic meaning. In material culture, as in other spheres, the two centers of taste were the Lower Yangtze cities and Peking. Qianlong and his predecessors undertook construction and production of public architecture and the decorative arts on a lavish scale and were responsible for creating many of the monuments and treasures of this period. The literati artistic achievements of the stressful seventeenth century, though never equaled in the eighteenth, were, as we have seen, integrated and diffused in the Qing as part of a broader and less troubled elite culture. Just as innovations in drama and vernacular fiction became established as part of a nationwide urban culture, so regional cuisines, fashionable apparel, and elegant homes were made part of the common vocabulary and experience of a wider elite.

The broad divisions of China into dry cropland and irrigated lowlands underlay traditional divisions in staple foods: gruels, breads, and noodles made from wheat, millet, barley, and sorghum in the north; glutinous and nonglutinous rice in the south. The development of upland farming on the peripheries in the middle Qing added a third set of basic foods that made an immediate impact on Chinese diet (but not cuisine): maize, sweet potatoes, and white potatoes. The diet everywhere and for most people consisted primarily of cereals. Chicken and pork were luxuries, and as a consequence protein came mostly from beans and fish, while vegetable oil (including that of the recently introduced peanut) was an important source of essential fats. Fresh vegetables were available seasonally in colder climates and more abundantly in southern regions.

Regional and seasonal dietary patterns constrained those of modest means, but in the eighteenth century marketing networks provided an expanding variety of foods for the well-to-do. Emperors consumed delicacies imported from all over the empire and abroad, while some wealthy families enjoyed elaborate cuisines that combined subtle flavors and rare ingredients. Most householders lived on moderate and less varied diets. Peasants did not eat meat except during festivals, a time when everyone was supposed to enjoy special foods and eat until full. Even the relatively wealthy merchants in the Chinese community at Nagasaki, Japan, had a daily diet of rice with pickles and vegetables, supplemented with meat or fish twice a day.

Like every preindustrial cuisine, Chinese food was marked by distinctive seasonal and regional delicacies, but the circulation of officials and travelers through the empire and the increase in sojourners in the major cities spread consciousness and appreciation of different foods. One characteristic of Qing city life was its opportunities for eating out.

Restaurants catering to regional tastes served banquets for all levels of clients. It was probably in the eighteenth century that the American red pepper became established as a landmark of Hunanese and Sichuanese food. In Muslim restaurants, located throughout China, believers could observe religious prohibitions against eating pork, while others could sample beef and lamb dishes of Central Asian origin.

Tea was, of course, a universal beverage, and teahouses were to be found in most central places. A multiplicity of varieties, from the strongly fermented Puer tea of southern Yunnan to the light, fragrant, green teas of the Lower Yangtze, satisfied the tastes of different regions and social classes but also developed national constituencies. Chinese wine, always served warm, was likewise made and sold everywhere. Although perhaps not everyone was in the habit of drinking wine with every meal, as were nine out of ten families on the remote Penghu islands (according to the 1770 local gazetteer), it does appear that alcohol had become a regular part of the diet of most people. A great many varieties made from a range of grains were available, but only a few became nationally known—Fenjiu, a distilled liquor prized by Shanxi merchants, for example, or Shaoxing, a milder, sweet wine championed by its sojourning clerks and officials.

The Chinese had eagerly adopted tobacco smoking in the late Ming and had already made it a national habit. Most people smoked it in a water pipe, but elites (possibly instructed by foreigners at court) began to take snuff. The snuff bottle, a small container made of some precious material (porcelain, glass, jade, and so forth) and carried on the person, was a Qing innovation. (See plate 5.) The eighteenth century also saw Chinese begin to be addicted to opium. Long used as a medicine and aphrodisiac, crude opium (*madak*) was first mixed with tobacco and smoked in the seventeenth century by Chinese in Southeast Asia and then along the Southeast Coast and in Taiwan. Conversion to smoking pure opium seems to have occurred by the 1760s, and during the late eighteenth century the habit spread along the trade networks out of Fujian and Guangdong among transport workers, soldiers, merchants, and officials. Attempts to prohibit the drug (once in 1729 and repeatedly in the early nineteenth century) failed to dislodge opium from its new place as a food substitute, painkiller, and source of cheap pleasure.

The Chinese repertory of tools for mining, metallurgy, agriculture, food processing, textile production, transport, housing construction, and domestic chores does not appear to have changed significantly in the early and middle Qing—unlike in Europe and the United States, where a machine-tool industry that would speed industrialization was emerging.

But the printing and distribution of illustrated reference works, almanacs, and manuals of many sorts did make traditional techniques available throughout the length and breadth of the empire.

In clothing, the major textiles—silk, cotton, and hemp—had been known for some time. It was in the seventeenth and eighteenth centuries, however, that cotton became universally available, displacing less satisfactory materials (ramie, hemp, or bark cloth) and no doubt resulting in a major increase in comfort and convenience. Silk was no longer required for tax payments, and, stimulated by demand from appreciative foreigners, a range of weaves became available to others besides the rich.

The Manchus brought with them a tradition of nomadic apparel that was not only reflected in the mandatory queue (which necessitated a man's forehead being shaven and his hair braided at the back of his head) but was also incorporated into court dress. A closely fitting jacket that was slit to allow riding in the saddle, with tight sleeves to keep out the wind and cuffs to protect the back of the hands; trousers to provide protection from the horse's flanks; riding boots and fur-lined caps—these were now official garb. As in previous eras, the designs of all official and ceremonial garments were based on traditional cosmological symbols; rank was indicated by color, embroidered insignia, and jeweled knobs on hats. An elaborate code was issued in 1759 in an attempt to regulate the ceremonial dress of officials. Manchus adopted Chinese clothing in their private lives, and their large-footed women soon learned to wear platform shoes that simulated delicate bound feet. (See plate 4.) Ming-style clothing continued to dominate informal wear, wedding attire, theatrical costumes, and robes for priests and temple images.

The characters in the novel *Dream of Red Mansions* display not merely their considerable wealth but their imperial connections (the author came from a Han banner family) in their clothing: beautiful silks in an array of dazzling shades, boots and capes lined with exotic furs, and gold-and-pearl earrings. And yet, despite the imperial monopoly on the finest embroideries, silk weaves, and rarest gems (often given away as gifts), conspicuous consumption among the well-to-do was as common in clothing as in food and entertainment. Among the upper elite, changes in the length of the coat or width of the hat were dictated by fashion as the styles of the trend-setting elites of Peking, Suzhou, Hangzhou, and Yangzhou were gradually diffused to urban and mercantile elites of other cities. Sumptuary laws attempted to regulate the dress of officials and degree-holders but, given the large number of social climbers, were

PLATE 4. Ornate and richly textured cloisonné enamels were extremely popular during the Qianlong reign and reflect the prevailing elite taste of the era. The cloisonné figures shown here represent a Manchu and a Chinese woman, both of high social status. Although the Manchu woman's hairstyle is decidedly more elaborate, she is wearing platform shoes to make her large feet look less ungainly by comparison with the elegant and tiny bound feet of her Chinese counterpart. Reproduced from the Metropolitan Museum of Art, gift of Mr. A. W. Bahr, 1954 (54.154.2ab).

probably effective only with regard to court dress. The supply and demand for expensive clothing were impossible to control.

Like clothing, styles and taste in jewelry, porcelain, and other goods were influenced by demand from literati, rich merchants, and the throne. Jade, theoretically an Imperial Household monopoly, became available on a new scale in this period. Thanks to trade routes through the Southwest, wealthy consumers in Peking and the Lower Yangtze quickly acquired a taste for the rich green colors of Burmese jade. After Xinjiang with its major deposits of jade was incorporated into the empire in 1759, a substantial illegal caravan traffic soon grew up; in 1773 the monopoly was abandoned, and this most highly prized of rare materials was bought and sold on an unprecedented scale.

Imperially run factories turned out decorative objects in glass, metal, lacquerware, wood, ivory, and porcelain as well as jade. In the imperial kilns at Jingdezhen, Jiangxi, the expanding market was reflected in the wide variety of objects of daily use that were made of porcelain— lanterns, screens, chairs, vases, ceremonial objects, and boxes and containers of all kinds. In style, too, we see an eclectic taste founded on a wide-ranging familiarity with earlier periods, knowledge acquired through collecting (private and imperial) and scholarly inquiry. Early Qing monochromes imitated Song styles, but added new colors (purple and black, streaked flambé); like other collectors, the Yongzheng emperor ordered that antique bronzes and jades in the palace be used as models for new shapes. Motifs from one medium were borrowed and used to enrich others: the textures of silver, stone, laquerware, and wood were imitated in porcelain; brocade patterns were used for porcelain borders. The consumer demand for new forms, colors, styles, and textures was very great. This was an era when minor arts such as lacquer and cloisonné and a taste for the rococo flourished.

Foreign demand for Chinese porcelain in this period stimulated production and encouraged the manufacture of objects in foreign styles (bowls with coats of arms, etc.). Though made primarily for export, they also shaped Chinese tastes. The delicate translucent enamels on white background known in the west as *famille verte* and *famille rose* were creations of the Yongzheng and Qianlong reigns, the pink shade a studied imitation of European techniques. The milky white (*blanc de chine*) Dehua figurines from Fujian included Chinese gods as well as Dutch horsemen. The reddish stoneware teapots from Yixing (Jiangsu), on the other hand, were made in a variety of irregular shapes highly prized by literati both in Japan and China. In addition to the many kinds of elite porcelain, Qing kilns produced chinaware and stoneware in bulk for the ordinary person at home and abroad. The production of wares of different quality in the same factories assured a diffusion of designs and styles between classes and between localities within China and beyond.

Qing architecture, by contrast, shows little foreign influence. European architecture, transmitted by the Jesuits at court, was the model for a complex of buildings constructed at the summer palace by Qianlong (and destroyed in 1860); but, like the clocks and other gadgets brought by tribute missions, these buildings were largely curiosities, seen by a few, with little influence on native traditions. Instead, Qing architecture had much continuity with a long and conservative tradition that had emphasized harmony with the environment and cyclical rebuilding rather than permanent structures. Wood was the preferred building material, but the demand for lumber in the eighteenth century was so intense that it encouraged the substitution of brick and stone by the less affluent in Peking, and may have done so elsewhere. (One of the charges against Heshen was his extravagant use of the durable and finely textured *nan* wood of western China for his Peking residence.)

Qing emperors constructed a great many grand public buildings in and around the capital, at many national shrines, and in every important administrative center. This elaborate neoclassical style rejected Ming simplicity and was not remarkable for its originality, but it did provide models of traditional techniques and cosmological concepts throughout the empire. In these buildings, as in domestic architecture generally, we can see certain unifying ideas that underlie diverse forms.

Separated from the outside world by a wall, the Chinese house consisted of one or more courtyards between buildings that were usually one story high and one room deep. The layout, as Nelson Wu has noted, permitted "graduated privacy" from the public rooms near the gate to the private rooms at the rear.[10] The Imperial City inside Peking followed this pattern on an enormous scale: a series of concentric walls enclosed the Forbidden City, differentiating between the public halls where the emperor met with officials and envoys and the Great Interior that was open only to the emperor, his women and children, and eunuch servants.

Although peasant homes might have only a few rooms, the number of component hearths, which defined the *jia* units in an extended family, increased as one ascended the social scale. Size and solidity distinguished a landlord's home, walled to protect his wealth. Degree-holders' residences in the Qing could be identified by the ostentatious horizontal plaque and tall flagpole at the main gate. Walled houses, some built with towers at the corners to facilitate defense, became common in areas of high militarization, increasingly so during the nineteenth century. Unusual round multistory houses that emphasized communal solidarity were built by Hakkas. (See plate 8.) Multistory buildings were rare except in cities where crowding and high real-estate values prevailed over a preference for the ground level. One such town, not surprisingly, was Huizhou, which featured many of these two- and three-story merchant houses, usually with the front and back wings of a room facing a central courtyard.

In buildings, as in other aspects of material culture, the life-style once restricted to a few became popular among a great many in the eighteenth century. One manifestation of this trend were the garden villas constructed by late Ming and early Qing elites. They too were built according to traditional formulae but emphasized a more refined taste for irregularity, asymmetry, and surprise. Extensive gardens with pavilions, bridges, ponds, and winding walkways, shut off from the noisy world by high walls and planted with trees and flowers, dotted the major Lower Yangtze cities and inspired imitation elsewhere.

These gardens created a microcosm of the natural world within a controlled environment, arranging earth, rocks, plants, and water around the buildings in ways that (like poetry and painting) were replete with historical and literary allusions. Although the architectural arts were transmitted in an artisanal tradition, many literati designed their own gardens and considered them an expression of their character as well as their taste. Qing emperors imitated Lower Yangtze villas on a grand scale outside Peking and at their summer residence in Rehe, beyond the Great Wall. As wealthy families lost their riches and were forced to sell their homes and properties, others eagerly clamored to become the owners of famous sites. Some of these gardens survive today, but none achieved the enduring recognition of Prospect Garden in *Dream of Red Mansions*, inspired by the Cao family estate of the early eighteenth century but created in the imagination of Cao Xueqin.

By the beginning of the nineteenth century, the circulation of elites through the urban centers of eighteenth-century China had diffused to a wide population a variety of different but now familiar regional variations on common themes in buildings, clothing, food, drink, and entertainment. Mercantile, literati, and imperial patrons, using their considerable wealth, had created enduring examples of this common culture. The vitality of eighteenth-century urban culture persisted, surviving the social conflict and crises of confidence of the nineteenth and twentieth centuries.

LIFE-CYCLE RITUALS

Life for all Chinese was punctuated by special days that followed the rhythms of the lunar month, the year, and the individual lifetime. Occasions for relaxation, entertainment, visits, and feasts, these days marked the transition to new status, expressed pleas and gratitude for supernatural assistance, and reminded people of their identities as members of families, villages, and other groups. They were the quintessential expressions of popular culture, unifying Chinese of various social strata living throughout the empire. Indeed, one could say that performance of the crucial rituals of birth, marriage, and death in the prescribed manner was one of the key elements in popular conceptions of what it meant to be civilized, to be a Chinese and not a barbarian. We present here the normative rituals, bearing in mind that there were persistent subethnic and regional variations on these models; current research does not make it possible to say much about how these rituals were changing in the Qing period.

Weddings and funerals were unquestionably the two most important life-cycle rituals in China. Although birthdays were occasions for festivities for the elderly, most people simply counted themselves a year older at each new year. The first formal celebration of a child's birth came at the end of one month with special dishes and the giving of gifts by friends and relatives. This was the point at which a child would be officially counted in the family register; boys would be assigned "milk names." Infancy was in general an anxious period for parents, since mortality was very high for children of all classes. The child who survived infancy remained at risk until the danger of smallpox was past.

For boys and girls the transition to being a productive adult was gradual, but there was no period of adolescence, and the shifts from infancy to adulthood went unmarked by ritual or public display. The age of six or seven, however, was an important turning point for both sexes, marking for boys the onset of formal schooling, the removal from maternal to paternal authority, and the conferral of a formal name. For girls, footbinding began at this age, the tight painful binding of the toes and wrapping of the feet to keep them the small size deemed desirable for wives. The onset of puberty was indicated by a change in a daughter's hairstyle and decreased mobility outside the home; formal instruction in the arts of cooking and sewing, if it had not begun earlier, started now. For boys, the transition to work at the father's occupation also began gradually at a young age, even among the elite for whom schooling started at home. Sexual maturity, once marked for men with the capping ritual that had died out by Qing times, was now signaled only by marriage. Even courtship, although a subject for folksongs and plays, took place within the strict confines of arranged marriages.

Although there was much variation in local custom, most young people were engaged and married in their late teens. The formal preparations were negotiated through a matchmaker; the betrothal was marked by an exchange of gifts between the two families and considered as binding as a wedding. Because of their importance in raising or lowering the social position of a family, marriages were arranged with great care. Surname exogamy was observed, differences of status were closely considered, and the boundaries between religious or ethnic minorities firmly defined. Marriage itself was a transaction between families, not individuals, and involved a further exchange of property (both dowry and brideprice) and the ritualized transfer of the woman to the home of her husband's family. The wedding was an occasion for both families to win local prestige through lavish entertaining of relatives and friends.

In the course of a lifetime, there were various causes for the occasional celebration. Boatmen would celebrate the successful completion of an arduous voyage, scholars the passing of the examinations, parents their child's recovery from a serious illness. For adults who had passed fifty or sixty years of age, birthdays became a cause for joy and (particularly among the elite, it appears) were remembered with gifts, feasting, and entertainment. (The birthday extravaganzas of Kangxi and Qianlong—and the latter's mother—surpassed those of the local gods and may have set the style for Manchu nobility and high officials.)

Although ordinary government officials had formal ages at which they were expected to stop work, retirement from farm or manual work was probably involuntary on the part of most men, who had to earn a living or contribute to the household coffers for as long as possible. The abdication of the Qianlong emperor in a great ceremony on New Year's Day, 1796, was as exceptional as his occupation. The marriage of a son or birth of a grandson may have been a private signal for a woman's retirement from childbearing, but she would just be entering on the most glorious period of her life, when she ruled the household as matriarch. For the well-to-do, old age was the reward for a youth spent in diligence and obedience to elders; for others, it was a painful and insecure period of life.

A funeral was an even more important ritual than a wedding for a family in Qing times. Because of the centrality of filial piety in this culture, the mourning of a child for a parent took ritual precedence over other demands, and one did not marry, take exams, or contribute to community festivals while in mourning. Washing the corpse, placing it in the coffin, receiving condolences, chanting for the soul of the deceased, moving the coffin to the graveyard, and constructing the grave itself were all carefully prescribed by custom. Expenditures were supposed to be high (as a sign of respect for the deceased), and extravagance was generally encouraged. Most of a family's network of friends and relations came to pay condolence visits and present gifts. For close relatives, funeral clothing and ritual defined what Maurice Freedman has called "the hard core of Chinese agnation."[11] After death, the spirits of deceased relatives (represented by wooden tablets) were cared for by their descendants on a daily basis, supplemented by offerings at the grave at regular intervals, and given special attention on the anniversaries of the death.

The death of the father usually meant a restructuring of family relationships. If the man was poor and left young or infant children, his *jia* was in great economic danger, since it lacked adult labor power to till fields or engage in other work. The widow would probably have to hire laborers to do the farm work, but most small farms could not be maintained with this added cost. The death of a father in a richer household brought other threats: a young widow would be vulnerable to attempts by her brothers-in-law to take her husband's share of the estate away from her sons and force her to remarry and leave the family. In households with two generations of adults, the father's death signaled the division of the family property when the sons finally became heads of households in their own right. This division, a crucial stage in the household cycle, was marked by none of the ceremony associated with individual rites of passage.

In general terms, clothing and hairstyle were the standard markers of new or special status. Women changed their way of wearing their hair at puberty and marriage. The shaving of the forehead and braiding of the queue, in addition to being an initial symbol of Manchu rule, seem to have indicated a boy's progression to adulthood. Men and women who left their families to become monks or nuns shaved their heads entirely. During mourning, men were expected to unbraid their queue and forego any shaving as a sign of grief. Special clothing was worn by a corpse, bridal couple, nun, priest, monk, and of course officials. The distinctions between Han and non-Han were similarly marked by hairstyles and clothing.

Weddings and funerals were family affairs, and their ceremonial locus was the main hall of the home where the ancestral altar was located. Relatives and the personal acquaintances of the family were invited and cemented these ties with gifts. While there was usually a religious specialist at a funeral, a wedding was performed without any professional in attendance. No government validation or participation was necessary for either ritual. These crucial transitions—including betrothal and the birth or adoption of a child—were instead announced by the family to the ancestors and to the local earth god (and through him the celestial bureaucracy).

Both weddings and funerals showed considerable differentiation according to the status of the individuals concerned. Deviations from the major form of marriage, as, for example, when young girls moved to their future husbands' homes as "little daughters-in-law" or when widows remarried, were, like the funerals of the unmarried or underage, celebrated with truncated ritual and only modest display. The amount of money expended also varied widely. Imperial life-cycle rituals became public events, although the casual involvement of the populace was not encouraged. Imperial rituals also revealed thorough acculturation and adoption of Chinese norms by Manchu rulers. Kangxi's marriage at the age of eleven in 1665 was performed in a largely Chinese style. And after Shunzhi's death in 1661, when the emperor's orders that his corpse be cremated were obeyed, Qing emperors and their consorts were buried in the Chinese mode; indeed, Qing mourning observances were slightly more stringent than those during the previous dynasty.

Imperial ritual extravagance set a model for others to emulate. Yangzhou salt merchants flaunted their wealth in lavish weddings and funerals that involved huge processions and hundreds of guests. The government obliged even its soldiers by paying special allowances for these occasions (twice as much for funerals as weddings). Landlords called upon tenants for service at weddings and funerals. Merchant guilds frequently made provision for storage of the coffins of sojourner members and had charitable gravesites for the indigent. Ordinary people, who might spend the equivalent of a year's income on these events, created marriage and funeral saving associations on which they relied for funds. The very poor were shamed by having to make do with the simplest of rituals and burying their dead in public graveyards.

ANNUAL FESTIVALS

It is not surprising that the Chinese calendar, whose promulgation and design had from earliest times been a function of the emperor, marked each year by the reign name of the current ruler. The eighteenth century of the Western calendar thus corresponded to the period between the thirty-ninth year of Kangxi and the fourth year of Jiaqing (r. 1796–1820). A year was divided into twelve lunar months of usually thirty days each, with an intercalary month inserted every three years to keep the lunar and solar calendars in synchronization. The new moon fell regularly on the first of the month, the full moon (whose bright light permitted evening activities) on the fifteenth; each month was also divided into three periods of ten days each. Each day consisted of twelve periods of two hours each. Official calendars were issued in the tenth month of each year. They were probably the basis for popularly printed almanacs that also included information about religious holidays and noted for each day what activities were auspicious and inauspicious.

In the Ming and Qing periods this calendar, unlike that of Christian

Europe, had no scheduled day of rest. In earlier eras leave had been given to officials once every five or ten days, and in the Tang and Song dynasties there had been fifty-three or fifty-four holidays during the year. The number of holidays had been continually reduced, and, although the new-year break was lengthened to fifteen days in compensation, the Qing really observed only three major holidays, universal for all classes: New Year's, the fifth day of the fifth month, and the mid-autumn festival. The emperor himself adhered to a rigorous schedule of work. If he was conscientious (as eighteenth-century emperors were), for most of the year he was up and holding audiences with officials by 5 A.M. or 6 A.M., before breakfast; court officials were clocked in on a twelve-hour schedule, from 6 A.M. to 6 P.M. Artisans seem to have worked equally long hours, while the only constraints to agricultural work lay in the hours of daylight available.

Chinese daily routines were punctuated by festivals that followed the changing seasons and were defined by both the lunar and solar calendars. These rituals reflected and shaped agricultural and business cycles. Some were associated with the repayment of debts, guild meetings, or the renegotiation of contracts; others with the planting or harvesting of crops. The new-year's celebration dominated the winter, lasted for several weeks, and was a holiday from employment for virtually the entire population. Families (including deceased ancestors) were reunited, and friends and relatives exchanged visits. New Year's was traditionally a time of reckoning, even in the spiritual world, as the kitchen god was bribed in order to sweeten his annual report to the Jade Emperor on the household's behavior. It was the one time when everyone tried to have meat on the table, in dumplings in North China and in other delicacies elsewhere. The lantern festival on the fifteenth day of the first month, when everyone went out into the streets to see the lantern displays, symbolized the end of the holiday and was one of the rare occasions when women of all classes were permitted to walk about in public. During the solar festival in the spring known as *qingming*, families again cemented links with their ancestors and one another by visiting and cleaning their graves. *Duanwu* (the fifth day of the fifth month) was a time for wearing certain prophylactic objects as the heat of summer approached, as well as for competitive community boat races on rivers and canals. The protracted Ullambana rites to appease the spirits of the untended dead that lasted (unofficially) most of the seventh month were a counterpoint to the family-oriented new-year holiday of the winter. These festive but worrisome rituals involved everyone in communitywide activities and necessitated the services of Buddhist monks and Taoist priests. The arrival of autumn was signaled by the moon-viewing mid-autumn festival of the fifteenth day of the eighth month, commemorated with moon cakes, while the double ninth (the ninth day of the ninth month) called for picnicking on a hilly spot with a view.

Intertwined with this cycle of holidays were the birthdays of China's many deities, whose celebrations prompted temple festivals and fairs. Although the worship of some gods had become standardized by their inclusion in the official pantheon, China had hundreds of deities, each with its own birthday (and some with more than one celebration a year), and so there was no single sequence of rituals in which the entire country shared. Each village, town, and city had its own set of important dates. At most temple festivals the community visited and made offerings to the god, watched the plays put on for the deity's benefit, and generally enjoyed the lively atmosphere.

Some ritual celebrations were generated by crises in the lives of communities. When there were devastating epidemics or droughts, officials led the populace in special penitential rites to seek relief. At long intervals, special rites of thanksgiving were performed in local temples by communities to thank the gods and request continued protection.

Although the constituencies of most temples were residential or occupational groups of a limited size, temples to the same god often celebrated on the same dates, and certain temples had in the course of time become pilgrimage sites that attracted tens of thousands of visitors annually. At the temples on Putuoshan, an island off the coast of Zhejiang, for example, thousands of pilgrims came to worship the goddess Guanyin on the nineteenth day of the second, sixth, and ninth months.

Taishan, the sacred mountain in Shandong, was the site of a spring pilgrimage. A twentieth-century observer commented:

> Every day during the spring pilgrimage season . . . is marked with the arrival of several thousand country folk. The red-bordered banners, carried by the venerable leaders of each band, indicate that they come from villages all over the face of eastern China. . . . on the home journey the pilgrims always load themselves heavily with souvenirs in the way of shrubs from the sacred mount, alpenstocks with dragon heads, dolls and whistles for the babies, and pewter amulets or earrings for the wife at home.[12]

Mount Tai attracted emperors, literati, and male and female pilgrims. The women often came riding by twos on wheelbarrows; the better-off rented a mountain chair to carry them up the steep slopes to the summit, with ingots of paper money tied on the chairs "to advertise their meritorious intentions toward the gods." At the principal temple, the Palace of the Princess of the Azure Clouds, pilgrims threw their offerings into the main altar room through barred doors, believing that any that landed within the room and not on the porch were accepted by the goddess and her two female associates.

The celebrations of annual holidays and gods' birthdays had much in common with weddings and funerals. All were a respite from work, an excuse to enjoy many kinds of popular entertainment, and were times when traditional restrictions loosened. Women went out of the home more readily; gambling, shopping, drinking, and eating were encouraged; music filled the air, and there was much to look at. A sense of abundance reflected the real redistribution of wealth within the community that took place as the richer members contributed proportionately more to community festivities.

Children learned the rudiments of popular culture as they looked at temple decorations, the gods and their retinues on parade, the priests in their embroidered robes. The legends and quasi-historical stories associated with special days were retold to each new generation: the feats of the warrior god, Guandi; the piety of Mulian who journeyed to hell to save his mother; the virtues of the poet Qu Yuan commemorated in the dragon-boat races; and so forth. The associations between certain colors, foods, and directions of the compass, the distinctions between male and female behavior, the relations between generations—all were illustrated in ritual actions and thus handed down over the centuries.

Festivals themselves generated the need for specialized goods. Small industries throughout the country produced the ritual paraphernalia essential to these events: paper spirit money, candles, lamps, special food offerings, incense pots, banners, gods' statues, coffins, catafalques, shrouds, sedan chairs, and parasols. Special stores dealt exclusively in religious and ceremonial supplies: the production of new-year pictures and popular woodcut illustrations of the gods of happiness, emolument, and longevity was concentrated, for example, in Suzhou and several North China counties. Many people, especially those without regular work, depended on the sporadic employment and charity that accompanied public processions and feasting.

Although the basic unit of participation in these festivals was the household, not the individual, we have seen that many rituals celebrated and defined larger groups—"families" of affines and agnates, lineages, native-place associations, temple organizations, occupations. Where rival groups lived side by side (e.g., lineages, guilds, religious or ethnic minorities, even offices of the government), some rituals accentuated their differences and provided a framework for competition. At the same time, loyalties within groups at different levels of organization (e.g., neighborhoods within towns or villages, families within lineages) were cemented by the need for cooperation and collective endeavor. When loyalties competed, priorities could be defined; the centrality of family values in this society, for example, was emphasized by the suspension of all other activities at the time of the new-year holiday.

As we have noted, many of these rituals also marked the changing seasons of the year. Most festivals had some food or special product with which they were associated—the peonies of the late spring, charms purchased for the fifth day of the fifth month, moon cakes of the mid-autumn festival, chrysanthemums of the late fall, *laba* porridge of the eighth day of the twelfth month, matched couplets and god posters of the new year. Indeed, there seems to have been an annual cycle of foods (different from place to place) loosely correlated with other festivals and the availability of the foodstuffs that gave variety to the diet. Certain games and sports were also associated with particular seasons and festivals—autumn cricket fighting in Peking, or spring dragon-boat races in central and south China. Festivals not only advertised the availability of seasonal goods but also promoted their sale. In less commercialized areas, temple fairs substituted for markets. In cities, these festivals were the occasion and place for the sale both of seasonal items and goods for which regular demand was weak (pet dogs, crickets, pigeons, and so forth).

Among the urban elite, an interest in the foods, flowers, and entertainments of the changing seasons may have been deemed more dignified than the worship of deities popular with the vulgar masses. In a Suzhou temple on the birthday of the dragon god of Dongting Lake, the prominent local families set up displays of glass lamps and flower arrangements in the temple where they gathered in the evening to sing, listen to music, and talk; ordinary people could only look on from afar, hanging over the railings erected to keep them out. Demand grew for decorative seasonal paintings and porcelain statuettes of deities with national reputations and comparatively high status, such as Guanyin or the god of longevity (for which the kilns of Dehua, Fujian, had recently become well known), a demand that seems to reflect elite absorption (and appropriation) of traditions associated with the lower classes.

The continuity of gods and the names of festivals over the centuries has masked both regional difference and temporal change. The same rites were performed by social groups that were unlike one another or were different from what they had been a century before. More important, rites with the same names were in fact carried on in very different ways in different places and at different times. As Robert Weller's work on the rites of the seventh month has shown, the place and the meaning of the feeding of the hungry ghosts within this ritual was altered considerably as society in Taiwan changed in the nineteenth and twentieth centuries.[13] We might expect, for example, that the emphasis on competitive boat races as part of the *duanwu* festival was not equally strong all over China (we know that not all communities held them) and may have become prominent in places where competition between urban organizations was becoming more controlled. In the absence of further research, it is difficult to see exactly what changes were taking place during the eighteenth century. In general terms, there appear to have been long-range trends toward the standardization of festivals from the top by the elite and by the state, as well as toward the creation of urban organizations that emphasized cooperation rather than competition.

STATE RITUAL

Although state rituals were performed by a very few, they drew on the popular repertory, established the highest standards for these ceremonies, and reflected the seriousness with which ritual was regarded in Chinese society. No treatment of China's cultural system would be complete without consideration of this essential component of government. For the truth is that the Qing state was not a secular institution; rather, its legitimacy depended on assumptions about the ties between the Son of Heaven and the cosmos, and on his crucial role in creating harmony between human society and the natural and supernatural world. Expressions of order in the universe, such as the creation of a calendar and the recording of the movements of stars and planets, were, together with the recording of human events, state functions administered by the Board of Rites.

Anyone who has examined the detailed records of individual reigns, the *Veritable Records*, will have noted the impressive number of ritual events in an emperor's schedule of work. The "grand" or first-rank state rituals were those performed in the capital at the Altar of Heaven, Altar of Earth, Temple of the Ancestors, and the Altar of the Land and the Harvest: sacrifice at these first-rank altars required the personal participation of the emperor. The grand sacrifice to Heaven was the first ritual act performed by the Manchus when they entered Peking in 1644; it was so fraught with political significance and so intimately linked with the imperial institution that for anyone else to worship Heaven was seen as an act of high treason. The accession of each new emperor was marked by his performance of sacrifices to Heaven and Earth, symbolic acknowledgement of the notion that "the power to govern was not an affair among men, but an arrangement between Heaven and the ruling group."[14]

The state ritual calendar marked the seasons of the year. The emperor worshiped Heaven at the winter solstice and Earth at the summer solstice; sacrifices to the imperial ancestors took place each quarter and at year-end, and sacrifices to the Altar of the Land and the Harvest once a year. Each sacrifice disrupted normal routines and required a three-day period of sexual abstinence preceded by ritual bathing. During this period, the whole court abstained from wine, meat, and strong-smelling vegetables like garlic. For the participants, no mourning was to be observed during this interval, no sacrifices performed, no music played, no invitations to feasts issued or accepted. Animals "without blemish" were selected for offerings: at the grand sacrifice to Heaven, for example, fourteen bullocks, a large number of sheep, and many pigs were among the offerings. Sacrifices of the first rank were marked by performance of the "three kneelings and nine prostrations" on the part of the emperor and other participants. Like everything else, the number of sacrificial offerings, degree of ritual action, and number and rank of participants in the rite were carefully graded. Correct performance was essential to ritual effectiveness.

The spirit tablets of the emperors and their consorts, beginning with Nurgaci, were placed in the Temple of the Ancestors, the Taimiao, located in the palace grounds just south of the Wu Gate. Worship here symbolized the emperor's rightful place in the imperial patriline as well as his role as exemplar of filial piety. As in ordinary households, there were regularly scheduled rituals during the year; individual ancestral tablets would be brought out for offerings on the deathday. Imperial ancestral tablets were also placed in the sacrificial halls of the emperors' tombs in the two imperial cemeteries located in the mountains northeast and northwest of Peking. In order for the spirits of deceased emperors to participate in the ceremonies at the Altar of Heaven and the Altar of Earth, additional tablets were kept at those locations and brought out for the grand sacrifices, where they were placed second only to the tablets for Heaven and Earth.

The state religion observed at the highest, imperial level extended all the way down the administrative hierarchy to the level of the county. There the county magistrate was expected to make offerings to his spiritual counterpart, the city god, and seek his cooperation in ensuring local peace and prosperity. He also conformed to a highly formalized schedule of ritual offerings to deities in the official pantheon, performed rites on imperial deathdays, and led the community in seeking relief from natural disasters.

These imperial and official rituals were directed toward communities defined by the state (the empire, the ruling house, the bureaucracy, the degree-holders). They were also distinguished by their reliance on written procedures for ritual and music, procedures in which great attention was given to the rank and position of the participants. These rites eschewed the use of Taoist or Buddhist professionals, did not include any of the ecstatic behavior associated with the mediumship or spirit possession common to many popular festivals, and relied on government employees as ritual actors. Ritual responsibilities were treated with great seriousness by emperor and bureaucrat alike. During the eighteenth century, members of the literati did intensive research on the rituals of "the ancients," not only to perfect official ceremonies but also to standardize ordinary rites, especially those of the uneducated populace and non-Han communities. The guides and handbooks they wrote (and that others simplified in more popular manuals and almanacs) disseminated orthodox procedures and helped create ritual consistency among classes and in different parts of China across time. Bureaucratic standards came to permeate most ritual ideals. At birthdays, marriage, and death, clothing and transportation for men, women, and gods were supposed to be like those of an official.

VALUES AND BELIEFS

On the basis of our analysis of different elements in the eighteenth-century cultural system, what can we say about the values and beliefs shared by persons of different status in Qing China? As *Annales* historians have discovered in France, the shift from study of concrete behavioral patterns and on-the-ground institutions to values and beliefs is extremely difficult to make, and cannot be accomplished with any degree of certainty. The following speculations are offered in the hope that they will provoke the research and analysis required for illumination of this vital yet neglected topic.

Perhaps the most basic value that spanned diverse social strata and even groups marginal to Han Chinese society was identification with a model of Chineseness that was already broadly disseminated in early Qing times. Han Chinese, from officials down to peasants, identified their culture with civilization. Non-Han peoples on the peripheries of the empire were called barbarians, some of whom were "raw," wild and unassimilated, others "cooked," partially accustomed to civilized values and behavior. To be Chinese was to be a member of a superior civilization: ethnographers studying overseas Chinese communities, as well as contemporary anthropologists studying outcast groups, have commented on the pervasiveness of this sense of identity, which crossed regional and socioeconomic lines.

But what was entailed in being Chinese? Some might associate this identity with the written language that had linked the educated elite of this culture for millennia. Even the illiterate peasant had a profound reverence for the written word—written in Chinese characters of course—if not a passing familiarity with it. The near-magical power of writing was certainly common to Taoist rituals, imperial edicts, legal contracts, and fine calligraphy, while written materials were a shared language for educated people from across the empire. Despite differences between dialects that were virtually separate languages, being Chinese seemed to involve some commitment to the unified and standardized written character.

The classical formulation for Chineseness identified clothing, diet, and ritual as key components. China's superior textile technology had long since become a hallmark of Chinese culture. The Chinese rejected the dairy products that the nomads ate and took pride in a culinary tradition that considered good eating essential to good health and placed eating at the core of community solidarity. Above all, to be Chinese was to value ritual and to follow tradition, especially in marriage and funerals.

Implicit in the centrality of ritual was a confidence in the linkage between external behavior and internalized values, an assumption by now so ingrained in Chinese culture that performance without belief could be seen to suffice. In a ritual, correct actions were thus more essential than the feelings of the participants. Individuals with widely different educations and background could invest the same ritual with different meanings. Ritual thus subsumed and harmonized differences even as it educated. Community rites cut across class and were not categorized as being associated exclusively either with the elite or with the masses, thus forming the basis for a truly popular (in the sense of pervasive) shared culture. Chinese followed Confucius not only in this faith in ritual but also in the core values expressed in such ceremonies: the asymmetrical and hierarchical relations between ruler and subject, father and child, husband and wife.

Proper behavior expressing orthodox values was associated in Confucian thought with a properly ordered and stable society presided over by a ruler who was in harmony with the cosmos. Harmony, order, and stability were goals not just for the state but for individuals as well. To the Chinese, civilization consisted of imposing order onto chaos, transforming societies in which individuals wore no clothing, "knew their mothers but not their fathers," and made no social distinctions.[15] The enemy of order was *luan*, internal confusion and chaos. Not something imposed from the outside, *luan* was the disorder that could arise within the state, the community, the household, or the individual when ethical norms and correct ritual were not followed. The desire to promote order and prevent *luan* permeated Chinese society from top to bottom; most agreed that the nonviolent inculcation of values through a broadly educational effort, rather than reliance on coercion, was the best method of promoting order. Using the same paternalism with which children were socialized in each household, officials and literati attempted to indoctrinate the citizenry, beginning with an emphasis on proper action in a familial, social, and ritual context, because orthopraxy was seen as a means to promote orthodoxy among uneducated people. Crucial bulwarks against *luan* were the patrilineal family and the state.

By Qing times, filial piety meant a commitment to the patriline, living and dead, so profound that it affected not only behavior but also, as we have seen, many political and social institutions. Family identity was primary and central, and, as we have noted, individualism weak and undeveloped by comparison with the West. The concern with individual salvation that was so important in many Christian and Muslim societies was stunted in China. An emphasis on individual conversion was found primarily in heterodox sectarian religion, and it remained an anomaly in a culture where most religious activities were collective rituals and where salvation was muted by belief in cycles of karmic rebirth. Chinese were expected to seek individual fulfilment in carrying out the social roles and obligations learned in childhood. A crucial source of order was thus unity, loyalty to the group against the threatening outsider. Another was orthodoxy, the upholding of agreed-upon norms; deviations should be corrected, or at least ignored.

Family metaphors permeated the bureaucratic state: the emperor was called the Son of Heaven, the county magistrate the father-and-mother official, and yet the bureaucracy also presented a powerful alternative model for structuring social relations. The tension between particularistic and universalistic criteria for achievement, between public and private concerns, persisted of course, but acceptance of control based on objective yet correct standards and of a high-degree of impersonal regulation was a hallmark of the eighteenth-century citizen's world view. Chinese took for granted the existence of this centralized state that administered a large empire and promoted Confucian norms, and government service was still the most prestigious career. It was no coincidence that the world of the gods was an otherworldly bureaucracy in which objective merit and personal pleas could both bring blessings.

Like the individual whose attempts to order his world were sometimes theatened by fate, so disunity in the state could also be caused by external disaster, but by Qing times the resilience of the state, even in the face of rapid social and economic change, was well established. At the level of both household and society, there was a pervasive confidence that almost anything could be achieved given the right combination of talent, connections, and luck. This was a complex society that promoted entrepreneurship and managerial skills at every social level. "Poverty comes not from [spending on] eating or clothing but from inadequate planning"—peasant proverbs like this testify to an emphasis on initiative and enterprise that complemented fatalism and resignation.

A belief system that de-emphasized personal salvation and stressed the collective patriline, that valued ritual and behavior based on venerable Confucian precepts concerning the sources of order in society and the cosmos, and that encouraged individuals to work hard and improve their lot in life—these are major elements found not just in the eighteenth century but in traditional Chinese society generally. The eighteenth-century exposure of Han Chinese to non-Han minorities merely drew the latter into the powerful orbit of Chinese culture. Even the doubts about the foundations of classical education that were planted by evidential scholars in the minds of their contemporaries grew very slowly into disbelief and rejection.

Despite intensified contact with other ways of doing things, confidence in Chinese core values seems to have been unshaken. A growing minority found this complacency cause for alarm, but it would only be later, with exposure to the technologically advancing and equally self-assured culture of the West, that Chinese would begin to question in earnest the superiority of the culture of the Middle Kingdom.

PART TWO

*Change and Diversity in
Eighteenth-Century Society*

4

Social Change

Having set the stage and described in general terms the contours of Qing society and culture, we shall now look even more specifically at the diversity in this society and at the changes most characteristic of the eighteenth century. In this Part we explore first the eighteenth-century expansion and diversification of the Qing economy that was the foundation for so many social changes, then the demographic increases of the period and the related processes of social differentiation and social mobility. Next we consider in detail the various constellations of social problems and institutions found in each of China's macroregions. The book closes with a reappraisal of eighteenth-century trends and their implications for the nineteenth century.

ECONOMIC DIVERSITY AND GROWTH

The expansion of the Qing economy within and beyond China is so inextricably tied to changes in Qing society in the period that it must be considered in some detail. As the economy expanded and grew more diverse and more commercialized, the population increased and migrated into new regions, and society became more mobile and impersonal, more heterogeneous in some ways and more homogeneous in others. The Qing involvement in the world economy, on the other hand, was not marked by a comparable increase in awareness of the world beyond East Asia.

Throughout the Qing dynasty, agriculture contributed the dominant share of the national product; then as now, the vast majority of the people lived in rural villages and were primarily employed in working the land.

China had long since rejected the mixed-farming systems found in Europe that combined animal husbandry with cereal production and reserved a large amount of the cultivatable land in pasture. The Chinese concentrated on cereal production and substituted intensive human labor for animal power. But regional diversity, matching the wide extremes of climate and soil that existed within an empire about twice the size of Europe, produced a multitude of local cropping systems: an early twentieth-century survey counted 574 different rotation systems, and the earlier period was probably no different.

Broadly speaking, China proper could be divided into two zones. In the dryland cropping zone that dominated the northern plains, the major cereal crops were wheat and varieties of millet; south of the Huai River and the Qinling range the norm was wet-rice cultivation. Tillage practices, agricultural implements, grain storage, and the system of landownership varied enormously between these two zones. Northern dryland agriculture fought a short growing season and the twin enemies of drought and flood. Large fluctuations in the size of the harvest were common and periodic crop failures were a fact of life. Because of smaller yields, population densities were lower, and farm size had to be larger than in the south. The Qing imperial estates and lands appropriated for bannermen were concentrated in this northern zone, as had been the lands of the Ming imperial family. With the exception of these estates, tilled initially with servile labor but later with contractual tenants, tenancy was relatively uncommon. Landlords tended to be extensively involved in production, providing seeds, plough, and oxen for their tenants in exchange for a share of the harvest. Share cropping, the rent system by which landlord and tenant divided the risks of harvest failure, was more common in the northern zone than the southern.

The wet-rice cultivation system of south China was typical of East Asian rice systems in its ability to support very high population densities—average yields were much higher than for wheat or millet—and to reward intensive labor. China grew several subspecies of Asian rice in a large number of varieties adapted to specific soils, climate, and water conditions. Because wet-rice culture depended primarily on nutrients in the water and the timely supply of water, the creation and maintenance of irrigation systems, as we have noted, was essential. The high cost of this investment and organization paid off, however, in a much more regular sequence of harvests and in continuous cropping of paddies.

The abundant rainfall in south China and the widespread network of rivers and tributary streams that supported wet rice were also the basis for an efficient system of waterborne transport that enabled many localities to have ready access to markets outside their immediate vicinity. Many goods traveled along the rivers across macroregional boundaries. From the "rice bowl" of Hunan's Xiang River basin, rice was shipped downstream to the marketing center of Hankou and sold to other merchants who transported it down the Yangtze to large cities in the delta. Large rice yields and dense populations were found together with small farms, high rates of tenancy, and diversified agricultural systems that incorporated handicraft and by-industries into the farm economy.

Northern cropping patterns characterized North China and North-west China; southern patterns dominated the Lower Yangtze, Southeast Coast, Middle Yangtze, Upper Yangtze, Lingnan, and Southwest. Of the areas newly developed in the Qing, Manchuria was part of the northern zone and Taiwan part of the southern; the fragile Xinjiang oasis agri-culture, dispersed in deserts and grasslands, was quite different from either. Within each macroregion the intensive agriculture of the cores contrasted with the extensive cultivation of the frontiers.

Chinese Marxist studies of the "sprouts of capitalism in agriculture" have described the linkages between the agrarian economy and the commercial expansion of the eighteenth century. More commerce and mercantile investment in agriculture stimulated specialization in crops sent to market, both raw materials for the expanding handicraft industry and consumption goods such as tea, cane sugar, and tobacco. Profit enticed merchants, landlords, and peasants to buy or rent lands to produce cash crops, and many prospered. A new kind of managerial landlord, a commoner who used hired labor to farm several hundred *mu* of land, growing crops for the market, emerged in the early Qing. The influence of the market could be further seen in changes in forms of rent, improvement of the position of the tenant vis-à-vis the landlord, the rise of a wage labor force in agriculture, and the increasing use of land as a marketable commodity. In this view, the capitalist sprouts in agriculture increased the tendency toward commercialization and specialization and improved the lot of most tenants, while polarizing rural society into rich and poor.

Western-trained economic historians have tended to view the cap-italist-sprouts thesis with skepticism, but many of their studies agree in surprising measure on the main trends of Ming-Qing agrarian develop-ment, including the increasing complexity of the farm economy and the resultant heterogeneity of rural society. Most Western scholars also believe that landownership had become more dispersed in the early Qing and that large landlords were fairly unusual. (Even the large imperial estates amounted to less than 1 percent of all the land under cultivation.)

Many of the elements of this process of commercialization had appeared in earlier periods, particularly during the commercial revolution of the Song. Historians have been hindered by the lack of reliable quantitative measures from precisely comparing and thus distinguishing earlier phases of economic growth from the Ming-Qing spurt. They must turn instead to qualitative changes in the Chinese economy. China experienced a new and higher form of economic activity in the eighteenth century, as can be seen in the monetization of silver in the sixteenth century and the circulation of Mexican silver dollars in Qing markets, the appearance of new forms of multiple landownership rights and permanent tenancy, and the emergence of a labor market for agricultural workers.

Japanese, Chinese, and Western scholars all agree that, regardless of their precise origins (a subject still under debate), systems guaranteeing tenants permanent rights of cultivation first emerged in south Fujian in the late sixteenth century, spread in the eighteenth century through the wet-rice cultivation zone, and could also be found in many dryland cultivation systems. Multiple layers of ownership made landlord-tenant relations more distant, physically and socially, generally benefited the tenant, and, by providing security of tenure, improved his incentives to maintain soil fertility and increase productivity. There is also widespread agreement that even when permanent tenancy did not exist, most tenants were better off because they were now legally treated as commoners rather than as servile dependents.

The general shift from servile to contractual labor in agriculture is one of the many social consequences of these economic changes that marks a contrast with earlier eras; this shift paralleled and encouraged a slow trend from Ming times toward elimination of fixed statuses and increased mobility of labor and land.

We must also stress the limitations of the new eighteenth-century developments in agriculture. Land sales and mortgages, for example, show the frequent persistence of customary checks on the theoretical mobility of land. In many localities, a landowner had first to offer the land to his kinsmen before he could sell it to an outsider. An unusual study that examines contracts for the same plot of land over several decades in eighteenth-century Fujian shows that complete alienation of the land from an owner frequently stretched over decades. A longitudinal study of an estate on Taiwan comes to similar conclusions: the size of the estate was always changing in response to changes in the size of the domestic labor force, but the transactions were primarily between agnates: in other words, "land changed hands frequently but within a limited social sphere."[1]

The post-sixteenth-century boom also created new layers of rural markets that linked villages more firmly than ever before to the commercial economy. The majority of transactions in the early Qing continued to take place within regional systems, but there was also a significant expansion of interregional and national trade in bulk consumables such as grain, tea, cotton, and silk. The Yangtze River brought rice from interior areas downstream, while the delta also began to serve as a processing center for consumer goods, importing raw cotton from North China via the Grand Canal and exporting finished cotton cloth as well as local silk. Handicraft textiles, produced in rural areas, passed through merchant hands before being sold back to peasants, who bought cloth with money earned from selling grain. Shanghai—long before its discovery by Westerners—became a thriving entrepôt for coastal trade. Thousands of boats brought wheat and soybean products (beans, oil, and meal for fertilizer) from Manchuria and North China, while others sailed north with sugar, earthenware, and tea. The commercial profits from serving as a national entrepôt and manufacturing center thus gave the Yangtze delta the economic foundations that underlay its political and cultural preeminence.

The most dramatic innovations in eighteenth-century economic institutions such as native banks and new fiscal instruments came at the end of the century and were responses to the needs of the expanding long-distance trade for credit and the safe, easy transfer of funds. Native banks (as they were called by foreigners in the nineteenth century) accepted deposits, made loans, issued private notes, transferred funds from accounts in different regions, and performed many other functions essential to local and long-distance trade. Private notes payable in silver or in copper cash were issued by these banks, by money shops specializing in money exchange, and by pawnshops. Promissory notes, issued by native banks on behalf of merchants and payable in five to ten days, facilitated the purchase of large quantities of goods, and money drafts and transfer accounts helped merchants move resources from place to place. By the early nineteenth century, paper notes may have constituted as much as a third or more of the total volume of money in circulation. Thus, the demands of large-scale long-distance trade had, without government participation, inspired merchants to transform the monetary system from a bimetallic regime to one in which paper notes supplemented copper cash and silver.

Similarly, customary law evolved outside the formal legal system to expedite economic (and social) transactions. Legal developments also reflected an increasing need to do business with strangers. Reliance on written contracts for the purchase and mortgaging of land, purchase of commodities and people, and hiring of wage laborers became commonplace in the Qing period. Most eloquently, private (so-called white) contracts supplemented (and soon outnumbered) the red (that is, stamped) official versions registered for a fee with the local yamen. Business partnerships in mining, shipping, commerce, and agriculture could be formalized and protected through this increasingly vigorous and effective system of contract law.

The process of agricultural commercialization and diversification described above took place in different localities at different times. It was above all a gradual, long-term process that was initially stimulated by a shift in the focus of foreign trade from the Central Asian caravans to the ports of the southeast coast. European ships, arriving in Chinese waters in the sixteenth century, could carry more cargo in a shorter time more cheaply than the camel caravans of the medieval period, and the magnitude of trade between Europe and China rose substantially with the advent of waterborne commerce.

The foreign trade in which the early Qing domestic economy was increasingly involved had two major components: the exchange conducted by Chinese merchants who traveled on junks to ports in Southeast Asia, Japan, and the Philippines (part of Spain after 1583), and the expanding trade conducted across the Indian and Pacific oceans by European trading companies. The Chinese junk trade, handled primarily by merchants from Lingnan and the Southeast Coast, sent porcelains, cotton, and silk textiles to Manila in exchange for Mexican silver and carried ceramics, textiles, medicines, and copper cash to Southeast Asia in exchange for incense ivory, pepper, and rice.

Foreign trade with Europeans in the ports of the Southeast Coast was temporarily halted by the Ming loyalist resistance during the Ming-Qing transition. After 1684, when the imperial ban on maritime trade was lifted, Western traders gravitated to Canton and were finally confined to this port by imperial edict in 1759. The "Canton system" of trade that lasted until 1842 (the conclusion of the Opium War) specified that Europeans had to trade through the Co-hong, a group of firms who were given monopoly rights by the state to the trade in tea and silk but in return were held responsible for collecting duties, leasing factory space, and controlling the foreigners.

TABLE 2: Index of Foreign Trade at Canton, 1719–1833

Year	Foreign tonnage (thousands of tons)	Index*
1719–1726	2.803	100
1727–1734	3.178	113
1735–1740	4.968	177
1741–1748	9.093	324
1749–1756	11.620	414
1757–1762	10.199	364
1763–1768	15.344	547
1769–1775	16.537	590
1776–1782	16.158	576
1783–1791	25.013	892
1792–1799	22.731	811
1800–1807	24.689	881
1808–1813	20.309	724
1814–1820	25.591	913
1821–1827	30.493	1,088
1828–1833	37.507	1,338

Source: Louis Dermigny, *La Chine et l'occident: le commerce à Canton au XVIIIe Siècle, 1719–1833* (Paris: S.E.V.P.E.N., 1964), vol. 1, p. 204.
*Constructed using 1719–1726 = 100.

Between 1719 and 1833, the tonnage of foreign ships trading at Canton increased more than thirteenfold (see table 2). The lure was Chinese tea, which, as one eighteenth-century Frenchman observed, "draws European vessels to China; the other articles that comprise their cargoes are only taken for the sake of variety."[2] Until the Commutation Act of 1784 lowered the price of legal imports, continental European tea smugglers vied successfully with the British East India Company to supply Englishmen with what was becoming their favorite beverage. The export of tea increased steadily through the eighteenth century and by 1833 was at more than twenty-eight times its initial level. Exports of silk, the second-most important commodity and long a staple of Chinese export trade, also expanded through the first half of the century, when woven silk textiles were replaced by raw silk for the nascent European silk-weaving industry. The sale of porcelain, also a traditional export, declined during the seventeenth century, rose again after the rebuilding of the imperial kilns at Jingdezhen, but eventually also faced serious competition from European products.

The impact of foreign demand on the society and economy of the areas producing export goods was direct and important. Exports were, of course, only a fraction of either total output or the amount marketed within China: in the early nineteenth century, for example, tea exports may have represented only 13 or 14 percent of all tea produced and marketed.[3] But the significance of the trade cannot be measured solely in these terms. The imperial treasury, for example, profited directly from it: the post of Hoppo, or Superintendant of Imperial Customs, for Guangdong, created in 1685, was usually filled by bondservants from the Imperial Household who ensured the flow of surplus revenues into the Privy Purse. Additional and greater sums were presented to the emperor by the Hoppo and the Co-hong.

Western traders had in fact come to exert direct influence on the shape of the export-linked industries. In the course of the early eighteenth century, the British developed a system for the advance purchase of tea by which the British East India Company prepaid 50 percent of the agreed-on price for the next season's crop to the Chinese Hong merchants, who in turn advanced 70 to 80 percent of the purchase price to their suppliers in the tea-growing districts. This advance-purchase system provided security for tea producers and helped ease the perennial problems of liquidity in the expanding trade; the British were assured of supplies at a stable price. Fujianese who were Hong merchants in Canton responded by investing in tea-growing land in the Wuyi Mountains (Bohea Hills) of northwestern Fujian, thus profiting from both sides of the business.

The repercussions of expanding foreign trade were not limited to the merchants and producers involved in specific export commodities: prosperity was bound to stimulate local economies. In the silk industry, as we have seen, the effects of export demand were also reflected in higher prices. In the Lower Yangtze silk-producing center of Wujiang the price of raw silk rose by 86 percent in the first half of the eighteenth century, while the price of damask, for which foreign demand was declining, rose by only 30 percent.[4] The relationship between foreign trade and the money supply was even more complicated. Because the net balance of trade during the eighteenth century was in China's favor, it was the steady annual inflows of New World silver in enormous amounts that financed this commercial development and economic growth.

The Chinese economy had long been based on a bimetallic currency system, whereby copper cash was used for daily purchases and silver for larger business transactions. In the sixteenth century, silver had become the medium in which most taxes were calculated and paid, and this practice continued in the Qing. Copper cash was minted, silver was not.

The exchange ratio between these two money metals was highly vulnerable to fluctuations in supply that had immediate effect on all citizens. Although paper money was originally invented in China, some unsuccessful early Ming experiments had made it unpopular, and the Manchu government soon abandoned its attempts to issue paper currency. The notes issued by private firms, discussed above, were relatively uncommon until the late eighteenth century.

The economic expansion of the eighteenth century was thus matched by rising demand for increased amounts of the money metals, not only to accommodate the growing population but also to serve the needs of increased market activity. Because silver was primarily obtained from abroad, fluctuations in this trade had a direct impact on the domestic money supply. The so-called Kangxi depression of the 1660s and 1670s, when the price of rice and other commodities fell, is attributable to the imperial ban on foreign trade, aggravated by withdrawals of silver from circulation to build up reserves in the government treasury. Resumption of foreign trade in 1685 had brought in silver imports direct from Europe and Central America: the monetary silver stock may have tripled in the period 1644–1830, and perhaps ten million Spanish silver dollars a year were flowing into the coastal ports of Fujian in the early Qing. In the eighteenth century Spanish silver dollars became a common unit of account, first in Canton and thence in ports of the Southeast Coast and Lower Yangtze. By the 1780s, prices of commodities in Suzhou were frequently expressed in silver dollars instead of in the domestic unit of account, taels (ounces) of silver.

The Kangxi depression ended with resumption of foreign trade, but it was succeeded by inflation in the value of copper cash as the supply of this metal failed to keep pace with demand or with silver imports. In the early decades of the eighteenth century and in the 1730s and 1770s, prices of copper relative to silver were high, and the actual rates of exchange were far below the official standard (one thousand cash to a tael of silver). The low copper:silver exchange was beneficial for many landholders, since small sales of grain were generally conducted in copper cash while the tax was calculated in silver. But the shortage of this money metal also had a dampening impact on economic growth. The copper inflation spurred the government to be conciliatory toward potential Japanese copper suppliers; it also stimulated state promotion of mines in the Southwest, which after the 1730s were able to provide sufficient copper to meet China's needs for the rest of the century. This success in maintaining a supply of both silver and copper to feed the voracious domestic demand lasted until the dramatic reversal in the balance of foreign trade in the 1820s. Such success may also have had the effect of persuading the Qing court that they were well equipped to deal with the consequences of this new degree of involvement in a market that extended far beyond China's borders.

The eighteenth century witnessed a real improvement of China's economic base, which went well beyond rehabilitation to new levels of gross agricultural output and volumes of domestic and foreign trade. These substantial economic achievements of the high Qing had a wide variety of social consequences, perhaps the most far reaching of which was an unprecedented increase in population.

DEMOGRAPHIC TRENDS

The tripling of Chinese population is probably the most frequently noted feature of Chinese society in the eighteenth century. Qing peace and prosperity made possible not simply a recovery to Ming levels but con-tinuing growth thereafter. We have noted some of the circumstances that facilitated this increase: the improved status of the peasantry, the growth of commerce, effective public measures for coping with natural disasters, better agricultural yields, expanded acreage, and diffusion of improved agricultural technology. Although population growth in turn encouraged colonization of new lands and stimulated demand, scholars have viewed the overall impact of this population increase on China in generally negative terms. In time, competition for land and jobs became sharper, landholdings shrank, prices rose, and the state's control over this huge citizenry diminished. Most historians would agree with Ping-ti Ho's asser-tion that "by the last quarter of the eighteenth century there was every indication that the Chinese economy, at its prevailing technological level, could no longer gainfully sustain an ever-increasing population without overstraining itself."[5]

We shall consider in greater detail in the sections that follow the effect of population increase on stratification, mobility, and social organi-zation generally, but here let us look more closely at the population growth itself, examining it in terms of birth and death rates, age and sex distribu-tion, and the structure of households.

Reliable population figures from China's past are rare. For the first century of Manchu rule, government tax figures (the most accessible sources) registered not population but corvée units known as *ding*. After 1741, and more effectively after 1775, officials were supposed to record the age, sex, and household of every person, but the population continued to be underreported. Members of non-Han minorities (who were majorities in some parts of the empire) were entirely omitted from most records. China does not appear to have the detailed village-level population data that existed in contemporary Western Europe and Japan. Our knowledge of Qing demography thus comes from these problematic government totals, as well as male-oriented lineage genealogies that are disproportionately from the wealthier strata in the Lower Yangtze, a few handfuls of scattered local data, and several detailed twentieth-century surveys. It is tempting but dangerous to borrow life tables created from Western European data (and thus associated with a disease structure different from China). In the discussion that follows, we survey Qing demography at this writing and point out seeming trends and interesting areas of further research.

Surely no single premodern government anywhere in the world ever attempted to rule a populace larger than the three hundred million (or more) under Qing rule in 1800. By contrast, Russia had about forty million people in 1800, Japan about thirty million, and England eleven million. The scale on which the Qing state had to operate would have imposed constraints even had the population been stationary. The sheer size of this eighteenth-century population has tended to overshadow appraisals of actual rates of increase. In fact, Chinese rates of growth peaked at about .8 percent per year ca. 1800 before declining to .6 and then .4 percent in the first half of the next century. Contrary to the impression given by most Chinese historians, these were, by comparison with other contemporary societies, by no means unusually high rates, and were comparable to those experienced by quite a number of unindustrialized European countries.

The nature of this demographic growth has not yet been clearly explained. Preliminary indications suggest that much of it was due to decreases in the death rate, resulting from the absence of warfare and major natural disasters during the eighteenth century. (It may be indicative of increased life expectancy that the formal age for retirement from the government bureaucracy was changed in 1757 from fifty-five to sixty-five.) Some eighteenth-century data suggest mortality rates of about twenty-five to thirty-five per thousand population, with an average male life expectancy at birth of at least thirty. Statistics on almost two hundred imperial offspring show that princes (exclusive of the eventual emperor) lived to an average age of thirty-one and princesses to age twenty-five.[6]

We know little about the actual causes of death in this society. Infant mortality was high even among those with considerable resources; of the Kangxi emperor's fifty-five children, twenty-two died before the age of four.

The three emperors who reigned in the eighteenth century each lost between 50 and 60 percent of their sons before age fifteen. Tuberculosis was common; smallpox was particularly feared as a childhood killer, but vaccination, usually by implanting in the nose scab-extract from persons with the disease, became a common practice among well-to-do families during this period.

Mid-Qing reductions in mortality coincided with increases in fertility. Birth rates are affected by a variety of factors: age and incidence of marriage and widowhood, frequency of sexual intercourse, length of breast-feeding, use of contraception and abortion, and so forth. The religious concern with maintenance of the patriline over the generations combined in China with relatively high rates of infant mortality to put a premium on all children, especially sons—up to 20 percent of couples were heirless[7]—and create marriage patterns that encouraged high birth rates.

Marriage was early (at age seventeen or eighteen for women, twenty-one for men), arranged entirely by parents, and virtually universal for females. Polygyny was encouraged and occurred in some 10 percent or more of marriages.[8] By contrast with Japan, we see little evidence of deliberate attempts to plan and limit family size.

Nevertheless, the actual fertility rates for traditional China (largely projected back from this century) seem to have been rather low—by age fifty most women had borne about 5.5 children—and demographers have been at a loss to explain why. Was the reason the prevalence of infant mortality and infanticide, both of which went unrecorded? In most societies before the late nineteenth century, medical knowledge was simply too primitive to be effective against disease, the major killer. We know from the studies of other cultures that the death of children before age two was extremely high, and there is no reason why China should have been exempt from this fact of premodern life. Contemporary Chinese writers also discussed the prevalence of infanticide among poor families. Indeed, some philanthropists tried to discourage infanticide by endowing orphanages in the seventeenth and eighteenth centuries. In both cases, by removing children from family records, infant mortality and infanticide would artificially lower statistics of marital fertility.

Different forms of marriage also had direct consequences on fertility. We do know from studies of Chinese populations in the late nineteenth and early twentieth centuries that major marriages were the most fertile, and women who married as concubines or as "little daughters-in-law" the least so; but we do not know for the eighteenth century precisely how many marriages fell into each type. (In major marriages, the only form recognized by Chinese marriage ritual and the normative ideal in the society, the bride moved into her husband's household as an adult, transferring her allegiance from her natal family to the family and ancestors of her husband. In minor or "little-daughter-in-law" marriage, a girl was taken into the household at a very young age and reared by her future mother-in-law. In the third type, uxorilocal marriage, a man moved into the home of his wife's parents and agreed to let one or more sons bear the wife's surname.) As in other preindustrial societies, the demand for agricultural labor affected seasonal fertility rates, and male sojourning may have reduced fertility.

Further research will be necessary before we can understand the impact on fertility of Chinese ideas about conception. Medical treatises intended for well-to-do families and doctors present recommendations that would lower fertility: women should not have sexual relations before the age of twenty, the optimal male age for conception is thirty, the sexual act for procreation should take place only at certain propitious times. While some treatises recommended nursing a child for two years (which would have decreased the fertility of the mother), others assume that a wet nurse will be hired (which would raise a mother's fertility by removing the infant from her). Erotic novels, prints, and scrolls, produced in great volume in the late Ming, were outlawed with only limited success by the more puritanical Qing rulers. This literature refers to an extensive array of potions, foods, perfumes, and spells designed to heighten desire and improve performance, and it reflects an openly sensual urban culture in which a variety of nonprocreative sexual acts were common. Elite Buddhist, Taoist, and Confucian ideas all stressed the dangers of excessive sexual indulgence. Men were consistently counseled to control ejaculation in order to preserve the semen and prevent the sapping of male essence by the female. In popular culture, the blood of women was seen as polluting, and menstruation, childbirth, and sex were in some sense dangerous to men and an affront to the gods. People were expected to abstain from sex on religious holidays and during mourning. Nevertheless, we cannot tell if such normative behavior was so commonly observed as to reduce marital fertility significantly.

In England and Japan birth rates fluctuated as a result of shifts in the number and age of women who married. In China there was relatively little variation in the age of marriage, and spinsters were virtually unknown (only a few percent as compared with 10 percent or more in Europe). Occupations for unmarried women were few and of low status; male homosexuality, although not uncommon, served only as a supplement and not an alternative to marriage. On the other hand, an apparently higher mortality rate among women created a sex ratio that left many men unable to marry, especially since well-to-do males took more than one spouse. Official sex ratios for the eighteenth century (which do underreport women) are in the range of 120 males for each 100 females. Even with the considerable male bias of the data and systematic undercounting of women, there is little doubt that there were more men than women in China at almost all age levels.

The support of a daughter-in-law who would remain in the household and bear sons to continue the patriline was more desirable than that of a daughter who was destined to marry out. Families therefore preferred to raise sons, not daughters, and female infanticide was apparently a common (perhaps the most common) way of adjusting family size. Infanticide meant finer tuning in family planning than the more indiscriminate and hazardous techniques of abortion. It is possible that the sex ratio became somewhat less imbalanced with prosperity, and that, in consequence, more men were able to marry in the course of the eighteenth century. But it is not unlikely that 10 percent of males never married, most of them among the poor.

Ordinarily, women worked only within the home: the popularity of foot-binding as a sign of social status meant that many women would have been disabled for field work or work that required physical mobility. (The practice of tightly wrapping the feet of young girls, folding under most of the toes until they rotted away, dates from the Song period; men found these two-to-four-inch feet highly erotic.) Marriage was the lot of virtually all women. If a woman was lucky, her family provided a portion of the family estate as dowry, giving her honor in her husband's household and the likelihood of better treatment from his mother. If she was unlucky, she might enter a wealthy household as a maidservant or concubine or be sold into prostitution. Women were entirely dependent on male relatives in their old age.

How much, if at all, did increases in births contribute to the eighteenth-century population increase? To the extent that prosperity may have encouraged the survival of more females, somewhat earlier marriage, and perhaps more major marriages, birth rates may have increased. This increase in population was apparently expressed both in more new households and in the expansion of existing ones. Although twentieth-century data suggest that the average Chinese household was actually rather small—between five and six persons—the cultural ideal remained larger, "five generations under one roof." Unlike premodern Europe, which had a similar average household size, China had what John Hajnal has called a joint household system in which (ideally) marriage came early and married couples lived with the groom's parents and did not form new households until the death of the older generation.

Even male sojourners who left home to seek employment elsewhere returned home to marry and left their wives in the parental home. As a result, China had more joint (as opposed to stem or nuclear) households than Japan or Europe; Arthur Wolf has asserted not only that in the course of a lifetime "almost everyone experienced life in a complex family" but also that "the potential for large family size was present everywhere and needed only the slightest encouragement to realize itself."[9] If life expectancy increased during the mid-Qing, households all over China, especially those experiencing prosperity, were likely to pass through a joint phase in the family cycle. Prosperity would permit parents to pay the brideprice or dowry needed for a wedding a few years earlier and thus encourage even earlier marriages and longer childbearing years. In regions where new lands were being opened to settlement, on the other hand, we might expect that more young men left home early to set up new households elsewhere, thereby leading to an increase in the total number of households. Single male pioneers in minority areas, too poor to marry at home, may have found non-Han women for wives.

The estimated mortality rates for traditional China, borne out by some scattered data, suggest that about 35 percent of the population was under the age of fifteen and 7 percent over sixty. If infant mortality declined in the eighteenth century, a small baby boom may have occurred late in the century (when rates of increase peaked), one that would have necessitated a shift of resources toward the young. Because Chinese society did not rely on age-graded institutions as a common form of social organization, it was probably better able to handle this sort of fluctuation in the age distribution. However, that generation born in the 1780s and 1790s—a time of shrinking access to resources—would have been mature heads of households when the Daoguang recession of the 1820s and 1830s struck, and they may have been particularly hurt by it.

The larger, more complex households that resulted from Qing population increase were disproportionately among the wealthy. Stevan Harrell has posited that wealthy men "married earlier, married younger women, married or brought in as concubines more women and more fertile women."[10] But we do not in fact have very good information on the average number of concubines possessed by a wealthy man. The genealogies used by demographers only list concubines who gave birth to sons, and the figure of about two women (wives included) per elite adult male is probably too low. This segment of society grew faster than the less well-to-do and swelled the size of the non-degree-holding elite defined (as we think appropriate in this period) by control of wealth. Clustered in the regional cores of the older macroregions, these complex families also symbolize the transience of worldly power, as the custom of equal inheritance among sons ensured fragmentation of wealth in each generation and contributed to downward mobility.

Except for Manchus, we know even less about demographic trends among non-Han minorities than we do about the Chinese majority. Gains in subsistence levels through adoption of some New World crops such as corn and potatoes were offset by the steady encroachment of settlers into tribal lands, accompanied by fighting and perhaps death from unfamiliar diseases. More contact meant more intermarriage, usually between Han men and minority women, which probably prevented some minority men from marrying at all. The actual marriage customs of such minorities diverged not only from Han Chinese but also from one another and produced distinctive demographic patterns whose study has barely begun. In Tibetan society, to mention simply one example, fraternal polyandry (where a woman married a set of brothers) was common, and younger sons were systematically sent into the celibate priesthood.

Although historians have concerned themselves rather little with the differential impact (by time, place, and class) of Qing population increase, they have been more interested, for good reason, in the impact of more people on the overall well-being of Chinese state and society. We shall consider below in more detail the ways in which this society adjusted to and tried to cope with the tripling of population in four generations, examining not just the role of the Qing bureaucracy but other institutions as well. As background to that discussion, let us first consider the mechanisms by which the state might have been able to affect the rise or fall of population.

It is important to realize that in China the influence of formal political and religious institutions on demographic trends (and hence their control of such trends) was slight, especially as compared with Europe. There, Christian ideas banning polygamy and promoting chastity, celibacy, and individual consent in marriage significantly influenced marriage and birth patterns. By contrast, the monastic communities in which Chinese Buddhist monks and nuns resided had long since been stripped of significant wealth or secular authority; the Taoist establishment was even more atomized and impotent. Neither had much influence on Confucian family values.

The generally powerful Chinese state did not challenge the widely accepted belief in the importance of the family and desirability of many offspring. Adopting the Confucian notion that the family was the paradigm for the state, the Qing glorified, supported, and strengthened the family institution and the family relations that were a central part of Confucianism: the reciprocal but hierarchical father-to-son, husband-to-wife, and elder-to-younger-brother relationships. The state praised filial piety, rewarded chaste widows with certificates of merit (permitting their names to be inscribed on monumental arches), and erected temples honoring the chaste and the filial. Susan Mann's work shows that the Qing raised widow chastity to new heights of social prestige. The virtually total authority of the male head of the family over the household and the general submission of women to men were upheld by the legal codes.

Chinese society encouraged or at least tolerated sexual license for men. Female infanticide, while criticized, continued to be practiced. Divorce and concubinage were private matters implicitly sanctioned by the cultural insistence on male heirs. Even the failure to bear children was a matter of concern only to relatives and to the gods (who were frequently petitioned for assistance).

As women, children, and the infirm were considered dependents of the family head, so responsibility for care of the disabled and needy was left largely in family hands. Figures from late eighteenth-century Manchuria (probably exaggerated but nonetheless significant) indicate that 6–9 percent of adult males were reported blind, deaf, dumb, or mentally ill, a considerable burden on their relatives. Although Buddhist monks undertook some welfare activities, and Qing emperors directed that orphanages and homes for the indigent be built at government expense in each county, public institutions did relatively little to relieve relatives of primary responsibility for family members.

Although the Chinese government had few ways of directly influencing fertility, it could and did reduce mortality by promoting peace and prosperity. Qing rulers were aware of some of the implications of a growing population. In 1793 the Qianlong emperor reflected on what he mistakenly thought was a tenfold increase in population within the last century. Grateful that (as he saw it) domestic peace and internal colonization had sustained this growth, he met concern about diminishing resources simply with a call for greater efficiency and frugality. Government policy was directed toward coping with the consequences of improved mortality and fertility, not toward reversing these trends.

Chinese values and institutions, in short, were well adapted to increasing birth rates to take advantage of improved economic opportunities, but they were relatively unsuited to containing such growth. Given these family values and the insistence on universal marriage, only infanticide and the crude mechanisms of disease and death intervened in a Malthusian manner to check population increase.

Perhaps an even more significant difference between China and Europe was the fact that in Europe population growth was soon followed by the economic transformation associated with industrialization. The Chinese economy was not transformed during the nineteenth century, and, although population growth did slacken and mortality rose during the prolonged period of rebellion in mid-century, total population remained between three hundred million and four hundred million. The race between population and resources would begin again in the twentieth century, and by the 1980s an industrialized economy and revolutionized institutions and values would struggle to cope with a population of more than a billion.

HEREDITARY STATUSES

In the eighteenth century the forces of change so far described put pressure on the hierarchy of Chinese society and on those institutions intended to promote social order. To examine this interaction, we shall look first at the tensions between fixed statuses and social mobility and then at the consequences of geographic mobility for life on the internal and external frontiers of the empire.

To understand stratification and mobility, we need to understand the nature of the Qing elite. Although the peasantry was the largest component of Qing society, even modern social historians have tended to concentrate on the top of the pyramid, paying particular attention to the problem of how to define and demarcate the elite.

While most scholars agree that the Chinese elite enjoyed a concentration of political power (office holding), economic power (wealth), social power (prestige), and what might be called cultural power (education), there is less consensus about which was primary. Historians such as Chung-li Chang and Ping-ti Ho focused on political power and examination degrees (the prerequisite for office) as the sine qua nons of elite status. For this group, they use the term *gentry*, borrowed from European history.

Their view excluded certain members of the ruling minority, such as uneducated bondservants or eunuchs, who exercised real political power. Very fine status gradations were made within this group based on levels of degrees and access to office, although the primary social distinction lay between the upper degree-winner, who was eligible for office, and the *shengyuan*, who was not.

The gentry as defined by Ho and Chang was a small group, consisting, with their families, of less than 5 percent of the population.[11] Marxist historians, by contrast, have emphasized control of the means of production and defined elite status more broadly to include not just educated degree and office holders but wealthy landlords and businessmen. Such a definition has the advantage of calling attention to movement into the literati by the nouveaux riches, intermarriage between merchant and literati families, cooperation between officials and powerful local families, Manchu-Chinese collaboration in government, and the general interpenetration of the various status hierarchies so typical of this period.

Of course, identification of individuals as members of the Chinese elite depends very much as well on which political and social stage we place them: attempts to distinguish national, provincial, and local elites suggest that at the national level the office holder and degree-winner were preeminent, joined by only the very wealthiest and most distinguished merchants. As we move from Peking down to provincial capitals, prefectural cities, and county seats, degree-holders become increasingly rarer, and we are forced to use broader and broader definitions of elite status to study local leaders. In the village, leadership might be provided by a semiliterate owner-cultivator or by a landlord with little schooling.

We have here eschewed the term *gentry* in order to avoid the misleading implications of the English model. We have adopted instead the broader concept of *elite*, believing that in the Qing period any concentration of education, political influence, social status, or wealth tended to be used to attain similar power in the other spheres. In the eighteenth century, the lines between types and levels of status within this elite became increasingly blurred. While an orthodox education, office holding, and the higher examination degrees remained markers of elite status, respect was also accorded to men of leisure whose wealth (however acquired) enabled them to adopt an elite life-style.

Many studies of the Chinese elite have been concerned with the question of social mobility and have been anxious to show that China did (or did not) make possible the kind of transformation of status by dint of personal effort not only prized by Westerners but upheld as a virtue in

Chinese culture as well. Because most analyses of social mobility in Qing society have concentrated on the degree-holding portion of the elite and have narrowly defined mobility as movement in or out of this group, they may have neglected the important place of hereditary status in this society and given a misleading impression of the possibilities for dramatic change of status. Studies by Japanese and Chinese historians that have seen a trend in this period toward increased stratification and greater inequality, on the other hand, may have exaggerated the impermeability of status barriers.

In our view, the economic growth of the eighteenth century was accompanied by a general expansion of opportunity, increased occupational differentiation, and a dissolution of formal and informal barriers to social mobility. Wealth was the essential prerequisite of elite status, yet entrance into the upper levels of the elite did grow more and more difficult even as it became easier to get rich. These trends developed most rapidly in the cities and regional cores but reached even into China's peripheries. In the newly settled frontiers, the absence of old established elites had by the end of the century permitted the emergence of a particularly fluid, unstable, and highly competitive society, poorly structured by the traditional mechanisms of hierarchy and social control.

Hereditary status groups were an accepted part of the social fabric in eighteenth-century China. At the pinnacle of the society, all descendants of the imperial line were clearly identified, their genealogies recorded and their activities supervised by the Office of the Imperial Lineage. This lineage, which grew to very large proportions, distinguished main lines (yellow sashes) from the collateral lines (red sashes) of more remote imperial ancestors. Early Qing rulers exercised firm control over the award of ranks within the twelve-tier nobility; under the Kangxi and Yongzheng emperors especially, demotions and deprivation of rank were not uncommon. Except in a few cases, moreover, rank was automatically lowered with each generation. Vestigial reminders of the Manchu past remained in the so-called Eight Great Families, princes of the first and second rank by right of perpetual inheritance who were descendants of the brothers of Nurgaci and his son Hongtaiji.

The banner system, a distinctly Qing institution that reflected the highly stratified preconquest society of the Manchus, segregated the new rulers and their followers from the populace and divided them into hereditary groups of Manchus, Mongols, and Chinese, each organized into eight banners. Banner membership was intended to be permanent and inaccessible except by birth or imperial fiat. Elsewhere on China's frontiers, in Tibet, among related tribes like the Lolo, even among the Mongols, rigidly two- or three-tier societies were the norm. In these frontier groups, headmen in the *tusi* (tribal headmen) and banner systems as well as Lamaist Buddhist and Islamic religious leaders occupied powerful hereditary positions.

Within China proper, membership in ethnic and religious minorities was also hereditary. In most cases, but especially for groups who were viewed as low in status (Hakkas or Muslims, for example), entry was usually by birth, and movement out was difficult. In theory, one of the firmest divisions in China's hierarchical society was the one at the bottom, which distinguished respectable commoners, called *liang min* (literally, "good people") from *jian min*, the "mean people." The latter category included remnants of aboriginal groups who had survived Chinese expansion and settlement and practitioners of occupations that included prostitutes, musicians, actors, and some yamen employees (gate keepers, coroners, runners, police, jailers). The laws forbade intermarriage between mean and good people; all mean people were barred from sitting for the examinations. Although new laws and the fluidity of eighteenth-century society ate away at legal proscriptions, strong prejudices survived.

The evolution of this particular cluster of mean occupations is not fully researched. Some groups, like the "shed people" (discussed in more detail below), seem to have been singled out because they were seasonal migrants and escaped normal household registration. But why, for example, was music consistently linked with degraded status? The supposed low position of the mean people also contrasts with the actual importance of some of these occupations. Indeed, it is difficult to reconcile the eager patronage of actors by literati or the popularity of the post of jailer among the well-connected subbureaucrats from Shaoxing prefecture with such supposedly lowly status. In fact, these must all have been relatively promising occupations in this period, attracting the poor and ambitious as well as those with hereditary claims.

In the 1720s, the Yongzheng emperor tried to remove the stigma from a number of despised local groups, who were to be permitted to change their hereditary occupations and register as ordinary commoners. Groups so identified and emancipated, perhaps in response to special interests, were the musician households of Shaanxi and Shanxi, the "fallen people" of Zhejiang, the hereditary servants of Huizhou and Ningguo prefectures in Anhui, the Tanka boatmen of coastal Guangdong, and the beggar households of Suzhou. Descendants of these people (and of entertainers and yamen employees), according to a law of 1771, still had to wait three generations before being permitted to sit for the examinations. But rapid social change ran ahead of even these more liberal laws; in 1786 punishments had to be spelled out for those people in mean occupations who were daring to take the exams themselves.

Servitude in a variety of forms was commonplace at all levels of Qing society. Among the Manchus (like other non-Han groups), human beings were seen as a basic and easily transferable form of wealth, more important than land. Control of another person's labor power was one of the signs and privileges of success. The Manchus had enslaved prisoners of war and used them not only for domestic service but also to till fields. After the Qing conquest, those personal servants of the ruling family (the bondservants) had become part of the powerful Imperial Household Department. North China peasants whose lands were seized by the Manchus technically became servants of the Imperial Household and were used to cultivate the imperial and banner estates. Together with bondservants they constituted the largest part of the servile population in early Qing society. In the eighteenth century, as we have noted, servile field workers were supplanted by contractual tenants, and domestic service performed by persons who had sold or mortgaged themselves became the most common form of Chinese servitude.

Servitude actually involved an exchange of control for security. For poor people it represented an opportunity of last resort. In the mid-seventeenth century, as in other hard times, adults had sometimes voluntarily commended themselves to the protection of others, while in periods of high demand for such labor, people were frequently kidnapped and sold in distant markets through middlemen. Some sales were for short-term servitude: this was the case for prostitutes and in some regions for maidservants. Other transactions permanently altered the status of the individual and his descendants. The Qing code outlined the rare conditions under which a slave could be released from servitude, and provisions for emancipation increased through the eighteenth century. But, like mean people, such ex-slaves suffered lingering discrimination.

Most slaves either inherited that status or were sold as children by their parents. One clear mark of servile status for males was the lack of an independent household registration: slaves and servants were listed under their master's name. Females, not being in the patriline, were sold more readily and cheaply than males (standardized written contracts recorded the particulars), but they did have some hopes for mobility. A female servant might begin with lowly household chores, be promoted to personal maid, and then be installed as a secondary wife—a process that occurred as easily in the imperial family as elsewhere. Female slaves were sometimes used by their owners to bind free males to that status: a man who married a female slave became a slave himself. Men in servile statuses were unable to change their status as women could, except for infant boys purchased to be adopted as heirs.

In Qing law persons in servile statuses were classed with the *jian min*: their relationship with the master and his kinsfolk reflected the inequality of their position. Servile tenants were not free to move or leave the land and of course domestic servants were considered chattels. The criminal code reinforced this inequality (as it did other unequal relationships) by varying the punishment with the status of the offender, not the crime itself. An act committed by a slave against the master was thus much more harshly punished than the same act committed by a master against his slave.

But the mere fact of servitude said little about an individual's economic status and power; in fact, it was entirely possible for persons of servile status to wield authority and accumulate wealth in Qing society. Some bondservants accompanied bannermen into battle and won degrees and office as a result of prowess on the field; the powerful Imperial Household Department was largely staffed by bondservants; in Huizhou, trusted hereditary servants were raised as companions to the master's son and relied upon to transact family business. Even within servile statuses we can see clear hierarchies of privilege, wealth, and power. Among the servile tenants of Huizhou, for example, the households specializing in providing bodyguarding services were the elite, while coffin bearers occupied the lowest echelons. Bondservants in the Imperial Household Department can actually be classified into four ranks; the small elite at the top was both rich and powerful, while those on the very bottom were the slaves of the elite bondservants. It was thus possible, and not uncommon, to have several layers of servitude coexisting within a household or organization. The household staff of a wealthy official or merchant, were, moreover, a world apart from the hired gateman or domestic servant of a struggling rural licentiate or the indentured laborer of an ambitious peasant.

The role of domestic servants in the life of elite households is too infrequently analyzed by social historians of China. Servants performed a variety of intimate functions (nursing, bathing, feeding, dressing, procuring, and so forth) for their masters and mistresses. In addition, the line between servant and family member, as the ambiguous term *jiaren* (which could mean either) suggests, was blurred and very permeable. Personal slaves who accompanied their mistresses into the husband's household might well serve as the nurse of the heir and thus occupy a position of respect in the next generation. The tension between mother-in-law and daughter-in-law was mirrored in the relationships between the personal servants of these women, relationships that were complicated by the other cross-cutting alliances tying these servants to the male members of the master's household. Those who have read the great eighteenth-century novel of elite life, *Dream of Red Mansions*, will know just how complex the currents and undercurrents of master-servant relations could be in a well-to-do establishment.

Household servitude in its various forms was not only an important avenue of social advancement but also a crucial mechanism in the creation and maintenance of a common Chinese culture. Because servants were usually from poorer families and poorer (even non-Han) areas, preferably from beyond one's own community, the personal interaction in households with servants regularly promoted the blending of cultures and traditions—expressed in foods, dialects, and folklore—from different regions and classes.

The diminution of servile field labor and its replacement with contractual forms of tenancy ranks with the emergence and widespread use of hired labor as one of the major social and economic phenomena of the early Qing. We do not in fact know precisely how widespread servile field labor was in the Ming and earlier periods: historical work suggests that the great estates in the Ming period did use such labor but that the farm economy also included many small owner-cultivators. In the early Qing, however, the use of servile statuses to do farm work diminished noticeably. Tenancy was no longer a sign of unequal status: *liang min* who entered into contracts with landlords were in theory their social and legal equals.

Even more tangible evidence of the changes in the social structure comes in the heightened importance of long-term and short-term hired labor. The emergence of labor markets in the early Qing in urban and rural areas testifies to a significant increase in physical and social mobility. From the late Ming through the Qing, we find large farms managed by landlords who relied primarily on combinations of hired laborers. Long-term workers, employed typically by the year, would be supplemented at periods of harvesting or planting with men hired by the month or by the day. The cost of maintaining the labor force during slack seasons was thus shifted from the landlord to the worker. In exchange, through enactments in 1761 and 1786, workers were legally freed from servile status and became part of the respectable commoner population, in theory at least, protected by law from gross abuse by the employer. Best of all, they were free to take advantage of the expanded labor market and change employers if they wished.

Although fewer servants who lived outside the households of their owners were bound to them by a web of personal obligations, older, more "feudal" forms did survive in some localities. In three notorious prefectures in southern Anhui (Huizhou, Ningguo, and Chizhou), servile tenants existed until 1949. There, whole villages of such tenants, clustered around the lineage village of the master, were fixed in rigid relations of permanent tenancy accompanied by a variety of demeaning but obligatory services. The servile tenants were differentiated from other tenants in that they "lived in the master's houses, tilled the master's lands, and were buried in the master's mountains."[12] In addition to paying rent, they guarded the master's graves, took care of his ancestral hall, acted as his bodyguards, and performed music and drama at his weddings and funerals.

Servants and retainers were a symbol of status among the wealthy. As the number of wealthy people increased in the course of the eighteenth century, the demand for servants and slaves must have also risen. Families experiencing downward mobility and persons from areas of considerable poverty continually replenished the supply of servants to the rich. In such times, the transfer of people from one region to another, often from country to city, was probably accompanied by some improvement in their standard of living as well as by pain and loss. Among those at the bottom of the social scale, the line between servants and other groups of low status was quite blurred. Criminals were frequently awarded as slaves to high officials or frontier soldiers, and children were sold to be actors and prostitutes as well as servants.

Not all hereditary statuses were as permanent as those of the slaves, mean people, or ethnic minorities. The award of hereditary ranks and titles to eminent generals, officials, and imperial relatives by the Qing throne created special lines of descent that were somewhat less extensive and enduring than under earlier dynasties. Nevertheless, in a few special cases the ennoblement and its privileges were retained undiminished for many generations—as by the Taoist Heavenly Masters of Jiangxi or the descendants of Confucius and his disciples (the Kongs, Mengs, Zengs, and Yans) from Shandong.

A great variety of hereditary professions characterized by their monopoly over certain occupations existed in Han Chinese society. Such hereditary trades included the extremely wealthy salt merchants and the official merchants appointed by the emperor for the lucrative copper trade with Japan, as well as the more ordinary licenced brokers in other commodities, soldiers in the Green Standard Army, and those special occupations in which secret recipes and rituals were crucial (brewers, dyers, doctors, navigators, Taoist priests, etc.). Such occupations were usually inherited by only one son in each generation and did not restrict the mobility of family members into other trades. These specialized professions nevertheless mirrored the more general expectation that sons would succeed to the jobs of their fathers. Despite the long-term trend away from fixed statuses that had begun in the ninth century, the idea that status was inherited was apparently still pervasive even as the dream of upward mobility grew in power.

The tension between inherited status and the increasing importance of wealth in determining status is also revealed in the theoretically sharp but increasingly blurred demarcation between professionals and amateurs, particularly in the arts. Music was both the indispensable accomplishment of a gentleman (Confucius had identified it as such) and the profession of degraded persons. Although distinctions were made on the basis of a social hierarchy of instruments that ranged from the silk-stringed zither, played by the literatus (and depicted in plate 3), down to the horn and drums that accompanied weddings and funerals, there was an important area of ambiguity in ensemble music that could be performed by gentlemen or by low-status professionals. In painting, the distinction between the literati painter and the lower-status professional was more subtle, and in many instances it seemed determined not by the genre or style of the work but by the social origins of the artist. Certainly this was the case in the allied field of drama: consider the early Qing literatus Li Yu, who earned his living from touring the provinces with a drama troupe at one point in his life, yet was always treated as an equal by the officials who paid him for his services. As we have noted previously, in the eighteenth century the line between amateur and professional grew even fuzzier, as more men of elite background earned a living by their writing and their painting.

In sum, the fact of inherited status (whether privilege or burden) was commonplace in this society, and apparently widely accepted as a normal state of affairs. Even within closed status groups, however, there was often opportunity for advancement. Formal examination quotas aided Hakkas as well as merchants and bannermen, military campaigns afforded chances for promotion, and the resources and support of powerful owners gave servants scope for the exercise of entrepreneurial talents. The Manchus, who were committed to a hereditarily stratified society, may have encouraged the acceptance of such statuses, and a general reliance on hereditary claims may actually have buffered the trend toward dissolution of social barriers that accelerated in the eighteenth century.

SOCIAL MOBILITY

The drive for upward mobility was encouraged by the pervasive belief that it was possible for a humble peasant boy to become the first scholar in the land and advisor to the emperor. This belief, reiterated in proverbs, plays, and stories, together with an ethic that emphasized education, hard work, good deeds, and the improvement of one's material condition, combined to produce a powerful dedication to advancement. Economic growth and the increase and dispersal of population in the Qing both reduced the intensity of government and elite control over the society and provided the wealth that spurred education and upward mobility. Ideas about reincarnation, geomancy, and fate rationalized the failure and downward mobility that striving could not prevent.

The goal of the upwardly mobile, and still the most prestigious career in Qing society, was that of the scholar-official. Once the prerogative of an aristocracy, by the seventeenth century academic degrees and government positions were essentially open to merit; families had to renew their claims with each generation.

A variety of factors did, of course, tend to favor the relatives of successful literati, and even studies that do not (as they should) include in-laws as well as uncles and cousins in their definition of relatives, conclude that the majority of degree-holders had degree-holding relatives. The once mighty *yin* privilege (the right of high officials' sons to purchase low-level posts) and the special examination quotas for the sons and nephews of incumbent officials did survive in the Qing as remnants of hereditary advantage. Scholar-official families had not only the motivation but also the wealth necessary to support their sons during the long decades of study and preparation required for the examinations, to hire good tutors, purchase books, subsidize travel to the examination sites, and, above all, to forego the income that their boys might have earned in commerce or in some other endeavor. Equally important were other benefits that scholar-officials provided their offspring: the manners and culture of a refined person; marriages with families of similar or higher status; the resources of lineage and native-place organizations during the critical early stages of a career; and patronage networks for more rapid career advancement. Studies indicate that it was quite possible for lineages to produce holders of degrees and office for many generations and indeed over several dynasties.

It was, however, characteristic of Qing society that anyone with sufficient wealth could buy into this elite, using money to subsidize education, befriend the right people, and purchase available degrees and office. The demographic benefits of wealth (more surviving sons) made the odds on examination success over many generations more favorable, but they also threatened perpetuation of elite status by fragmenting the patrimony. As increased competition lengthened the time required to obtain a higher degree, family strategies for achieving and preserving high status had to give increased emphasis to commercial investment and estate management. This diversification of corporate resources led different members of the same household and lineage to follow commercial and scholarly careers, and precluded a neat bifurcation of scholar-officials from mercantile households.

Because the eighteenth century brought more opportunities to acquire wealth, the size of the elite, broadly construed to include literati, merchants, and rich landlords, no doubt grew in absolute terms and as a percentage of the total population. But neither the examination system nor the formal bureaucracy was allowed by the throne to grow as fast as the pool of aspirants. The number who could pass the metropolitan and provincial examinations to obtain the *jinshi* and *juren* degrees required to hold office was limited by quotas that did not keep pace with population. Competition to enter the upper elite was thus increasingly fierce in the latter part of the century. Under such circumstances, those who achieved degrees and office took special pride in their appurtenances—the banners and plaques of the degree-holder, special court robes, personal gifts from the emperor, and so forth. Social distinctions at the top became more finely graded: one's place on the palace examination, the highest rank attained in office, postings to desirable locations, and access to the emperor all counted in evaluation of status among the national elites.

At the same time, other developments (some a result of this increased competition) led to an expanded definition of what a respectable career was. High degrees and government office, becoming so difficult to obtain, were no longer seen as the only acceptable form of achievement. The demand of incumbent officials for personal aides had multiplied as the tasks of governance expanded, and the posts of private secretary became relatively prestigious and highly specialized careers in themselves, as well as back doors to office. Directorships of the growing number of schools and academies—and, more important, scholarly research on the many projects sponsored by rich patrons—provided employment for those who could be satisfied with a life outside government. The evidential scholarship that dominated intellectual life in the Yangtze delta and Peking in the eighteenth century encouraged men to withdraw from politics into textual research. For the wealthy, a gentlemanly life-style and skills in the arts of painting, poetry, and calligraphy became important badges of membership in the elite.

Upwardly mobile newcomers spent money from land and especially business to acquire the symbols of an elite life-style. The elite could be recognized by their printed genealogies and imposing ancestral halls; they were buried with considerable pomp in well-sited and elaborate graves. They traveled in special carriages, accompanied by a retinue of servants, and dressed fashionably in elegant clothes of expensive silks and furs. They lived in choice urban neighborhoods (but usually had country estates as well) in large compounds enclosing private gardens where they gave select parties featuring rare delicacies and special entertainers. Elite men lived in large extended households with many servants and multiple sexual partners. Their daughters were frequently educated and were trained to manage the finances of large domestic establishments; they were also used to create affinal alliances with other elite lines. The men were trained in the classics, and they collected books, antiques, and other rare objects; they painted, played the zither, wrote passable poetry, enjoyed the theater, food, wine, women, and sometimes young men. They had long fingernails, never performed manual labor, treated officials as social equals, and were exempt from physical punishment. Honor, wealth, learning, numerous progeny, and long life (sometimes with the help of ginseng and other expensive drugs): the hallmarks of the good life were all simultaneously displayed in the life-style of China's elites.

These attributes of elite status (rather than degrees or office) were now available to anyone at the right price. Once the casual possession of old elite families, this style of life was enthusiastically adopted by the nouveaux riches and upwardly mobile who came to dominate urban culture in the eighteenth century. Their quest for social respectability and the appurtenances of the good life was reflected not only in satirical novels of the period such as *The Scholars* but in many popular plays as well. Very limited sumptuary laws and the willing patronage by the throne of some of the most ostentatious of the newly monied families (such as the Yangzhou salt merchants) only encouraged conspicuous consumption.

Anxiety over status at all levels no doubt underlay the availability of opportunities for mobility. The fear of families at the very top that status seeking was undermining the social hierarchy was probably exceeded only by the desire of the ambitious and the wealthy for acceptance. And, given the demographic reality, the inability of those at the very bottom of society to reproduce themselves, and the all too successful ability of the elite household to increase in size, downward mobility was not only a fear but a patent social fact.

Fortunately for social stability, it was not just at the upper levels of the elite that socially acceptable careers were becoming more numerous. A variety of lower status elite careers also developed as attractive routes for the upwardly or downwardly mobile. The lower degrees (military as well as civil) became more desirable in their own right, especially in communities where higher degrees were rare. Small-scale business and managerial landlordism produced enough wealth for people who had no expectations of rising higher to pass the entry-level examinations or even to acquire the *jiansheng* degree by purchase. Writing plays and novels, as we have suggested, had already become a purposefully Confucian pursuit in the seventeenth century. Editing examination essays, serving as clerks in government offices, carving seals and inkstones, practicing medicine, and specializing in geomancy all provided occupations for the literate, the moderately well-to-do, and the status conscious. The emerging trend— against which the reformist policies of the Yongzheng emperor had been only temporarily successful—toward the involvement of local gentry in government, their assumption of responsibility for tasks such as dispute mediation, tax collection, public welfare, and supervision of schools and irrigation, can also be seen as an enlargement of career opportunities for lower- and middle-level elites. We should not be too quick to assume that these men were frustrated by their lack of higher status rather than satisfied with the niches they had carved out for themselves.

The possibilities for upward mobility for those at the very bottom of society were far more limited. Those individuals and families who were dependent on and part of the households of the rich were far more likely to have opportunities to enrich themselves and change their status. The people whose lives were most hopeless were those without a community to assist them and with no established claim to regular work. Both the city and the frontier beckoned as places of opportunity, despite the hazards, and daring and hardy young men were sometimes able to make new lives for themselves there.

Those at the bottom of society were quite likely to die without offspring. Many low-status occupations were ones where marriage and children were necessarily rare. Prostitutes, eunuchs, monks, soldiers, and convicts were far less likely to have natural families, and even despised groups were circumscribed in their choice of marriage partners. Poor diet, insecurity, dangerous and demanding labor, reduced access to marriage partners, vulnerability to the elements, illness, and injury combined to make it difficult for poor girls to live to bear children and for poor boys to marry and have surviving sons. The greater mortality of both individuals and family units meant considerable turnover and weaker social institutions among the urban and rural poor. The size of this social stratum must have varied with time and place, but one would expect to find the largest concentrations of the poor in cities (to which they were attracted for employment but where mortality was high), overpopulated areas, and depressed regions.

ASSIMILATION OF MINORITIES

Even before the Qing period, China had already assimilated (and, more than anyone would admit, been altered by) a variety of non-Han cultures. Over the centuries, Chinese thinkers had come to define a sequence of progression from chaos (the state of barbarian societies) to civilization that involved the acquisition of agriculture, clothing, writing, ritual, a complex social hierarchy, and the other concomitants of the Chinese way of life. Possession of these traits separated Chinese from their non-Han neighbors. As the seventeenth-century thinker Wang Fuzhi wrote, "Alas! What clothing represents to Man is indeed great! What brings it respect is that it is the repository of righteousness; and what brings it love is that it is the storehouse of humaneness. It is the axis of good and evil; the principle of life and death; the control between order and anarchy; the distinction between civilized and wild beings."[13]

The Chinese had long believed that barbarians, if properly encouraged, would willingly abandon their native ways for the superior culture of the Chinese. Ethnic minorities were distinguished more by clothing, food, language, customs, religion, and social structure than by race. As they interacted with Chinese settlers, they began to be evaluated by their degree of cultural assimilation, using the binary opposites *sheng* ("raw," "uncooked," i.e., wild), and *shu* ("ripe" or "cooked," meaning civilized or sinicized). We see this shift in classifications of Taiwan aborigines, who in the 1680s were divided into "local barbarians" and "savages." By the early eighteenth century, after several decades of contact with Chinese, an official like Huang Shuqing, appointed as supervising censor of Taiwan, called the aborigines "cooked."[14] Some ethnic minorities had societies that were rigidly stratified and highly self-conscious; others had loose, fluid social structures with weak boundaries. Some had preserved their distinctiveness through isolation, strong religion, or successful adaptation to environment. For others, frequent migration had worked to blend and blur differences between neighboring groups. Hakkas and Chinese Muslims, both Han groups, were nevertheless sufficiently different in customs to be treated with a similar combination of apprehension and disdain by other Chinese.

Because the ruling bannermen were themselves a multiethnic, largely non-Han group, Qing emperors showed, as we have noted, considerable concern for other minorities. They were sensitive to the destructive effects of Chinese culture and at times tried to block its advance into frontier areas. On the other hand, they themselves acculturated rapidly, championed high culture, and promoted it vigorously in traditional ways. In the end, both steady assimilation and a persistent pluralism characterized their empire.

Qing rulers were most concerned about preventing the assimilation of the Manchus. They actively tried to preserve Manchu clothing and customs, compelled the use of Manchu in government documents, recorded oral histories and wrote books in the language, and physically quarantined Manchuria and banner garrisons from Chinese neighbors. Nevertheless, the move of many bannermen to Peking in the 1640s was decisive in severing their roots, and they adapted to urban life with seeming ease. They became enthusiastic patrons of brothels, gambling houses, and theaters, oblivious to repeated imperial prohibitions of such activities. By mid-century, Chinese bannermen were already being encouraged to register as ordinary citizens, a path with burgeoning appeal to Mongols and Manchus as well.

The dynasty used similar methods to protect and isolate other minorities in the eighteenth century, but a variety of contrary policies and processes considerably weakened the impact of these measures. Population increase and the extension of the market economy promoted Han migration into tribal territories. The establishment of local government, schools, and examination quotas encouraged minorities to "come and be transformed." In Central Asia, Lamaist monasteries became the nuclei of new towns. Moreover, the Chinese state through its local officials attacked as improper or dangerous many aspects of native society: the bearing of arms, private justice, conspicuous ceremonies, lewd customs, and the like. Native power structures were systematically co-opted and neutralized; in Inner Asia the selection of religious leaders (especially the Dalai Lama and the Panchen Lama) was controlled so that men hostile to Qing interests would not emerge. Hereditary minority leaders thus became more impotent, more closely tied to the Qing state, and therefore less responsive to their own subjects, who were powerless to oust them. The dynamics of Qing rule combined with pressures toward assimilation to weaken and destabilize these communities.

A variety of middlemen were instrumental in the process of incorporating minority groups into the Chinese system. Partially sinicized groups—Chinese bannermen, Chinese Muslims, aborigines, monks and lamas, frontiersmen with native wives—were conduits for Han culture on the frontiers. Frontier towns were filled with Chinese merchants, soldiers, and immigrants. Merchants in particular acted as what twentieth-century critics have called the agents of Han cultural and economic imperialism. The lure of rare and valuable commodities (jade, ginseng, camphor, precious metals) attracted entrepreneurs who often organized local production and promoted trade. The monetization of frontier economies and the slow spread of the market drew non-Han peoples into a relationship of greater dependence with these Chinese traders. Native demand for Chinese goods was often greater than the supply of exportable local products. Tribal peoples therefore bought on credit and were encouraged by merchants to mortgage land and property; a cycle of indebtedness was soon set up that was usually destructive of native society.

The measures that (deliberately or not) promoted the acculturation of non-Chinese peoples within the empire were least successful when minorities were most isolated, had access to adjacent unassimilated groups, and possessed strong indigenous cultures. State repression and violence between Chinese and minorities broke the resistance of some people but had the contrary effect of raising ethnic consciousness at the same time. Many tribal groups were able to make some accommodation with the Qing state and its economy without surrendering their identity or independence. But tribal peoples in the Middle Yangtze, Upper Yangtze, Taiwan, and Southwest were increasingly assimilated, as were some (but far fewer) Mongols and Tibetans. By the end of the century, Chinese bannermen and many Manchus were legally but not culturally distinct, and some small groups within China (the Jews of Kaifeng and the Albazian Russians in Peking) had been assimilated completely and disappeared.

Cultural change was overwhelmingly one-way. It is true that the Manchu vigor associated with hunting and horses and physical exercise had some allure for the Chinese officials who attended the Manchu emperors during their summer sojourns (annual in the Qianlong reign) at Rehe, north of the Great Wall. Nevertheless, most Chinese elites who traveled or were posted to tribal regions returned convinced of the superiority of their own civilization; furthermore, they usually persuaded minorities of the correctness of this view.

FRONTIER SOCIETY

Frontier development was a major motif of Qing rule. During the eighteenth century, population pressure and the new food crops introduced from the Americas had encouraged the poor and ambitious to move out of China's plains and river valleys into the hills and mountains. For the most part, these large-scale migrations were encouraged by the government, which, as we have seen, provided aid, initial tax exemptions, and protection against native tribes. As we show in greater detail below, virtually every macroregion experienced frontier settlement and growth during this century. Immigrants moved to Taiwan and Manchuria despite government prohibitions; they flocked into the Yangtze hills, the Han River highlands, the mountains bordering Jiangxi and Hunan, and into Guangxi and the Southwest; they repopulated the Sichuan basin, moved into the western foothills of the Tibetan plateau, and followed Qing armies into Xinjiang.

The society of the frontier was shaped by the distinctive characteristics of its economy. Indigo, tea, and timber, the dominant plants of the traditional hill economy, were all perennials or long-lived plants that required long-term cultivation and encouraged stable settlement patterns. New frontier settlements (with the exception of Taiwan and Manchuria, which grew traditional cereals) relied on New World annuals—maize and potatoes—that encouraged slash-and-burn agriculture. Thus, the new hill agriculture of the eighteenth century meant quick exploitation of the soil and abandonment of the plot when yields fell; soil maintenance and fertility were ignored. As a result, the immigrant farming population was mobile and scattered (the texts frequently refer to these hill dwellers pejoratively as "shed people," because of the flimsy structures in which they lived). Furthermore, the lure of the frontier was not simply free land but precious metals, rare herbs, skins and furs. These attracted individual pioneers and gangs of workers who joined the colonists and the hired laborers employed in more traditional mountain industries. The extractive nature of both frontier agriculture and industry had its costs in denuded

PLATE 5. Tobacco from the New World was consumed by Chinese elites in the form of snuff, while ordinary people smoked it in pipes. Snuff bottles, a distinctively Qing product, appear in a wide variety of materials; this bright yellow porcelain one dating from the Qianlong period is shaped like an ear of corn. Maize, another New World crop introduced into China in the late sixteenth century, was still exotic to many Chinese in the eighteenth century, even though it was fast becoming a staple food for migrant farmers in the highlands of central and western China. Reproduced from the Metropolitan Museum of Art, bequest of Edmund C. Converse, 1921 (21.175.390).

hillsides, rapid and drastic soil erosion, and the silting of rivers and consequent upset of the delicate hydraulic equilibrium downstream.

The frontier societies that emerged in the eighteenth century all over China therefore tended to have a similar character. New settlers frequently came from many different localities, usually as single males or small family units. Early frontier populations probably had a highly unbalanced sex ratio and an age distribution that was skewed in favor of young adults. Social organizations formed on the frontier were correspondingly different from those in areas of longer settlement. The government was far away and there were few representatives of the established elite; communities were heterogeneous and society must have been relatively free and egalitarian.

But frontier societies were also societies of violence. Some areas were peaceful, such as the mountainous periphery bordering the Southeast Coast and Lower Yangtze where the shed people intermarried with the aboriginal people and were enrolled on tribal registers, but many localities saw intense conflict between new settlers and the original inhabitants. Armed confrontations between Han and non-Han tribes punctuated the century. Moreover, immigrant society itself was highly militarized. To the light hand of local authority was added the explosive demographics of a population with a large proportion of rootless and footloose young men, organized into peer groups and free from familial restraint. Riots and attacks on employers and officials were a common occurrence in the mines and forests where such workers collected. Immigrants preferred to live and work with others from their native place, and thus violence frequently erupted between rival subethnic groups. Indeed, violence was a recognized mode of upward mobility in untamed areas. The counterpart of the literatus, a product of the educational facilities of the large cities in the core, was the bully who, with his gang of armed protectors, dominated this frontier society (and was sometimes the founder of the local elite families of the nineteenth century).

Frontier society changed as the eighteenth century brought maturation and further development to the raw new settlements. This phase was marked by government attempts to collect taxes systematically, establish military garrisons, and enforce more local order, but without technological improvements in transportation, the rough terrain continued to hinder these efforts. In addition, so long as the economy was dominated by extractive industries and an exploitative slash-and-burn agriculture, important segments of the population remained mobile and difficult to control. The process of converting the frontier into settled society had occurred in different areas at numerous points in Chinese history. What made this particular transition difficult was the new technological basis of the economy of the peripheries, the rapidity and scale of the colonization, and the coincident inadequacy of the central government.

Here on the peripheries, where the environment was new and hostile, the state at its weakest, and the presence of the elite at its most sparse, China faced a considerable challenge in the eighteenth century. Could ways be found of organizing people into communities that would provide them with protection, solidarity, and peaceful and predictable forms of interaction with neighbors, yet still integrate them without violence into the national culture and state system?

The solutions that were developed in the Qing were only partially successful in meeting this challenge. The state was unwilling and unable to tap potential revenues to finance an extension of the bureaucratic structure out into the peripheries and down to the villages. Traditional elites did somewhat better. Scholar-officials helped raise the cultural level on the frontiers, mostly through education, but themselves gravitated to the macroregional cities, if not to the refined worlds of Peking, Suzhou, Nanjing, and Hangzhou. The prestige of degrees and office persuaded ambitious local families to try to replicate elite social organizations as best they could. Merchants were by far the most effective cultural and social force for integration on the frontiers. Drawn to remote areas by the opportunities for profit, they settled down in towns and markets and brought with them institutions such as the *huiguan* that not only regulated trade and organized social relations but sponsored cultural activities as well.

In those areas where elites seldom traveled and commerce was weak, ordinary people were left to their own devices; in the hills and mountains outside the cities, they responded both predictably and creatively. They stretched kinship into same-surname organizations, built temple associations on native-place and subethnic ties, adopted new religions, and formed their own occupational groups. Most of these organizations were relatively parochial in their orientation and emphasized exclusivity as much as inclusiveness. The violence of frontier life encouraged this trend, the economic downturn in the early nineteenth century exacerbated it. When closure set in, solidarities were the source of both security and hostility.

The tendency toward heightened boundary drawing was a dangerous one for most of China in the nineteenth century. Social tensions mounted in intensity and culminated in massive rebellions led by ethnic groups, religious minorities, fraternities, and outlaw gangs. Fortunately the national networks that had been built and maintained by merchants and gentry were strong. Elites worked with the state apparatus to restore order and rebuild the government in the late Qing. The price for their victory was high, however, and China would not experience the degree of social integration seen in the eighteenth century again until the middle of the twentieth, when a new set of institutions was introduced.

NEW ASSOCIATIONS

The eighteenth century witnessed a proliferation of social organizations based on an increasing variety of institutions. New economic opportunities, urbanization, migration and travel, social mobility, and sheer population increase had all called for institutions that were flexible and capable of expansion. The Chinese responded by continuing to build not purely on the most venerable basis for affiliation, patrilineal descent, but also on a variety of voluntary ties—fictive kinship, religion, patronage, similar occupation, and common residence. We can see these organizations (described in chapter 2) contributing both to integration and to conflict at all levels of society and throughout the empire in the eighteenth century. But by the end of the century men who belonged to groups that were beyond the control of the elite became organized to threaten the Qing order. Most of these groups were first active in peripheral areas, and all shared a common characteristic: the ability to provide an organization and identity to individuals who were poorly incorporated into more traditional, elite-dominated social institutions.

Ethnicity had been a basis for separatism from earliest times, but the organizing capacity of the many Qing ethnic minorities was shaped both by their internal social structures and by the nature and degree of their incorporation into the Qing state. In general, minority communities were small and widely dispersed, and distinctions among them were finely made; language and customs varied, and suspicion of the outsider discouraged solidarity. Few institutions existed to unite these disparate communities, and the Qing state certainly tried to use its system of local headmen to prevent collective action. Nevertheless, as we shall see in more detail in chapter 5, the inexorable advance of Chinese into minority territories in the eighteenth century sparked uprisings that left heightened ethnic consciousness as well as devastation in their wake.

Subethnic identity, the solidarity created among some Han Chinese on the basis of native-place ties, was an important organizing principle among migrants to new places and in frontier areas generally. Common dialect, familiar gods, and kinship relationships could be used to make a temple or village organization into a vehicle for common action. When such identities became entrenched among heterogeneous populations, as they did in parts of Taiwan, the Southeast Coast, and Lingnan, other loyalties (as, for example, the commitment of community leaders to local order or even to the dynasty itself) might become secondary and they could easily instigate sporadic or even endemic violence. The Hakkas of south and central China, who had long been perceived as different because of their distinct customs and dialect, had developed in response an unusual sense of solidarity. The famous Taiping rebellion, which began among Hakka converts to a new kind of Christianity in southeast China in the

1850s, swept through the Middle Yangtze, and held the Lower Yangtze city of Nanjing for over a decade, heralded the greatly magnified power of ethnicity combined with religion, a power that almost ended the life of the dynasty.

This same combination had also fueled the Muslim rebellions of the early Qing. Sufi sectarianism, a populist and reformist strand of Islam, had first been introduced into Central Asia in the fifteenth and sixteenth centuries, as missionaries converted nomads and townsfolk. Sufi teachers set up residence in the towns, owning land and schools and maintaining hostels for believers who proselytized as they traded. By the Qing, several saintly families of the influential Naqshbandiyya order had become power-ful local potentates in the towns along the trade routes in Xinjiang. This mystical brotherhood emphasized religious and political activism and venerated the tombs of saintly teachers. Competition between rival lines led to rebellion in Xinjiang in the 1750s and sparked the Qing conquest of that region.

In the eighteenth century, a new Sufi school, the New Teaching, spread from the Middle East. As the New Teaching found followers in the Muslim communities of Northwest China, tension arose between its adherents and the Old Teaching followers over doctrinal points, in par-ticular whether their practice of "remembering God" should be done vocally or silently. In 1781 violence between rival Muslims was quelled by the Qing, who arrested and subsequently executed the militant New Teaching leader Ma Mingxin. The Qing also suppressed a second uprising in 1784 that aimed to avenge Ma's death, and the Qianlong emperor banned the new sect in China and introduced a more stringent policy toward all Muslims. These uprisings, spurred both by an increased religious fervor and by conflicts with Han neighbors, foreshadowed the more successful Muslim rebellions of the 1860s.

The eighteenth century also witnessed the growth of another kind of conversion-oriented religious faith, this one indigenous to China: White Lotus sectarianism. The White Lotus religion had emerged in its modern form in the sixteenth century and had continued to attract adherents in subsequent centuries, primarily but not exclusively in North China. Sect members had their own scriptures and worshiped a supreme female deity called the Eternal Mother. Sect communities were originally intended to provide a quasi-clerical life for devout lay men and women. In the late Ming, these groups even enjoyed elite patronage and considerable popu-larity. But the millenarian promises of their scriptures, acted on by some believers, convinced the Ming and Qing states to ban the religion, and most of the time it was forced underground. Where opportunities existed to create public institutions, as among the boatmen on the Grand Canal who built shelter temples along their route in the early eighteenth century, White Lotus communities expressed themselves in conventional terms: they built temples and hostels, worshiped their deities, recited sutras for the dead, and made converts quietly. In general, however, the vigilant Qing state stripped the religion of a public infrastructure at every opportunity.

Under these conditions, the basic organizational principle in sect communities was the tie between teacher and pupil, which formed chains of individuals across time and space (a system also employed by the Sufis). The tie seemed an orthodox one, but the religion was not, and, even though it spread most easily along ordinary solidarities (kinship, residence, occupation), its extremely unusual openness to women as members and teachers betrayed the religion's heterodoxy. Communities, such as they were, consisted of very small groups of men and women (usually in towns and cities) who met to read and recite sutras and thus acquire merit. Proselytizers appear to have appealed most directly to individuals who were not part of existing social groups, recent immigrants or itinerant artisans, for example. By giving these people a network of connections, a common religious vocabulary, and justification for raising money, this voluntary religion was responding to the need for newer, flexible social networks that was characteristic of the middle Qing.

In the course of the eighteenth century, a slightly different type of sect teaching became popular, the product of a line of teachers from Shan county in southwestern Shandong. These Trigram sects, as they were called, emphasized healing, martial arts, meditation, and recitation of short formulae (rather than reading sutras). They appear to have appealed primarily to poorer, less urban, less educated men. Their popularity increased steadily during the latter part of the century in and around the North China plain.

Tensions between believers and nonbelievers, and particularly between sectarians and the state, were aggravated with the passage of time. In the 1770s, the White Lotus religion spread among the migrants to the Middle Yangtze, particularly to the Han River highlands. The implicit millenarian message became explicit: the Eternal Mother would deliver her devoted children from the chaos of the apocalypse sent to punish unbelievers. Rumors spread about the imminent arrival of the Buddha Maitreya (emissary of the Eternal Mother), and in the 1790s a rebellion was planned and initiated by separate sectarian cells linked across a large area by teacher-pupil ties and common belief. Terrain and government inefficiency (Heshen was in charge of the campaigns in the initial phase) made the rebellion difficult and expensive to suppress. Eventually put down a decade later, the uprising had still had the effect of heightening the consciousness of other sectarians about the millenarian promises in their religion.

Although White Lotus sectarianism enabled individuals in different areas to act collectively, in general terms the religion was fragmented and weak in its structure. Other rebellions (in 1774, 1813, and 1838, for example) foundered on the inability of scattered sect communities to overcome inherent divisions and to mobilize the population at large.

Along the Southeast Coast, we can see in the late eighteenth century the emergence of a new and remarkably successful form of social organization: the Triad fraternity. These fraternities were also built on preexisting affiliations—kinship, native place, and contractor-worker ties. To these bonds were added special rituals that bound fellow workers together by blending fictive kinship, discipleship to a monk founder, and sworn brotherhood (a practice common among men of all social classes but not usually involving large numbers of people in any one set). These were, nevertheless, multiclass associations in which the connections of the contractor or boss were used to integrate the workers into the economy. Although these fraternities were linked by secret lore, shared rituals of initiation, and an increasingly elaborate origin myth, in reality they were organized only into autonomous halls. They used a variety of names, most commonly Tiandihui (Heaven and Earth Society), but connections among halls were usually made, if at all, by the bosses.

Triad groups first emerged actively in the 1780s in Taiwan, then a distant periphery of the empire, and multiplied thereafter, especially among transport workers in south China. In the cut-throat competition that set in as Lingnan and the Southeast Coast plunged into depression in the early nineteenth century, the Triads were able to become the powerful predatory and protective organizers of a variety of Mafialike illegal operations in China and overseas. They reigned in an underworld that, freed from orthodox elite control, adapted to the times and provided a very effective organization for workers.

5

Regional Societies

Most descriptions of Chinese society have focused on China as a whole. Regional variations were overlooked in favor of generalizations that could hold true for the entire country. This approach has been most useful when applied to the society of the high elite, who by definition were molded by common careers and were active on a national level. The political borders represented by provinces only sometimes reflect the much more significant boundaries imposed by geography; moreover, the policies of the Chinese state rarely affected all regions in the same way—how could they? G. W. Skinner has more recently proposed that China be studied in terms of large physiographic "macroregions" and Chinese history analyzed as "an internested hierarchy of local and regional histories."[1] Disaggregating the country into its functionally integrated subunits also makes it possible, he has shown, to identify macroregional cycles of development and decline and so refine our understanding of national trends.

This macroregional framework has been criticized by some scholars, but we have found Skinner's system very useful for our purposes, believing as we do that China's enormous size and diversity do call for systematic dissection. We have used the macroregional vocabulary selectively, ignoring some of Skinner's views (most notably the slighting of interregional activity) and adding Taiwan and Manchuria to the eight major macroregions as initially defined. (See maps.) We have, however, taken to heart his central theme and have in addition begun to examine his untested hypothesis that these regions were socially as well as economically significant.

Throughout the sections that follow, we also use the terms *core* and

138

periphery. Each macroregion, Skinner has noted, "was characterized by the concentration in a central area of resources of all kinds—above all in an agrarian society, arable land; but also, of course, population and capital investments—and by the thinning out of resources toward the periphery."[2] The notion of core and periphery as we use it (and indeed, as Skinner himself has used it) is not precise—we offer no listing of county units falling within each category—but we believe that these terms are an extremely useful heuristic device to remind us of the overriding importance, before the era of modern transport and communications, of location. The fortunes of localities rested on their access to the outside world; those with diminished access were more likely to be poor, politically impotent, and culturally backward. Whether a locality was in the core or the periphery made a real difference in the lives of its citizens.

Scholarly research has been very uneven in its consideration of China, and some areas have received a disproportionate share of attention. We know much more about the places that are well documented and important to national affairs like the Lower Yangtze, much less about the politically peripheral Northwest or frontier Manchuria. Although local history has become quite popular in recent years, its focus is often the county or prefecture. We have tried, given what is available, to provide a more balanced picture here.

A regional approach to the study of Chinese society in the early and middle Qing has greatly clarified our sense of the trends and processes discussed so far and has sharpened our understanding of the applicability of received generalizations. We hope to reveal how very different the social fabric of each of these regions was, but also, by noting common processes, to use events in one place to understand those in another. This approach should in any case bring home to the reader the pluralism and great diversity of the Qing empire and illuminate the very particular effects of the national trends we have been looking at. Just as national histories in the West are enriched by consideration of Europeanwide similarities and trends of the sort that come naturally to historians of the Chinese empire, so, we believe, can Chinese history be improved by consideration of the different cultural and social clusters that made up the empire—regardless of whether or not Skinner's macroregions prove to be the most effective units of analysis.

We shall begin with the two most important regions—culturally, economically, and politically—North China and the Lower Yangtze, and then shall consider the rest of central and south China before turning finally to the developing frontier regions.

NORTH CHINA

The North China macroregion was dominated by the plain that made up most of Zhili, Shandong, and Henan provinces and was ringed by mountains on three sides; swampy lands in the southeast made a relatively permeable border with the Lower Yangtze. Situated on the border with Manchu and Mongol territories, North China was a gateway for trade with northern Asia; its strategic location combined with its role as the political center of the empire to ensure that it was heavily garrisoned. Its rivers being largely unnavigable, the primary waterway in the region was the Grand Canal that connected Peking to the Lower Yangtze. Although the flat plain was subject to regular droughts and floods, the fertile soil produced a surplus of wheat, millet, and sorghum that could be supplemented in times of dearth with imports brought in on the canal. Contrasting sharply with the more prosperous plains were regions on the fringes, flood-prone Huaibei to the south and the undeveloped mountains of Shandong, western Henan, and Shanxi.

North China fell rapidly to the Manchus in 1644, but it was some decades before local order could be fully restored and the damages inflicted by late Ming rebels, especially in Henan, repaired. The designation of Peking as the capital (a status it had shared with Nanjing during the Ming) assured North China a central role in the nation and furthered the orientation of the region toward that city. The imperial presence had a palpable and generally salutary impact: roads and bridges, as well as palaces, temples, and hunting parks, were constructed and maintained at imperial expense, and the emperor took a keen interest in local affairs. The Qing hastened to repair the Grand Canal, and by 1687 it was again in operation, stimulating the commerce of cities and towns along its course. Economic growth and the creation of commercial ties between the capital and the rest of the empire were paralleled by the perfection of bureaucratic structures for centralized government and the emergence of Peking as a cultural center for the nation.

The eighteenth century was a period of peace in North China. Soldiers were mobilized on a large scale for the Inner Asian Zunghar campaigns in the Kangxi reign, but there were few major disturbances in the region itself before 1774, the date of the first significant White Lotus uprising. Population growth, rapid until 1780, spurred migration to regional frontiers, especially Manchuria. (For a more detailed consideration of Manchuria in this period, see the end of this chapter.) By the turn of the nineteenth century, growth had slowed, but the loss of government control on the peripheries pointed toward later crises.

It was North China that felt the impact of the large influx of bannermen from the northeast after the Manchu conquest; although many settled in Peking, they were assigned land nearby that had been confiscated from Chinese owners. North China had the highest concentration of Manchus outside of Manchuria and well over half of all bannermen, some of whom were stationed along the Grand Canal as tribute-grain boatmen. Despite their origins as hunters and warriors, the Manchus soon became China's most urbanized ethnic group.

Because all bannermen were part of the ruling elite and dependents of the emperor, they were guaranteed a regular income by the ruling house (in return, one might say, for their military service) but were not free to move or pursue other careers. In the course of the eighteenth century, Manchu society became greatly stratified. A small number of princes and associates of the imperial family enjoyed luxury and power for many generations. Some bannermen became successful officials and scholars, while more pursued careers as military commanders or employees of the Imperial Household. The great majority, however, became poor, indebted, and unemployed; prices rose faster than stipends, and many abandoned their lands for the city. Elaborate programs to make the banner land system work, repeated welfare grants, subsidies, loans, cancellation of debts, even permission for bannermen to join the Green Standard Army (in 1745) or to go back to Manchuria (1740s–1750s) were all unsuccessful. And despite imperial efforts to isolate Manchu communities, preserve Manchu language and culture, and to keep bannermen combat ready, many soon lost touch with their ethnic origins and acculturated to the society around them.

The majority of the Eight Banners actually consisted of Chinese and Mongols who had joined the Manchus before 1644. A secret report by Prince Yi, brother of the Yongzheng emperor, noted that in 1648 Manchus made up only 16 percent of the banner forces; 75 percent were Han Chinese, and 8.3 percent were Mongols. By 1723 the percentage of Mongols remained the same, Han Chinese declined somewhat to 68 percent, and Manchus increased to 23 percent.[3] In the early Qing, Chinese bannermen from Liaodong (Manchuria) were frequently appointed as civil officials. As bondservants to the imperial family, they also became high-ranking officers of the powerful Imperial Household organization. Like the Manchus, these other bannermen lived in or near Peking, where they tended to merge even more rapidly into the local population.

Other Central Asian peoples also resided in North China. The summer retreat at Rehe drew Tibetans, Mongols, and others who came at imperial invitation. Lamaist monks staffed monasteries there, in Peking, and elsewhere in the region. There were also regular visitors to Peking from China's other tributaries: Korea, the Ryukyus, Annam, Siam, Burma, and the Sulu archipelago, caravans from Russia, and even an occasional Western embassy.

Muslims were active in trade, particularly with north and west Asia. Members of Muslim communities in the cities were engaged in the horse and caravan trades, cart transport, butchering, and the restaurant business. In some ways acculturated to Chinese society, the Muslims nevertheless lived in their own communities organized around mosques; in Peking, they inhabited the less desirable urban outskirts. Kaifeng (in Henan) housed China's only known community of Jews, some five hundred families in 1670, even then declining in social prestige and distinctiveness but given a community focus by their synagogue. Peking had the only legally resident Westerners except for Macao—the Jesuits, Franciscans, and Dominicans kept at court by Kangxi and Qianlong as artists and technicians, as well as the very small Russian mission permitted by treaty.

The great majority of the inhabitants of North China were, of course, Han Chinese. Because there were few geographic or cultural barriers to physical mobility within North China, linguistic differences between the Shandong peninsula in the east and the Shanxi mountains in the west were ones of accent not dialect. The population of the region seems to have been highly mobile, and subethnic differences had long since been minimized. Geographic mobility in pursuit of employment may have put a higher value on affinal ties, for the strong competitive lineages found in south and southeast China were much less common here.

North China had a particularly large and diverse number of sojourners from other regions, almost all of whom were concentrated in Peking. These included officials in the metropolitan bureaucracy, candidates for the nationwide triennial *jinshi* and Shuntian prefecture *juren* examinations, expectant officials, merchants, and transport workers serving the capital by land and waterway. The most important of the interregional merchants were those from the Northwest, who traded in salt, vegetable oils, and tobacco, and had become de facto bankers to the central government. These Shanxi merchants (who are discussed more extensively in the Northwest China section below) also helped open up Manchuria and dominated the trade with Mongolia (tea and cloth for animal products) that ran though Zhangjiakou (Kalgan) and Peking. The book-

and-art market in the capital was run, not surprisingly, by men from the Lower Yangtze. North China, though, did export officials from the Imperial Household Department who ran government monopolies in all parts of the empire, from Urumchi in the far west to Canton in the south.

Commanding the resources of the empire, Peking imported goods as well as people and had become a national storehouse of treasures: silver, gold, copper, pearls, jade, the finest silks, porcelains, furs, rare medicines, paintings, antiquities, and of course weapons and grain, all flowed to the capital. Many of these goods were recirculated by the throne in the form of gifts to officials and expenditures for bannermen, imperial campaigns, and tours. The salt monopoly for Zhili and Shandong had salt flats near the sea and its headquarters in Tianjin. This monopoly was profitable enough to assure its merchants a luxurious life-style and success in the examinations second only to that of their counterparts in the Lower Yangtze.

The most important change in North China agriculture during the early Qing was the adaptation of cotton manufacture to the dry northern climate through the use of damp cellars for spinning and weaving. By the eighteenth century, the core of the North China region was second only to the Lower Yangtze in cotton production; in 1750, cotton, replacing grain, occupied an estimated 20–30 percent of all agricultural land. In the newly settled peripheries in central Shandong, glass manufacture, coal mining, and sericulture were developed as mountain industries. Yangliuqing (Zhili) and Wei county (Shandong) were two of the three national centers for the production of the woodblock prints displayed at the new year that attained widespread circulation after the seventeenth century. The Shandong peninsula also exported soybeans and benefited from the growing coastal trade that linked Manchuria with Shanghai and Amoy. Sorghum liquor was a widespread local industry. Between 1723 and 1730 more than four hundred new breweries were licensed in one prefecture of Zhili alone.[4] Late in the century, we find sweet potatoes being planted along the coast and attempts being made to reclaim marshy lands in the Huai basin with wheat and short-season rice.

Because of its numerous mercantile and literary sojourners, Peking housed many native-place associations. There were at least twenty-six *huiguan* before 1800, half of which represented Shanxi merchants; by 1875 there were 387 *huiguan* of various sorts, the highest number found in any Chinese city.

The many imperially sponsored literary projects that produced encyclopedias, dictionaries, histories, and catalogues made Peking an intellectual center in the eighteenth century to rival the Lower Yangtze. Many of the most important patrons in the early Qing were high-ranking wealthy bannermen like Prince Yu, a brother of the Kangxi emperor, but Chinese soon took on similar roles. The scholarly associations formed around Zhu Yun, who served in many educational posts in the 1770s, for example, were important to evidential scholarship generally, just as the different but not entirely separate networks created by the imperial favorite, Heshen, reached the length of the civil and military bureaucracies in the 1780s–1790s.

For Manchus, the banner system was the primary associational network. Despite a trend toward bureaucratization and reduction of personal ties between imperial princes and banner forces, the banner was still the residential and work unit, and the hereditary company commanders wielded authority over the personal and professional lives of their men. The influence and identity of the lineage survived intact within the banners, even in less extreme cases than that of the long-lived and successful Fucas, who produced five generations of illustrious (occasionally notorious) imperial favorites from Mishan (d. 1675), who served the Kangxi emperor during the critical early years of his reign, to Fukang'an (d. 1796), one of the Qianlong emperor's most able military commanders. The major routes of social mobility for bannermen were through the Imperial Household, the imperial bodyguard, or the civil and military examinations.

There was a huge government presence in Peking. The metropolitan bureaucracy employed at least ten thousand people, not counting clerks. Many of these officials (those of the fifth rank and below) could obtain their posts by purchase, and by the nineteenth century (and perhaps earlier) it was outsiders, natives of Shaoxing prefecture, Zhejiang, who dominated the central-government boards. North China as a whole had the largest concentration of banner armies, and the Imperial Household Department, still growing in size in this period, was itself a major economic actor in the region, being a landowner, moneylender, and merchant broker (in salt, rice, and the trade with the northeast). The constant movement of officials en route to the capital, the regular imperial journeys to Rehe and other areas, and the numerous channels of information available to the emperor kept him informed of local conditions. North China in return appears to have received more than its share of government funds—for price stabilization, waterway and road maintenance, and local defense, not to mention the regular salaries paid to bannermen and government employees. (When such salaries became inadequate, however, these pensioners became a liability.) Imperial willingness to spend large sums on Yellow River conservancy and Grand Canal maintenance in the corridor leading to the Lower Yangtze may also have encouraged corruption and malfeasance there (a problem that was to become particularly acute in the early nineteenth century).

Three important sacred mountains were located in North China and were the sites of regionwide pilgrimages. Mount Tai in central Shandong and Mount Heng and Mount Wutai in northeast Shanxi attracted imperial as well as ordinary pilgrims. Wutai, center for the Manjusri cult, had a substantial Central Asian clientele and housed many Lamaist monks. The Taoist White Cloud temple in Peking claimed a bureaucratic authority over Taoist masters of the Quanzhen school comparable to that of the Heavenly Masters of Jiangxi. Peking was the site of the elaborate annual calendar of imperial sacrifices, previously described, that were offered by the emperor on behalf of the nation in vast reserved areas (e.g., the Temple of Heaven) within the city. Two complexes of Qing tombs and one for Ming emperors were located in the hills near Peking.

North China was also the homeland for the White Lotus sectarian assemblies, although the religion had already spread well beyond this region. Transmitted through teacher-pupil ties and often concentrated in certain descent groups, this religion found adherents throughout North China, in cities and increasingly in rural areas. As we have noted, the eighteenth-century development of a sect that concentrated on simple meditation and vigorous martial arts by teachers in southwest Shandong enhanced the religion's appeal among the uneducated. Intermittent government prosecution accompanied sporadic but generally ineffective attempts at millenarian rebellion.

The many minority groups in North China were generally small in number, and ethnic and subethnic violence was much less marked than in other regions. The ordinary brawls and quarrels between Han Chinese and other groups were less likely to escalate into communitywide struggles in this area of close government supervision. Among the elite there were occasional riots linked with the examinations, especially the Shuntian prefecture exams that were such an important channel for upward mobility. The general peacefulness of local society during most of the century was gradually interrupted from the 1770s by a number of small White Lotus uprisings in the regional core, followed by a rise in armed smuggling and mounted banditry in the Huai River basin on the southern periphery in the first decades of the nineteenth century.

Settlements on the North China plain were characteristically small

nucleated villages. Many peasants around Peking were tenants of bannermen and paid rent to the Imperial Household Department rather than
taxes to the local magistrate. The real power on such lands actually lay in
the hands of stewards, mostly Chinese, who managed the land, found
tenants or hired laborers, collected the rents, and loaned out money. The
instability of harvests in North China, caused by floods and droughts and
the long history of settlement, helped shape a society in which tenancy
was relatively rare (except on banner lands) and the use of hired labor
common. Landlords were usually involved in the daily management of
their properties and not residents of distant cities; on banner lands, rents
were often in arrears. Except for bannermen, ordinary people enjoyed
considerable physical and occupational mobility, landownership was
unusually fluid, and vertical organizations weak.

One of the least urbanized macroregions, North China was dominated by Peking. A city of at least a million, the capital had a carefully
constructed symbolic layout, huge intramural areas given over entirely to
the imperial family, large banner quarters within the Northern City,
multiple layers of government, and, as Alison Dray-Novey has shown, a
wide variety of urban social services provided by the government (poor
relief, snow removal, firefighting, etc.). The northern portion of the city
had been taken over by bannermen, but the Southern City, where most
commercial activity took place, had a very popular entertainment district
of wineshops, teahouses (Huizhou merchants alone ran two hundred of
them in 1801), theaters, and brothels. Other important cities in the region
included Tianjin, Dongchang, and Jining, all located on the Grand Canal,
and Kaifeng and Ji'nan, both provincial capitals and regional metropolises.

In the course of the eighteenth century, the advantages enjoyed in the
first decades of the dynasty by men from North China in official postings
had given way to greatly increased competition for degrees and posts. The
Shuntian *juren* exams attracted wealthy men from all over the empire and
put native candidates at a particular disadvantage. Lower Yangtze academic networks soon dominated life at court and in the capital, but that
was the only region to outproduce North China in eighteenth-century
jinshi.

The Kong family of Shandong were a shining exception to the
generally undistinguished array of local elites. Descendants of Confucius
in the seventieth generation, this very large descent group counted more
than ten thousand members in twelve branches in 1700 and was virtually
enfeoffed in Qufu county. They had extensive landholdings, control of the

local magistracy, special exam quotas, and high social position. In 1684, the Kangxi emperor visited Qufu, had sacrifices performed at the temple to Confucius, listened to lectures on the classics presented by two descendants, and favored one of them, Kong Shangren, with office. The Confucian shrine managed by the Kong (and restored at great expense in 1730 by the throne) served as a kind of pilgrimage site for literati and emperors. The Kong were eclipsed in status only by the imperial house itself. The Aisin Gioro descent group was supported by a vast staff, had a large surplus of women and a special category of celibate men (eunuchs) to serve them, occupied great chunks of the capital city, and had its own private army. Celebration of imperial birthdays, marriages, and deaths supplemented the annual festivals in Peking.

Literati life and culture in this region was also centered in Peking. The book-and-antique market at Liulichang was at its peak in the eighteenth century, and Manchus and Chinese met in literary and social gatherings in the homes of high officials. The orthodox school of academic painting flourished at court, where officials were exposed not only to the imperial art collections but also to Western curiosities (snuff, clocks, watches). Manchu interests in hunting and horse racing found Chinese audiences. As we have noted, imperial patronage, together with large audiences of bannermen and sojourning merchants and officials, turned Peking into a magnet for theatrical groups from all over the country. In the course of the century, a succession of regional styles were popularized in the city. By the Daoguang reign, the foundations for "Peking opera" were already in place, supported by an increase in public theaters and the popularity of theater going as a social event. This lively urban culture of Peking was oblivious to Confucian disapproval or imperial proscription.

Cultural sophistication as well as political and economic power were concentrated in Peking and less well distributed in the region as a whole; the centrality of the Lower Yangtze, by contrast, was firmly based on a stronger and more diverse economy and a network of prosperous cities. On the other hand, as the seat of the capital, North China enjoyed considerable two-way traffic with most regions of the empire. The Lower Yangtze tended to be an exporter not an importer of culture.

LOWER YANGTZE

The Lower Yangtze macroregion encompassed southern Jiangsu, northern Zhejiang, and southern Anhui provinces and was the heart of the area Chinese traditionally called Jiangnan, "south of the Yangtze." The flat terrain of the Yangtze plain was ideal for irrigated agriculture. The delta was covered by a dense network of waterways that provided cheap transport and were linked with the north by the Grand Canal, with the west by the Yangtze River, and with the entire east coast (and abroad) by the sea. Location and topography made the Lower Yangtze the most urbanized and densely populated region in Qing China. Even its mountainous western and southern peripheries were relatively developed, and the hills of southern Anhui were the home of the nationally prominent Huizhou merchants. Through the eighteenth century, however, the settlement of the Yangtze highlands by shed people created widespread deforestation, soil erosion, and flood damage downstream in the delta. By the 1790s, officials tried to stop further expansion of highland agriculture, with no apparent success.

China's most advanced economic region, the Lower Yangtze recovered quickly in the late seventeenth century, despite the deflation of the mid-century and the occasional resistance to Manchu conquest such as provoked the 1645 massacres of citizens in Yangzhou, Jiangyin, and Jiading by advancing banner armies. The Qing imposition of law and order benefited the landowning classes by suppressing the potential for tenant uprisings, while the coastal evacuations of the 1660s prompted by pro-Ming resistance on Taiwan were fairly lightly enforced at Ningbo and other strategic coastal sites in the region. The first concern of the new rulers was to secure tax revenues from this wealthy area. That this was no easy task was amply illustrated in the Jiangnan tax case of 1661 discussed in chapter 1. By the late seventeenth century, the regional economy had made a comeback and was beginning another upward trend. After Lower Yangtze elites had aided the new rulers in defeating the Three Feudatories, they were rewarded with renewed access to national power.

The Lower Yangtze was an old and long-settled society whose inhabitants were mostly Han Chinese. Small lingering remnants of aboriginal groups did remain: some mean people, descended from Yue tribes, had become actors, peddlars, sedan-chair bearers, wharf coolies, and petty artisans, while the women specialized as marriage brokers and midwives. A large community of Muslims in Nanjing, where the first mosque had been established in the late fourteenth century, used their Central-Asian connections to trade in jade ornaments, felt, and leather goods. Compared with other regions, however, these groups played very minor roles in the society; the Lower Yangtze experienced few of the minority-related problems that were so common in virtually every other region in the eighteenth century. Low-status bondservants, who had expanded in numbers during the late Ming in the Lake Tai basin and elsewhere, were disappearing in the eighteenth century except in some remote areas.

The Lower Yangtze held a central importance for the dynasty because of its economic prominence and its leadership in literati culture. Although it was a prosperous agricultural region, with rice paddies dominating the landscape, we have already seen how the cotton and silk textile industries were developed, so that market towns like Shengzezhen in the Lake Tai region attracted sojourning merchants from Shanxi and Shandong as well as from within the Lower Yangtze. Grain importers themselves (the region sent tribute grain to the capital but did not produce enough for its urban population), Lower Yangtze cities served as national markets in grain and other commodities, collecting and distributing goods from as far away as the Upper Yangtze and Lingnan regions to North China and elsewhere. The Lower Yangtze also supplied elites all over the empire with fine luxury goods: Shaoxing wine, Hangzhou green tea, Yixing stoneware teapots, Huizhou inkstones, Nanjing silks, and books of all kinds. The preeminent merchants of the region were those from Huizhou in Anhui who had begun centuries earlier to build their nationwide network of trade in lumber, paper, and tea (products of their mountainous home area), then rice, silk, porcelain, and, most important, salt. Scholars as well as businessmen, Huizhou men had substantial influence on eighteenth-century culture, as we have often noted.

The Lower Yangtze's favorable marketing advantages brought not only commercialization of agriculture and a very dense network of central places but also prominence in the national bureaucracy. Wealth and traditions of scholarly accomplishment encouraged families to educate their sons for the civil-service examinations, and the Lower Yangtze achieved success rates in these competitions that were far higher than those of the other macroregions. The Lower Yangtze also exported officials and subofficials, not to mention private secretaries: six of the nine prefectures producing the largest number of *jinshi* in the Qing were in the Lower Yangtze. The highest places on these examinations went overwhelmingly to men from this area, and private secretaries and subofficials from Shaoxing were ubiquitous in the metropolitan and provincial bureaucracies. The tendency for elite households to move from rural areas into towns during this period was reflected in the distribution of Qing degrees: between 1796 and 1820, more than 80 percent of the provincial degree-holders from the counties around Lake Tai came from urban centers.

The Lower Yangtze's centrality to the Qing economy paralleled its crucial role in central-government revenues—it contributed more than a quarter of the land taxes—and brought it under close scrutiny from Peking. In addition to the regular army, there were banner garrisons at Nanjing and Zhenjiang, part of a Yangtze defense line, and a banner garrison in Hangzhou for coastal security. The dense population and large tax income necessitated a multiplicity of administrative units: under Yongzheng twelve counties in Jiangsu were split in half for better supervision, Suzhou was the only city in the empire to be the seat of three counties, and Jiangsu after 1760 was the only province with two financial commissioners. Extra personnel were needed to carry out the complex and (to officials) vexing governance of this economic heartland, particularly tax collection. In 1728 the Yongzheng emperor commissioned an exhaustive investigation of the region's (actually Jiangsu, Jiangxi, and Anhui) persistent tax arrears. Encountering stout resistance from local yamen clerks and runners as well as local elites, the investigators took two years to complete their work. They concluded that only about half of the ten million taels of tax arrears in Jiangsu were the result of delinquency by taxpayers; the remainder was the product of official corruption. But without a vastly expanded bureaucracy, capable of supplanting the informal management of taxes by local elites, even the Yongzheng emperor could not successfully implement tax reform in Jiangnan.

The Liang-Huai Salt Administration, headquartered in Yangzhou, was the largest single source of revenue in the salt monopoly; the Imperial Textile Manufactories in Nanjing, Hangzhou, and Suzhou employed hundreds of workers to produce silks for imperial use. Chinese bondservants were appointed as textile commissioners and directors of the customs houses dotting the Yangtze and the Grand Canal; they collected the rich revenues from trade for the emperor's purse and kept an eye on bureaucratic intrigues and public discontent. Furthermore, three massive extraprovincial government bureaus were imposed along the North China–Lower Yangtze corridor, each with large (and growing) staffs and substantial budgets—the Grain Transport, Grand Canal, and Yellow River administrations. Even in the early Qing these bureaucracies were loci for corruption and inefficiency, and they posed serious problems for the court.

The Lower Yangtze was also the recipient of imperial tourism and a certain amount of imperial largess: the Kangxi emperor visited its great cities on his six southern tours, and so did his grandson, the Qianlong emperor. The large-scale projects in the Kangxi reign to construct waterworks that would assure continuous canal traffic, defend against floods, and provide irrigation for adjacent lands generally benefited the area. Salt merchants were expected to contribute some of their profits to pay for local water control and southern tours as well as flood and famine relief, even for military campaigns elsewhere in the empire.

Close scrutiny of local conditions by bondservants, bureaucrats, and soldiers did not necessarily result in tight control of this extremely complex society. The Lower Yangtze had developed a multiplicity of social organizations that cut across kinship, occupational, and residential loyalties. Although this region produced more genealogies than any other, lineage organization was, especially in comparison with the Southeast Coast and Lingnan, only moderately developed. Exceptions to this generalization such as Tongcheng (Anhui) and Shaoxing (Zhejiang) were located away from the richest lands of the delta. But for many elites, kinship was only one of many grounds for association. The movement of elite households into cities and towns during the late Ming and early Qing probably diluted kinship ties, and many elite households may have, by deliberate design, sharply limited their obligations to poor agnates while expanding marriage alliances with other prominent county families. In China's patrilineal society, it was difficult for such affinal ties to be formalized, but they were significant nonetheless.

The economic environment also stimulated individuals to choose alternative channels of social organization. In addition to investing in lineage lands, Huizhou merchants contributed heavily to the support of public works back home: in one locality, they contributed more than fourteen thousand taels of silver over ten years to repair roads, build bridges, repair temples, and create rest stops along the road. Because waterways were essential to both agriculture and trade, a great deal of private as well as public effort was devoted to water control, and people of disparate surnames and backgrounds cooperated in these projects.

The large cities of the region attracted many sojourners who used kinship and native-place ties to organize formal and informal groups and tried to dominate a trade or monopolize a wharf. During the eighteenth century, guilds (*gongso*) began to increase in number and eventually (in the nineteenth century) supplanted the more parochial *huiguan* as the major group in urban markets. Of the forty-eight or more *huiguan* in Suzhou, for example, more than 62 percent were founded in the late seventeenth to late eighteenth centuries, while only 13 percent of the Qing guilds in the city were founded in that same period, and the majority date from the nineteenth century. These various elite-dominated organizations were tolerated by the authorities, who used them to help run the cities, but, as we saw in chapter 2, attempts by workers to organize in similar fashion were strongly discouraged. Officials and merchants both feared the explosive potential of combining economic interests with religious dissidence in heterodox associations such as the Luo sects found among the eighteenth-century Grand Canal boatmen. It was not until the nineteenth century, when elite control weakened, that such groups came into their own as genuine worker organizations.

The state was also successful in suppressing literati organizations that might meddle in politics. The Ming examples of the Donglin and Fushe societies, both of which had their nucleus in the Lower Yangtze, were sufficient to put iron in the Manchu policy against academy-based factions. Only officially founded academies were permitted; poetry clubs and informal networks were tolerated, but independent higher-level elite organizations did not develop until the nineteenth century. As long as groups remained atomized and specific in function, so that individuals' interests were split among a variety of groups, the state was content to follow a laissez-faire policy. It is significant that regional unity was discouraged by administrative boundaries that pitted province against province in the examinations. Dialect differences (Wu speakers in the delta, Southern Mandarin speakers to their north, and Anhui speakers on the southwestern fringes) also worked against easy alliances among elites.

Three cities dominated the market hierarchy in the Lower Yangtze. Suzhou, which during the period of recovery was experiencing the most rapid population growth and eventually reached a population of seven hundred thousand in the mid-nineteenth century, was the center for the national rice trade and for the cotton and silk textile industries. It had supplanted Nanjing, the former Ming capital, as the region's central metropolis. Hangzhou and Nanjing (their days of glory past) continued to function as regional metropolises. Below these three cities in the urban hierarchy was Yangzhou, a great shipping center on the Grand Canal, seat of the salt monopoly, and a key node in the Huizhou merchants' national network. According to Kong Shangren, who lived there in 1685, this city, which had been in ruins after the Manchu conquest, had already regained its prosperity and "was unquestionably the most vibrant city in China at that time."[5] Ningbo was a rising eighteenth-century entrepôt for coastal and overseas trade, especially with Japan. Shanghai, a local textile center, was emerging during the century as a major port for the junk trade in soybeans and grain that linked Manchuria and North China to markets in central and south China. The rise of Shanghai was a harbinger of the

PLATE 6. The barges of Lord Macartney's embassy to the court of the Qianlong emperor in 1793 traveled to Peking along China's inland waterways. This river scene of the Grand Canal at Suzhou, done by an artist who accompanied the British ambassador, shows the large and small boats in ordinary use. Prints like this helped feed European interest in China. Reproduced from an engraving by William Alexander held by the Library Company of Philadelphia.

changes of the mid-nineteenth century that would make it, not the older Lower Yangtze cities, preeminent in the region and eventually the nation.

In the early Qing, the Lower Yangtze market economy continued to penetrate deeply into rural villages. Handicraft production stimulated the rise of satellite centers for the silk industry near Suzhou on the shores of Lake Tai and around Huzhou and Jiaxing further south, where an elaborate putting-out system drew peasant women into weaving. A healthy market in imported rice became crucial to the region. Access to large markets meant that rural households were encouraged to earn additional income through handicrafts or to cultivate cash crops such as cotton, mulberry trees, or silkworms. Households also had the option of sending surplus sons into the cities for work. This was the market-oriented environment that produced the late Ming and Qing agricultural handbooks explaining how to weigh alternative occupations and land-use patterns for maximal profitability.

As elsewhere in China, the peripheries of this region were made more productive in the Qing. Some of the marshy lands of northern Jiangsu were drained and planted with winter wheat or newly developed short-season rice, although they continued to be subject to the chronic flooding of the Huai River system. Uplands adjacent to the Southeast Coast and Middle Yangtze received new migrants and by the end of the century experienced the problems with soil erosion that were common elsewhere.

Because Suzhou, Nanjing, and Hangzhou have been much studied, we know a great deal about their spatial organization, social composition, and economic functions. In the heart of China's most advanced economic region, enjoying optimal transport networks, these cities were at the heart of a burgeoning textile industry, were the major centers of quality book publication, and served important entrepôt functions for other inter-regional trade. Like other large cities, these had large populations of sojourners from without and within the macroregion: Huizhou and Fujian merchants, Ningbo and Shanxi bankers, as well as intraregional migrants filling craft and service specializations. What made them unique was their role as centers of literati culture.

If Peking had become the locus for imperially sponsored historical and literary work in the middle Qing, the Lower Yangtze cities were still the preferred homes of China's literati. The older urban areas in particular produced and attracted scholars and men of leisure: bibliophiles, scholar-printers, collectors, artists, poets, and writers. The demand for books was fed by this community, which also created and printed books for an educated audience and dominated quality printing outside government circles. Drama too flourished, especially in cities with large merchant populations: Suzhou was the Qing center of the *kunqu* style, there were numerous types of local theater, and the wealth of the salt monopoly made Yangzhou renowned as a drama town. Huizhou merchants were important carriers of dramatic fashions between the Lower Yangtze and other regions. The restaurants, teashops, taverns, and courtesans of these cities were famous throughout the empire, and the extensive gardens and villas of the urban rich were widely imitated.

Lower Yangtze scholars (whether at home or in Peking) were the leaders in virtually all realms of eighteenth-century scholarship. Textual research was supported by the rich library collections, coteries of scholars working in academies, and wealth derived from trade of this region. But the Lower Yangtze was also the center for other successful scholar-officials (from Tongcheng, for example) who defended the Song learning associated with Zhu Xi, as well as the home of many scholars who had given up official careers altogether. During the eighteenth century, as competition for degrees and posts became increasingly fierce, dissidence and alienation from orthodox literati values came to be more and more frequently expressed by members of the scholar class. Ming loyalism was no longer the dominant motive for distancing oneself from a bureaucratic career, but other themes that had been sounded in the seventeenth century were revived. The notion that government service sullied one's integrity, that the arduous preparations for the civil-service examinations stultified true intellectual development, and that examinations favored the dull over the talented were all common criticisms voiced directly and in fiction.

Some failed scholars attacked the mores of those in power; others retreated to pursuits such as literature, calligraphy, painting, and connoisseurship. Some were like Shi Guoqi, who gave up competing for a *juren* degree at age forty and turned to a combination of scholarship on the Jin dynasty (rulers of north China in the twelfth and early thirteenth centuries) and management of a cotton wholesale house in Huzhou. Provincial examination quotas that protected the bureaucracy as a whole from becoming a Lower Yangtze monopoly produced high rates of examination failure that diverted the creativity of educated men to the arts and to commerce, while also provoking a malaise with the status quo that would later become the basis of calls for bureaucratic reform.

The Lower Yangtze had virtually every type of rural settlement, from the isolated farmhouse to the nucleated village. Villages tended to be larger than those in North China and had shops servicing the farm population. In the core area south of Lake Tai, large villages were clustered on waterways only a few kilometers apart, with the largest settlements located at the confluence of streams. In the delta further east, houses were dispersed on man-made canals. The terrain throughout the core region was extremely flat, punctuated by grave mounds in fields and the occasional stone bridge.

Although there were very large landowners in this region of high tenancy, land was also owned by many who had relatively small holdings. Estates consisted generally of widely scattered parcels, and a typical tenant rented land from more than one landlord. These facts, coupled with absentee landlordism, undoubtedly worked in the tenant's favor by weakening landlord control. During the eighteenth century some localities developed the kind of permanent tenancy known as "two owners to a field" that gave the tenant the right to cultivate the plot and freedom to subrent or sell this right without the consent of the subsoil owner or landlord. The advantageous position of the tenant was partially a result of his contribution to the creation and maintenance of high-quality paddy; it was also a reflection of the difficulty many absentee landlords confronted in supervising their scattered holdings. Tenants were not necessarily poor; some were entrepreneurs who rented land to cultivate cash crops on a large scale.

The organization of work in such a commercialized region transcended the seasonal limitations that have confined many premodern farmers. Diversification and intensification in agriculture and handicraft production kept peasants occupied throughout the year. Migration to cities for work was convenient and was stimulated by urban prosperity. The subregional ties that dictated that Hangzhou's carpenters and cabinetmakers were Ningbo natives or that Suzhou's pork butchers came from Piling and its barbers from Wuxi, Jurong, and Dantu counties show the importance of the cultivation of institutional connections in determining sojourning strategies.

The Lower Yangtze was a heartland of Chinese Buddhism, containing many of China's great monasteries. This was the region that had produced the late Ming movement to rejuvenate and popularize Buddhism led by the monk Zhuhong. During the eighteenth century, the lay-Buddhist movement expanded, and the popularity of vegetarian sects of the White Lotus type in which members chanted scriptures and followed many monastic precepts testifies to the continuing power and adaptability of the religion. The most famous pilgrimage site in the region—one that attracted many outsiders—was Putuoshan, an island off the Zhejiang coast near Ningbo that was sacred to the goddess of mercy, Guanyin (Avalokitesvara). Putuoshan was on the major coastal trade route, and since the Tang period sailors and seagoing merchants had prayed to Guanyin for protection from storms and pirates. By the Qing, the island held more than a hundred temples, monasteries, and hermitages of the Chan Buddhist sect, some the recipients of imperial patronage. Mount Jiuhua was a regional pilgrimage site located on the south shore of the

Yangtze in Anhui, not far from Huizhou. Jiuhua's temples and monasteries were dedicated to Dizang (Kshitigarbha), the buddha of the underworld who leads souls from hell to the Western Paradise. During the pilgrimage season in the fall, boats brought filial sons to Jiuhua to get garments with Dizang's seal that would ensure that their aged parent could escape the tortures of hell. For literati, Mount Huang in Anhui, made famous by late Ming painters from Huizhou, became a favored tourist and vacation site.

Social conflict took two major forms in the Lower Yangtze during the eighteenth century. The first was the interlineage feuding similar to that found in Southeast China and Lingnan at this time (described in more detail below). *Xiedou*, the term coined to describe this collective violence, focused on control over water and occurred most frequently in east Zhejiang. In delta cities such as Suzhou, where rising handicraft production had created large groups of hired workers in a single trade and the labor market was fluid and unstable, artisans and workers fought with shopowners and employers over wages and the right to organize. Although not all of the conflicts suggest the emerging class consciousness ascribed by Marxist historians, there is no doubt that the workers did try to improve their status and win higher piece rates, and that shopowners and officials feared the threat to law and order posed by such large numbers of workers. Strikes and riots punctuated the decades from the late seventeenth through the eighteenth centuries in cotton textiles, silk, paper manufacture, and many other sectors.

Preeminent in the early and middle Qing, the nineteenth century brought more hardships for the Lower Yangtze. The deflation of the 1830s must have caused business to fall off in this highly commercialized region, smuggling and government demands made the salt monopoly less profitable, and the near collapse of the Grand Canal in the same period forced a reorientation of trading networks. The apolitical stance of evidential scholarship began to be strongly criticized, and scholars of other persuasions from other regions found new audiences. Even worse was yet to come. The Taiping rebellion of the mid-nineteenth century physically destroyed the academic infrastructure of Jiangnan, gave a considerable boost to rival merchants from other regions, and promoted the extraordinary growth of Shanghai at the expense of those cities occupied by the rebels.

No other macroregions could match the centrality of the Lower Yangtze and North China in the empire—not even the Middle Yangtze, Southeast Coast, and Lingnan, which each played important national roles in the eighteenth century. Although the Gan River basin in the

Middle Yangtze macroregion had long produced the wealth essential to political and intellectual power in China and its elites had shared the same world as their Lower Yangtze colleagues, the rest of that region was comparatively late in developing. We can see illustrated in the Middle Yangtze, to which we now turn, not only the world of national elites but also the consequences of greater isolation and the problems of frontier unrest that, although less typical of the two regions so far considered, were very characteristic of the empire as a whole.

MIDDLE YANGTZE

The Middle Yangtze macroregion consisted of more than eight hundred kilometers of the Yangtze River corridor plus the basins of four major Yangtze tributaries (the Han, Yuan, Xiang, and Gan rivers) and parts of nine provinces. One characteristic of the Middle Yangtze, by contrast with those macroregions so far discussed, was its fragmentation into several sharply demarcated subregions. Mountain ranges surrounded the region on virtually all sides, cut off each river system from the others, and thus encouraged separate subregional development.

One of these subsystems was the Gan River basin, which, although G. W. Skinner has decided it constituted an independent macroregion, we have included here. The special features of the Gan basin, located in Jiangxi, include its dialect (which resembled that of the Lower Yangtze), its continuing (though declining) role as an intellectual center, its successful extraprovincial merchant network, the concentration of powerful old families in the northern regional core, and the large numbers of Hakkas in the mountainous peripheries to the south and west. Another important subregion at the other end of the macroregion was formed by the Han River, whose highlands (comprising northwest Hubei, southwest Shaanxi, and northeast Sichuan) were to become a major trouble spot for the government during the White Lotus rebellion (1796–1805). Indeed, many of the mountainous areas in the macroregion were the sites of unrest. Han Chinese clashed with aboriginal Miao tribes through the eighteenth century in the mountains of west Hunan and the mountains separating the Xiang and Gan basins were locales of intermittent Hakka-Han conflict. Nevertheless, the fact that people moved rather readily across these mountains made macroregional boundaries rather porous, both economically and culturally.

The Middle Yangtze's central location and the suitability of its navigable rivers for long-distance trade kept the region open to the east and the west and provided an offsetting unifying force. The Gan River and its tributaries formed one of south China's rare north-south interior trade routes, linking the Yangtze with Canton. The Xiang River was a second north-south artery linking central China with Guangdong's West River, while the Han River system thrust deeply into Northwest China to make connections with Central Asian trade routes. The biggest artery of all was of course the Yangtze itself; it cut through the entire region and transported goods and people across all of central China from the mountains of the far west to the delta in the east. During the middle Qing, the city of Hankou became the center of an integrated macroregional economy that excluded only the Gan River basin (which remained oriented downriver to Lower Yangtze markets).

Rehabilitation was the major theme of the late seventeenth century in a region devastated by warfare from the 1640s into the 1670s. The first task for the Qing was to revive the agricultural economy by encouraging settlers to take up abandoned lands. As the regional economy recovered and expanded in the eighteenth century through large-scale migration into the Yangtze and Han River highlands, it became part of vigorous national grain markets. Problems with water control in the core and with increasing militarization and social unrest in mountainous areas marked the end of the century, but the general economic growth of the region was not interrupted until the deflation of the Daoguang reign and subsequent Taiping rebellion.

Recovery and expansion of cultivated acreage brought many new settlers into the best lands of the region, but, as the good rice land disappeared, migration into the peripheries was accelerated and the highlands received an unprecedented stream of colonists. As Shi Runzhang, a local official, wrote, "The Fujian coast has many vagrants, and Jiangxi governs many untended fields. . . . The vagrants come in herds, to sleep in the open and live on cold mists."[6] Some imitated minority tribesmen and practiced slash-and-burn agriculture, cultivating the fertile soil with new dryland crops such as maize and sweet potato and then moving on. Other migrants had technological expertise in mining, lumber, paper, and other highland industries. Marketing networks were developed for the sale and export of these cash crops downriver, while the need for labor often created well-trodden paths across the mountains into adjacent regions. Even as their own region was filling up, Huguang (Hunan and Hubei) peasants formed a large component of those resettling the Upper Yangtze, and both Huguang and Jiangxi men also pushed on into the Southwest and Lingnan.

Many of these migrants were Hakkas. This subethnic minority with its own distinctive dialect and customs had made the border area between the Southeast Coast, Lingnan, and Middle Yangtze macroregions their homeland, and they now emerged with heightened selfconsciousness from what S. T. Leong has termed their "incubation period." Hakkas responded to population growth in their own communities and to new opportunities in adjacent cores. They took their skills in highland agriculture and industry with them, but in the open society of the Middle Yangtze (with the exception of the western Jiangxi hills that marked the boundary between the Xiang and Gan basins) tended to abandon many of the markers of ethnicity preserved elsewhere and to blend into the sea of shed people and "wandering households." In western Jiangxi, the Hakka seem to have been sandwiched in between two hostile groups, the Han Chinese on the one hand and the aboriginal tribespeople on the other. They did not intermarry or live among the aborigines as they did in the Southeast Coast. Perhaps the local hostility was responsible for a high level of militarization: the locality saw several shed-people uprisings during the late seventeenth and early eighteenth centuries. Some Jiangxi shed people did so well that local elites felt threatened, and separate quotas were created in 1731 for those with twenty years' residence and landed property who wanted to sit for the examinations.

Another characteristic of the settlement of this region was the conflict generated by Chinese penetration into the non-Han areas. Yao tribes lived in the south Hunan hills, and the Miao in the west along the border with the Upper Yangtze. At higher elevations, these tribes lived by slash-and-burn agriculture; lower down, they tilled irrigated fields. They grew a variety of grains, and some New World crops like maize became progressively important in their economy during the century. They also produced cotton, indigo, and trees for timber, mined and manufactured iron tools and weapons, made elaborate silver jewelry, and were immediately recognizable by their embroidered and batiked clothing. Settlements were small, often surrounded by wooden stockades, and were the primary social units. The major event in the Miao calendar was a spring festival, held during the full moon, which provided the occasion for drink, dancing, games, and sexual license for young men and women, who lived together only after the birth of their first child. Subethnic groups did not intermarry and were differentiated by altitude of residence, mode of subsistence, and other cultural markers.

In these societies, small-scale feuding and violence were endemic. As in the Southwest, Han advance and the conversion of tribal territories into regular administrative units led to trouble, despite the government's establishment of charitable schools and special examination quotas. Conflict occurred sporadically throughout the century, and armed confrontations with the Miao took place in 1728–1730 in southwestern Hunan and again on a much larger scale in 1795 in west Hunan. (Western Hunan, which remained a Miao area, was highly garrisoned even in the twentieth century, when Fenghuang county was noted for producing army officers.)

The development of the regional core and particularly the Xiang River basin into a rice-surplus region was integrally linked to the management of water resources. The Yangtze and its tributaries experienced wide seasonal fluctuations in water levels and could suddenly be transformed into violent floodstreams. As a result, the hydraulic system of the whole macroregion was inherently unstable. When the Han River, Yangtze, and Dongting Lake simultaneously experienced high-water levels, disaster was imminent for the low-lying plains. Only persistent investment in water conservancy could help prevent such disasters, and for almost a century the Qing state financed the construction of a very large number of preventive dikes and water works.

With the rivers and irrigation systems of the Middle Yangtze managed by a combination of private and public leadership, the successful development of the region's economy rested on both rice and water transport. Rice, grown on the alluvial plains of the regional core, had become the region's major export product, sold to residents of the Lower Yangtze and Peking. As Hunan's rice economy grew, so did the Xiang River ports and rice-collection centers of Xiangtan and Hengyang. By the end of the eighteenth century, Xiangtan had some twenty li of extramural wharfs and markets stretching out along the river. Hankou, located downstream at the confluence of the Han and Yangtze rivers, experienced spectacular growth as an entrepôt for rice and other commodities.

The settlement of the Han River highlands in the northwest corner of the macroregion brought an increase in commerce on this river as well. Cotton, produced in the lower Han basin as the result of the active promotion of local officials, was transported upriver to the Northwest and eventually Mongolia. By the late eighteenth century, tea grown in Hunan was being shipped up the Han to Kiakhta for sale to the Mongols and the Russians. Mountain products produced for market in these highlands became crucial to the economy of the region. Iron, paper, varnish, wood oil, fungus, and turmeric (used in prepared tobacco and incense) were exports of the Han River highlands that moved downriver to Hankou.

Hengyang had become a center for similar cash crops as well as minerals, timber, tobacco, indigo, and seed oils.

Foreign trade was also important to the fortunes of Jiangxi and the Gan River basin. The customs house managed by the throne at Jiujiang, a major Yangtze port, had the highest quota for domestic transit taxes in the empire. In the early Qing, tea produced in northwest Fujian was sent south to Canton by a busy inland route through Jiangxi. Jingdezhen, the porcelain center near the Yangtze in northeast Jiangxi, had recovered with vigor from the devastations of the 1670s. In the early Qing, both the needs of the court and flourishing domestic markets were supplemented by the enthusiastic demand of Europeans for Chinese porcelain. New glazes were perfected, and at its peak in the late seventeeth century, the Jingdezhen porcelain industry was exporting several million pieces to European markets every year. Timber and raw materials were brought in in great quantity, and finished goods were shipped out through Jiujiang for the domestic market and along the Gan River system to Canton.

Middle Yangtze cities and productive centers naturally attracted specialized traders from other macroregions. Salt was imported by the Liang-Huai salt merchants based in Yangzhou; the salt merchants also controlled portions of the Yangtze River transport services, for salt barges making the four-month trip upriver to Hankou were then loaded with grain for the return trip to the delta. Rice markets were dominated by Lower Yangtze merchants, tea by Zhejiang and Huizhou traders, banking and trade with Central Asia by Shanxi-Shaanxi merchants. As foreign trade in opium and tea increased at the turn of the century, Cantonese merchants began to be prominent in Hankou.

Although Middle Yangtze merchants met with only mediocre success in their efforts to penetrate delta markets, they did establish themselves in their own region and in adjacent developing areas. The "Huang league" of Macheng in Hubei monopolized the cotton trade of the Han River system, and merchants from Jiangxi, their guildhalls dedicated to a deified Nanchang man of the fourth century, specialized in Sichuan salt, Yunnan tea, and timber (which they procured from the Upper Yangtze and the Southwest as well as their own region to meet a continually expanding demand). Jiangxi natives also seem to have run the textile industry in west Hunan.

Of the three largest urban areas in the region (Nanchang, Changsha, and the Wuhan tricity area), Hankou, one of the cities comprising modern Wuhan, was emerging as the preeminent Middle Yangtze city. Soon a major transshipment point for rice, salt, copper, and tea, as well as a host

PLATE 7. The Jingdezhen porcelain works in mountainous Jiangxi were
one of many large-scale imperially managed manufactories. Here a great
variety of porcelains were produced for use at court, by the wealthy, by
ordinary Chinese, and for sale abroad. The woodcut shown above is part of a
set prepared in the eighteenth century for imperial inspection. It shows
the porcelain being put into the kilns (at left and right) for firing. Since the
temperature of the kiln was highest in the front and lowest at the rear,
the porcelain to be fired was packed into the twenty-foot-long kilns according
to the glaze with which it was coated. Source: *Jingdezhen taolu* [The
Jingdezhen kilns], 1815 ed., Cornell University Library, Wason Collection.

of other commodities, Hankou had become, in the words of an early Qing
merchant manual, "the single greatest port for the collection and sale of
commodities in all of the empire."[7] The city's population, the great
majority of whom were male sojourners, grew accordingly, reaching two
hundred thousand people by mid-century and a million by 1800.

Among city residents, native-place ties were formalized in the pro-
liferating *huiguan* organizations. Though Hankou had but a single
huiguan in the early Qing, it had twenty-six by the end of the eighteenth
century (and many more thereafter). As the urban economy expanded,
these *huiguan* gave way to industrywide combinations aimed at monopo-
lizing trade. The Rice Market Guild in Hankou, organized in 1678 and

lasting into the twentieth century, was one of the early examples of a trade organization that embraced merchants from different regions. Major urban property holders, these large native-place associations built bridges, widened, straightened, and resurfaced roads, supported fire-fighting units, and provided public ferries and public schools. Welfare services, cultural functions, and even municipal defense relied heavily on the financing and leadership of the mercantile community. The dragon-boat festival on the fifth day of the fifth month structured urban rivalries through competitive boat races that the entire community enjoyed. As William Rowe's work has shown, developments in Hankou illustrate the more general trend for particularistic, nonbureaucratic organizations to deparochialize their membership, "identify their interests with that of a broader urban community," and cooperate in managing city business.

The Middle Yangtze was not free of the new type of industrial conflict found in the Lower Yangtze, but its workers were no more successful in creating their own organizations. The Ming system of reliance on corvée labor having been abandoned in the Jingdezhen porcelain factories, by the 1740s there were between two hundred and three hundred kilns there, employing about one hundred thousand workers. With its mass production, highly specialized division of labor, and many seasonal employees, this major industrial center was the scene of several strikes in the mid-eighteenth century. One, by the straw packers who prepared porcelain for shipment, was to demand more meat rations; another, in the 1790s, tried to make the official kilns restore the traditional mode of wage payment back to sycee (ingot silver) from the less valuable broken silver. Both strikes were speedily suppressed by the government; the straw packers were said to have subsequently donned white cloth stomach bands at work to commemorate a leader who was killed.[8]

By contrast with North China, the official hand lay lightly on the Middle Yangtze, and commercial centers were as important as administrative ones. There was a single Manchu garrison in the region and a relatively small Green Standard Army presence. Hunan did not even have its own governor until 1723. Despite its economic centrality, Hankou was the lowly seat of a subcounty magistrate under the jurisdiction of officials in nearby Hanyang. Changsha, the capital of Hunan and a marketing center on the Xiang River, was not the largest rice market in the province in the eighteenth century—that position was occupied by the upriver port of Xiangtan. Nanchang, the capital of Jiangxi, combined administrative primacy with dominance in the entrepôt trade because of its location on the Gan River, but nearby Jingdezhen was a major industrial city with no administrative status. The state did take an active interest in the intraprovincial grain trade in which this region played such a crucial role and, as Bin Wong has shown, tried to create a stable and orderly environment for such trade. Similarly, government officials took the lead in building dikes and managing irrigation projects. As elsewhere, the trend in both water control and granary management during the century, however, was for local elites to take over direction of these institutions from the state.

With the exception of northern Jiangxi, the Middle Yangtze could not rival North China or the Lower Yangtze in scholarly prestige. Jiangxi, the empire's prime scholarly center in Yuan and early Ming, ranked third after Zhejiang and Jiangsu in absolute numbers of *jinshi* produced. Jiangxi merchants were active in the Peking book trade, more local histories were written here between the Kangxi and Daoguang reigns than in any other province, and even the energetic censorship of Jiangxi libraries during the "Four Treasuries" project of the 1770s testifies to the area's involvement in national scholarly concerns. Hunan, by contrast, did not even have its own *juren* exams until 1723, and the eighteenth-century boom in Huguang bore academic fruit only slowly. Toward the end of the century the directors of the Yuelu Academy in Changsha shared their concern for statecraft and practical administration with students like the future official Yan Ruyi. Hunan's days of academic and political prestige finally came in the nineteenth century when natives such as He Changling, Tao Zhu, and Wei Yuan (and later Zeng Guofan) became influential leaders in national politics.

Urban elite culture in the Middle Yangtze reflected the shifting dominance of different merchant groups. As elsewhere (and particularly in Hankou), salt merchants from both Shanxi and Huizhou built guild halls and temples, and sponsored poetry societies, banquets, and theater. The once fashionable Yiyang style tunes of Jiangxi had long since been eclipsed, but in the eighteenth century Hankou became a center for the clapper music (named after the distinctive clappers used to beat out the rhythm) introduced by its merchant patrons from the Northwest. These merchants were in turn supplanted by the middle of the nineteenth century by merchants from Hunan, Ningbo, and Canton who had become the culturally dominant groups.

The Middle Yangtze region boasted a number of religious sites. The most famous was probably Mount Longhu, whose twin peaks on the border of three prefectures in eastern Jiangxi were the home of the Celestial Masters, the Zhang family who were the prestigious hereditary heads of Zhengyi Taoism. First enfeoffed with land in the eleventh century, more than fifty generations later, the Celestial Masters had extensive rental lands, an officially funded staff, income from the sale of incense and charms, the authority to issue the certificates of an official Taoist priest, and even the power to make appointments in the celestial hierarchy of the gods. Mount Wudang in northern Hubei had been extensively patronized by Ming emperors in the fifteenth century and continued to be an important pilgrimage site.

In the growing cities and rural settlements of the Middle Yangtze there were households in various stages of development, ranging from single male sojourners to small families attempting a new life to established and successful households in stable communities. In Jiangxi, for example, much of the substantial population increase toward the end of the century was absorbed in expanding households. As in other parts of China, most migrants relied on native-place ties and economic specialization to find a place in the new society, but, like the Upper Yangtze and unlike the Southeast Coast, subethnic identities were not sharply developed.

A variety of voluntary associations that cut across ties of kinship and native place grew and spread outside the cities as well. On the frontiers where the state's power had always been weak, such links were made not by elites but by others in the society, many of whom were not responsive to government authority. Toward the end of the century, a general lack of central-government control throughout the peripheries allowed both new organizations and armed groups to run out of control. The Triad society networks that had begun in the Southeast Coast spread west with transport laborers and migrants. A closer look at the Han River highlands, where another voluntary organization became prominent, will illustrate this phenomenon further.

In the densely forested mountains that sprawled over provincial borders, immigrants, bandits, and powerful local bosses had established new settlements by relying upon occupational connections as much as native-place ties. Frontier conditions necessitated local militarization. The profits to be made from smuggling salt from adjacent Sichuan, the demands for currency that could be met with counterfeiting, and the need for security that stimulated protection rackets all encouraged illegal activities. In the absence of established degree-winning families, leaders of armed gangs emerged as the highland elite. In the 1770s, bandit gangs (possibly of Hakka origin) known as Guolufei became active. Then, in the 1780s and the 1790s, many in the Han River highlands found in the White Lotus faith an organization and source of solidarity that overrode other differences. When population growth and the development of the local economy prompted the government to attempt to bring the frontier under closer supervision, the officials discovered and tried to repress the White Lotus sect. Thus they provoked an armed rebellion that lasted into the opening years of the nineteenth century, encouraged further militarization, and severely taxed the resources of the throne.

The state was also experiencing difficulty maintaining the water works on which the economic health of the region was based. Extensive settlement and population increase in Hunan, for example, had led to encroachment on Dongting Lake, as farmers diked off parts of the lake shore in order to plant crops in the fertile silt. Although embankment projects increased in size, government efforts failed to forestall continued encroachment, and as this valuable catch basin for surplus water was reduced, the delicate hydraulic equilibrium was endangered. Development of the Han River and other highlands had an equally upsetting effect. In order to plant new crops on the hillsides, settlers stripped the forest cover, and the denuded hills were soon subject to drastic soil erosion. Rivers filled with silt, and floods downstream became more frequent. The turning point in the hydraulic cycle came with the 1788 flood in Hubei: the Yangtze breached the dikes in more than twenty places, flooded the river basin as far upriver as Mianyang and as far downriver as Hankou, and drove the Han River back upstream and extended the disaster far upriver. Floods of the Yangtze and Han rivers punctuate the subsequent period.

The frontier problems experienced in the Middle Yangtze were also common in both the Southeast Coast and Lingnan, where they were compounded by heightened subethnic competition and highly developed and defensive lineage organizations. These coastal regions were, on the other hand, exposed directly to the maritime economies of Southeast Asia and Europe. Let us look first at the Southeast Coast.

SOUTHEAST COAST

The Southeast Coast entered the eighteenth century at a low point in its regional fortunes. Residents along the seacoast had suffered from the late Ming deflation and the forced evacuations of the 1660s; the subsequent ban on maritime commerce had struck another blow to trade. The coastal prefectures of Quanzhou and Zhangzhou had changed hands repeatedly during the forty-year struggle between the Manchus and first the Ming loyalist movement led by Zheng Chenggong (Koxinga) and then the rebellion of the Three Feudatories. Although it was never to regain its primacy in foreign trade, the Southeast Coast economy did experience substantial recovery after 1683 and expanded greatly during the eighteenth century, thanks to the development of Taiwan and substantial economic relationships with Southeast Asia.

The region consisted of the basins of several rivers running east across Fujian, south Zhejiang, and east Guangdong from the Wuyi Mountains to the sea. Mountain ranges isolated these river valleys and created four major subregional systems: the Ou River, whose delta was dominated by Wenzhou (Zhejiang); the Min River, whose delta city, Fuzhou (Fujian), was the regional metropolis; the Jiulong River system, containing Zhangzhou and Quanzhou; and the Han River, whose delta city was Chaozhou (Swatow) in Guangdong. These ports had a long history of involvement in interregional trade along the coast and overseas, and they opened the Southeast Coast region to contact with foreigners all along the rim of East Asia. Their prosperity contrasted sharply with the poor landlocked mountainous interior. Because the macroregion was further divided by mountains cutting through its center in a north-south direction, interior areas were oriented inland toward the Lower Yangtze, Middle Yangtze, and Lingnan, and boundaries were more fluid than one would expect from topography.

Despite competition from Canton and Ningbo, the region's ports continued to serve as important transshipment points, and their merchants dominated the trade along the coast and with Southeast Asia. In the late sixteenth century some seven thousand Fujianese traders were already traveling every year to Manila to meet the galleons from the New World, and they eventually set up their own community there. Chinese from the Southeast Coast (and from Lingnan) followed trade networks and settled in Siam, Batavia, Malacca, and Sumatra; when the British took over Singapore in the early nineteenth century, the development of tin mining took place with Chinese capital and labor from these two macroregions. Sporadic Qing attempts to restrict the expansion of trading networks overseas were weakened both by difficulties of control and by official recognition of the fact that in this region "half the population depends on navigation for a living."[9] During the eighteenth century there was a steady outmigration of individuals into other macroregions as well as to Southeast Asia. The population pressures in this region with limited arable land continued to channel people into fishing and trade, both of which were easily transformed into piracy as the government lost control over the coast in the late 1780s. The boom in opium imports sustained the local economy in the early nineteenth century, but the effects of the depression of the 1820s were acutely felt in a region so dependent on overseas commerce.

The Southeast Coast housed both minority ethnic groups and Chinese who spoke a variety of dialects. The Wuyi mountains were the home of the She, remnants of an aboriginal tribe related to the Yao who practiced slash-and-burn agriculture. Tanka boatmen of similar origin were also found in small numbers along the coast. Both the She and the Tanka were quite assimilated into Han Chinese culture. The She had migrated north in the late Ming and Qing from the hills of northern Fujian into southern Zhejiang; some even moved into the Lower Yangtze mountain districts farther north. In these hills, they cleared land, made terraces when the water supply made that feasible, and grew paddy rice, tea, and mushrooms. Their staple was the sweet potato. Perhaps this population movement was a response to the Hakka encroachment on their former homelands that took place over the same period. The two groups certainly interacted a great deal and came to share similar customs, most notably permitting women to work in the fields and not bind their feet.

Among the Han Chinese, language differentiated the five major subregions. The Ou River was the home of Wu-dialect speakers, people in the area of Fuzhou spoke Hokchiu (Northern Min), in the Jiulong basin Hokkien, and the Chaozhou area Teochiu; Hakka was the dominant dialect in the interior uplands along the southwestern periphery. The Southeast Coast's subethnic divisions were unmatched in their exclusivity, but the greatest tension existed between Hakka and other Chinese. This low-status group of early immigrants lived, as we have already noted, in the mountainous periphery of the region and specialized in tea, indigo, and trades such as timber, charcoal manufacture, mining, and stone cutting. Distinguished by dress, custom, occupation, and language, and despised by their neighbors, the Hakka occupied a marginal position wherever they lived. During the early Qing, as we have indicated, they left their overcrowded highlands and pushed westward into the Middle Yangtze, southwest into the Lingnan delta, and east across the straits into Taiwan.

The Southeast grew two crops a year on the coastal plain, one in the peripheral hinterland. Rice was the staple and competed with cash crops such as sugar cane and tobacco for the richest land. Limited paddy and the trend toward commercial crops combined with a large military establishment to make the Southeast Coast a rice-deficit area; its ever-normal granary quotas were among the highest in the empire. Grain had to be imported from Taiwan, the Lower Yangtze, and Southeast Asia in the eighteenth century, increasing the region's dependence on maritime trade. As cotton was replaced by crops like sugar cane, the macroregion began to import raw cotton from the north for local processing. New World food crops brought along familiar routes from Southeast Asia had been adopted in the region as early as the sixteenth century and contributed to the development of upland peripheries; the sweet potato joined taro, bamboo, and fish as part of the local cuisine. This macroregion had the dubious distinction of introducing opium, also discovered by sojourners in Southeast Asia, to the China mainland in the mid-eighteenth century and then disseminating it along domestic trading networks. As the smoking of pure opium became popular at the end of the century, Southeast Coast merchants shared in the profits of the illegal import trade.

A number of local products found national markets. Available timber in northwest Fujian had made Jianning prefecture a well-known printing center in the Ming, and paper merchants from adjacent areas were among the first from the region with a *huiguan* (established in 1739) in Peking. The pure-white porcelain figures of Buddhist deities and ceremonial objects from the Dehua kilns near Amoy, called *blanc de chine* by the Europeans, were widely sold in and beyond China from the late Ming through the early Qing, reaching their technical peak in the early eighteenth century.

Tea was one of the best-known exports, a product of the Wuyi Mountains (Bohea Hills) in northwest Fujian. (The English word *tea* is derived from the Amoy pronunciation.) Fujianese tea had lost its predominance in the Ming to Longjing and Songluo teas from the Lower Yangtze as popular taste shifted from powdered and cake to leaf tea, but Fujian continued to ship tea through Hankou for the Central Asian trade while also becoming a primary producer of fermented black tea for export to the West in the eighteenth century. (Tea began to be sold to the public in England in the 1650s.) Production increased almost sixfold between 1719 and 1762. In the decade 1760–1771, about 48 percent of the tea shipped out of Canton originated in Fujian. By 1800 this figure had risen to 69 percent. Demand for tea stimulated the economy of northwest Fujian, but the landlocked nature of this area prevented a wider economic impact on the region. Instead, the tea boom benefited the local economy in contiguous areas of the Middle Yangtze, luring itinerant workers into Fujian and creating a major tea market in northeast Jiangxi. Eventually, in the nineteenth century, the overland tea route was itself replaced by one going downstream to the treaty port of Fuzhou.

Recovering from the downturn in regional fortunes in the middle of the seventeenth century, Amoy (Xiamen) emerged as the center for both Zhangzhou and Quanzhou, a bustling port at which thousands of ships docked annually. "The richest city in the South [in 1786]," one scholar called it.[10] Not only did Fujianese businessmen reestablish their pivotal role in the coastal trade linking Southeast Asia with central and north China, but sojourning merchants controlled the expanding trade in rice, sugar, silk, and timber with Taiwan. Although Canton won a monopoly for trade with the West in 1757 and Ningbo for trade with Japan, Fujianese merchants sojourning in these ports participated in that profitable commerce. Several of the Canton Co-hong merchant families who became prominent in the late eighteenth and early nineteenth centuries were actually natives of Fujian, most notably the Pans (Puan Khequa) and the Wus (Howqua). These Co-hong merchant princes used surplus capital from the sale of tea to Westerners to invest in tea production in the hills of northwest Fujian. In the late eighteenth century, other Fujianese were still dominant in Japan, Korea, and in Southeast Asian Chinese communities.

Southeast Coast merchants ran trading companies and wholesale firms and were active in shipping. In order to avoid shipping bullion by sea, they improved their systems of credit. Amoy merchants trading across the rough seas to Taiwan, for example, balanced purchases and sales with their clients on the island only once a year. Trade imbalances, common with Taiwan, stimulated the development of specialized remittance agencies to provide the necessary transfer of funds. These business operations undoubtedly contributed to the evolution of the sophisticated customary law of contracts found in Taiwan in the nineteenth century. (Taiwan is treated separately below.) Even in the rural hinterland of northwest and south Fujian, Fujianese had devised sophisticated market instruments for renting draft animals and sharing animals through cooperative societies.

Fujian's role in the Ming loyalist movement had resulted in a strong Qing military presence there. Fuzhou, the provincial capital, housed a garrison of three thousand banner troops who were part of the coastal defense line. As of 1767, Fujian (including Taiwan) had the largest Green Standard force of any single province—more than sixty-six thousand men—and one of the most expensive. These standing armies saw major action in the eighteenth century only against rebels in Taiwan during the 1720s and 1780s and against Cai Qian and his fleets of coastal pirates in the 1790s.

The Southeast Coast had long been officially characterized as a very unruly region, and the trends of the eighteenth century confirmed this evaluation. Strong corporate organizations suppressed class conflict but magnified rivalries based on territory, kinship, and ethnicity. The Southeast Coast, like Lingnan, was well known as a region of unusually powerful lineages. These lineages owned common property, tried to dominate villages and even market areas, and were the vehicles by which local elites competed with one another for power and status. Lineages were often highly differentiated internally and dominated by the wealthier, better-educated males. *Fengshui*, or geomancy, the pseudoscience that sites structures so that they tap primordial energy pulsing through the earth, was taken very seriously here, and the custom of double burial characteristic of parts of south China (where a body would be exhumed and the bones cleaned and reburied) encouraged wealthy households and lineages to vie with one another in the geomantic pursuit of good fortune. For individuals who lacked the protection and support of a strong lineage, one recourse was to produce fictive genealogies and create kin groups by fusion, a testimony to the efficacy of this form of social organization for local aggrandizement. Others relied on the corporate property and organizational structure of community temples. In the course of the eighteenth century, this tendency toward vertical organization into rival blocs increased, as did the violence that accompanied sharp competition.

In this increasingly closed and competitive society, the little-daughter-in-law form of minor marriage was quite common. It minimized affinal ties and eliminated the payment of a brideprice. Because the bride was raised in her husband's household from childhood, the normally tense relations between mother-in-law and daughter-in-law that hindered domestic peace were relaxed.

Southeast Coast society also produced one of the major new forms of social organization to emerge in the Qing: the Triad-style brotherhood. First appearing in the late 1760s in Zhangzhou prefecture, these distinctive men's associations became known to the government during the Lin Shuangwen rebellion on Taiwan in the 1780s and soon spread among transport workers and traders. We have seen how, by the early nineteenth century, Triad societies had been exported to the Middle Yangtze and Lingnan, and how they had provided a framework for illegal activities such as smuggling, racketeering, piracy, and banditry that were becoming more and more of a problem for the government.

Fujian's terrain encouraged high levels of population density and urbanization in the regional core. Indeed, the Southeast was among the three most highly urbanized macroregions by the mid-nineteenth century. Fuzhou dominated the northern part of the coast, and Chaozhou the southern, its rising prosperity stemming in part from the advantages gained in the Southeast Asian rice trade when a local man became king of Siam in 1767. Fujian's cities housed many landlords who had left their rural villages to enjoy the cultural amenities and security of the cities.

Fujian, which ranked first in production of *jinshi* per capita in the Ming, had slipped to eighth place by the eighteenth century. Cultural tradition, mercantile wealth, and lineage support for examination preparation undoubtedly helped the Southeast Coast, but academic decline in Zhangzhou and Quanzhou left Fuzhou as the premier literati center. Scholars from the region were not active in the type of evidential scholarship popular in the Lower Yangtze. Fuzhou's Aofeng Academy, founded in 1707, was well known instead for adherence to stricter orthodoxy. Like Canton and Hunan, the Southeast Coast gave rise to new schools of thought in the nineteenth century. A strong commitment to local dialect made natives notorious in national circles; the Yongzheng emperor commented that "of all the officials of every grade who come for audience, it is only those from Fujian and Guangdong who when they speak have accents so strong that we cannot understand them."[11] The emperor's attempt to improve the *guanhua* (the dialect used by officials) of Fujianese and Cantonese by founding Orthodox Pronunciation Academies (a continuation of efforts in the Kangxi reign) met with little success, however.

Fujian's cities were not free of the fractiousness that characterized so much of the society. Factional rivalries among the cities' elites could become enduring divisions. In Quanzhou, for example, the earth-god cults were organized territorially into two rival groups that even in the twentieth century still held separate rituals and festivals in commemoration of an early Qing quarrel between two cliques, one supporting Shi Lang (the pacifier of Taiwan) and the other supporting the Hanlin academician Fu Hongji. Elites competed for prestige by petitioning to construct impressive memorial arches to commemorate accomplished or virtuous members of their families, and Fujian was known in the seventeenth and eighteenth centuries for the formal public suicides by childless widows whose demonstration of devotion to husband and concern for chastity excited awe and admiration.

Terraced hills and villages within a short walking distance of one another dotted the rural landscape of this region, testifying to intensive land utilization. A trend toward absentee landlordism was accompanied by permanent tenancy and multiple layers of landowning rights. Alongside permanent tenancy and fixed rents in kind there were lingering remnants in certain localities of labor services and semiservile dependency. Yet, in contrast to the disorder of the late Ming and the early nineteenth century, the eighteenth century saw almost no large-scale movements of rent resistance. Landlord-tenant relations remained relatively low key and were subsumed by more powerful lineage and ethnic rivalries that cut across class differences.

Walled villages became more common during the eighteenth century as many rural areas became militarized. In southwest Fujian, from the Kangxi period on, the beleaguered Hakkas built multistory round or rectangular residences, with defensive outer walls, that were inhabited by many families and contained livestock pens and worksheds, "rather as if the whole village were built together in one building, with the addition of communal guest halls, ancestral halls, and the like."[12] (See plate 8.)

Walled villages and Hakka fortresses both express the social tensions that stimulated the communal feuds called *xiedou*, first reported in the early eighteenth century along the coast of south Fujian. Lineages or community temples would mobilize their poorer males into armed bands, finance fights with revenues from corporate property, and plan the campaigns from the ancestral hall or temple. Weaker groups banded together against stronger ones, and elaborate alliances based on possession of a common surname or territorial confederations were mounted for violent confrontations. Local officials, not knowing what to do when so-called good people, even local elites, were participants in these struggles, were easily persuaded to turn a blind eye to the proceedings. *Xiedou* were endemic in the nineteenth century and have been cited as signs of "a period of closure" being experienced by the region at the time. Such conflicts, however, had appeared first in an era of expanding settlement and competition for new resources.

Officials had difficulty enough controlling the elites in the regional core, but these problems were compounded on the periphery where, as on other frontiers in the empire, residents were beyond their social and cultural—as well as political—reach. There shed people struggled to make a living: some who worked in timber won permanent-tenancy status (the "two owners to a mountain" system); others grew hemp, indigo, or were seasonal migrants in mountain industries that required temporary hired labor and large numbers of transport workers (tea, tobacco, paper). The growth of Triad organizations and the popularity of opium smoking among these people in the late eighteenth century reflect both their need for social solidarity and the weakness of the government in these areas. The piracy that plagued the region at the end of the century presented corresponding problems at sea, where local familiarity with coastal coves and ports (as well as winds and waters) placed official navies at a disadvantage.

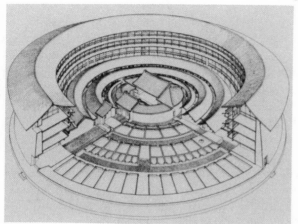

PLATE 8. The multistory fortified house shown above deviates considerably from the one-story, single-family dwelling that was typical of most parts of China. These multifamily residences found in Lingnan and the Southeast Coast reflected the high level of militarization resulting from Hakka feuds with their Chinese neighbors. Readily defensible and able to withstand seige, the fortified house included pens for livestock and facilities for grain storage as well as an ancestral hall and living quarters. Source: Liu Dunzhen, *Zhongguo gudai jianzhu shi* [History of China's ancient architecture] (Peking: Jianzhu gongye, 1984), p. 329.

Migrants take their gods with them. One of the most popular deities in the empire was from this region: Mazu, Empress of Heaven (Tianhou). Mazu had originally been born in Putian, Fujian, and as a god she came to symbolize native-place loyalties for Southeast Coast sojourners. The cult was intimately linked with sea transport, for the Empress of Heaven protected boats from disasters of all sorts. Temples to Mazu in the major cities of other macroregions were often financed and built by Fujianese merchants, although she was also popular in Lingnan and supported by Cantonese merchants away from home. In recognition of her wide following, the Qing court adopted Mazu into the official pantheon in 1737.

Fujian was also an important Buddhist center, with many old and wealthy temples. Its most famous monastery, the Yongquan temple on Mount Gu near Fuzhou, dated from the tenth century. Popular sectarianism also found adherents here in the Qing. The late Ming Religion of the Three Teachings preached by Lin Zhaoen in coastal Fujian may have laid the groundwork for such faith. A variety of sects venerating the late Ming patriarch Luo Qing had spread into Fujian from Zhejiang, and, with a community based on mastery of religious texts and practices, found a clientele in both city and countryside.

As we have noted, the Southeast Coast shared a number of characteristic social organizations and problems with its neighboring region to the south, Lingnan. Both were localities with strong lineages and traditions of unruliness (from the perspective of the court). Being areas of strong out-migration and competitors with one another for overseas trade, both regions faced more toward the sea than toward Peking. It would not be until the nineteenth century that their sojourning merchants would become significant groups, culturally as well as economically, within the empire.

LINGNAN

Lingnan, like the Southeast Coast, had adhered to the Ming cause and suffered for it. The attempt by Zhu Yuyue to establish a government in 1646 was quickly blocked by Manchus, and although Zhu Youlang lasted longer, he was no more successful than his predecessor and like him brought down his coterie of loyal Cantonese scholars. In 1650 the populace of Canton fiercely resisted a ten-month siege by Manchu armies, who retaliated when they captured the city by pillaging and killing an estimated seventy thousand citizens. The 1660s saw implementation of the order to evacuate the coast, which was a major event affecting the delta. But the dynastic transition brought benefits as well as punishments for Lingnan. Coastal and foreign trade revived, and in 1757 Canton was designated the sole port for trade with Europeans. The licensed Co-hong merchants grew fat on this profitable if perilous trade (firm bankruptcies were an intermittent phenomenon) until the Opium War and the resulting Treaty of Nanjing (1842) opened up other ports for trade and brought a depression to the Lingnan economy. But in the eighteenth century the massive lineage and ethnic feuds that were to erupt and unsettle rural society lay still in the future. Lingnan basked in prosperity.

The Lingnan macroregion was comprised of the two provinces of

Guangxi and Guangdong (minus its three easternmost departments) and consisted of the drainage basins of three rivers, bounded by mountains and high plateaus. Guangdong itself was separated from Guangxi by a mountain range that cut the latter province off from the sea. All of Guangxi's commerce flowed downstream into either Guangdong or, to the north, to Hunan.

Lingnan's markets, economy and society were heavily influenced by its location and its river systems. Guangxi's few cities were located on the Yu River and its tributaries, which cut through the mountains of the province in an east-west direction. Lingnan as a whole was dominated by Canton, the city that sat astride the confluence of its three navigable rivers in their flow to the sea: the West River, whose tributaries linked the delta to the Xiang River in Hunan and frontier regions in Guangxi; the North River, which led eventually to the mountain pass linking Lingnan to the Middle Yangtze; and the East River, which penetrated deeply into north-east Guangdong. Its southernmost location at the fringe of the Qing empire made Lingnan a great port for maritime trade, while its distance from Peking and its complex mixture of aboriginal and subethnic Han Chinese groups made its culture different and sometimes difficult to control. A mild climate permitted triple cropping of rice and high productivity in the alluvial lands, especially the delta of the Pearl River, which flowed from Canton south to the sea. Agriculture was much poorer in the more remote river valleys that laced the hilly terrain, and there were sharp contrasts between the prosperous delta and the rest of the macroregion.

Lingnan had a very heterogenous population, "the result of 2000 years of intermixtures among the Zhuang (Tai), the Yao, and the Han Chinese people from the north who themselves are an intermixture."[13] The indigenous Tai peoples (the Zhuang and the Li) were plains and valley agriculturalists who had already either been assimilated into the Chinese population or forced south to Hainan Island or westward into Guangxi. The Yao, who had originally resided on the fringes of the Lower Yangtze and Southeast Coast, had been pushed south by the Chinese settlement and moved across Guangdong from east to west. By the early Qing they were concentrated in western Guangxi. There, like many other minorities, they lived in the hills, practiced slash-and-burn agriculture, and were largely isolated from the Han Chinese population. During the reign of the energetic Yongzheng emperor, attempts were also made to accompany Chinese migration into Guangxi with assimilative policies toward the aborigines, including the replacement of the tribal chieftains with regular

Chinese administration and the opening of schools teaching Chinese language and values to aboriginal children.

Eighteenth-century migrations added further ethnic complexity to the region. Although some Guangdong peasants were attracted by opportunities in the Middle and Upper Yangtze, many new settlers also came into the province. The most conspicuous newcomers were the low-status Hakkas. As we have already noted, in the seventeenth century the Hakkas moved out of the hills of the Southeast Coast, settling in east Guangdong and in the rich Pearl River delta, where their sense of ethnicity was heightened by the hostility of the local people. In the delta the Hakkas became tenants on lands owned by Cantonese lineages. By the mid-eighteenth century, delta society included both the Hakkas and the Cantonese (called Punti or "locals" in Cantonese), who were predominantly farmers; Tanka boat people of aboriginal extraction (but long since assimilated), who were treated as mean people by their neighbors and specialized in fishing and shipping; and Muslims, who were urban traders. The northern and western peripheries also received many new migrants. There was a major influx of Hakka farmers into the river valleys and in-migration of another tribal group, the Miao, who were fleeing Chinese military pressure in west Hunan. Sharp differences in dialect were an accepted fact of life (there are still at least six major groups in modern Lingnan); indeed, dialect differences were major social markers in Lingnan society, just as the distinctive Cantonese dialect itself set off this locality from the rest of the empire and defied the Yongzheng emperor's efforts at language standardization among the literati.

The society of Lingnan was thick with highly structured and complex social organizations. The delta was the stronghold of extremely self-conscious patrilines, a few tracing residence back to Song times but most dating from the Ming and early Qing. In this competitive environment, the lineage had become a vehicle through which groups fought for political and economic dominance and the strong subjugated the weak. Peace and prosperity during the late seventeenth and eighteenth centuries stimulated competition for land, control of periodic markets, and local influence. Prominent lineages vied to create newly reclaimed land, called "sand fields," which benefited from tax exemptions for three years and were extremely profitable for pisciculture and paddy rice. Dominant lineages generally had their own paramilitary forces, maintained roads and bridges, and controlled the territory around their home villages. In the late Ming they had already been able to impose their own system of permanent tenancy. Here tenants were virtually servile in status and resided in satellite villages in hereditary positions of subordination. Success bred imitation, and it appears that in the Qing this kind of lineage organization as well as the appurtenances that elsewhere were exclusive markers of the elite (halls, genealogies, elaborate graves) were much more widely adopted in Lingnan than in most of China.

Geomancy was particularly useful in the fiercely competitive society of the Canton delta as a way of explaining success and failure in impersonal terms. The practice of double burial encouraged a concern with the alignment and location of graves, and geomancy was thus harnessed as a weapon against rivals, to turn the luck of a competing household, village, or lineage. It could also mask tensions within tightly knit groups (for example, between brothers or cousins) by expressing them in burial practices whose ethic was every man for himself.

Temples and shrines served both as social unifiers and dividers. Worship of a popular goddess such as Tianhou, Empress of Heaven, could be used by a dominant lineage as a symbol of its power over satellite villagers. In some multisurname villages, hostility among surname groups might result in an absence of communitywide events; life would revolve around activities conducted by each descent group, and there would be residential segregation of surnames and very little intermarriage. Other villages housing several lineages of roughly equal stature might emphasize community solidarity, with joint support of temples and community worship. Even in such cases, of course, individuals were keenly aware of their own descent lines, which linked them to communities outside their own. The influence of the lineage model can also be seen in the widespread reliance upon the corporate estate, a lineage institution, to raise funds for community purposes.

Dominant lineages were located in the countryside, and their maintenance of power demanded continued rural residence. Up the central place hierarchy, localized lineages were subsumed by higher-order ones, which had corporate estates uniting a set of component lineages, often located in a market town but sometimes encompassing several counties. By the late Qing, reflecting a long-term trend toward deparochialization of formal institutions, the major kinship-linked organization in Canton was not the lineage but the clan, organized on the basis of fictive descent among persons sharing the same surname, which served urban literati with an institutionalized basis for common action and promotion of examination candidates. In the "four counties" part of the delta, new social practices emerged (for example, the purchase of heirs) that were a reflection of the prolonged sojourning strategies of emigrants.

In areas where territories were not under the firm control of a dominant lineage, alternative bases for alliances were used. The Hakkas who took up tenancies from Cantonese lineages in the eighteenth century first lived in apparent harmony with their landlords, even in the same villages. As Hakka farmers prospered, they began buying land. Conflicts between Punti tenants and Hakka landlords, or Hakka tenants and Punti landlords, separated the groups into hostile camps, and each began to establish single-ethnicity villages that were walled for defense. (Hakka houses and villages were built in the multistory model created in the Southeast Coast, see plate 8). Violence there was, in great abundance, as the numerous criminal cases deposited in the Board of Punishments indicate. But in the eighteenth century, there was little collective, organized action along class lines against high rents or the illegal measures of landlords. Instead, group conflict involved different surnames and ethnic communities. Eventually, these conflicts would erupt in the large-scale sustained violence of the West River region in the 1850s.

The Cantonese-speaking boat people (whose neighbors called them Tanka) had few kinship links beyond the extended family and no lineage organizations whatsoever. Landless, they lived their whole lives on boats, often clustered in "boat cities," and worked in fishing and water transport. The boat people regarded certain fish as sacred, and in this and other ways signified their distance from their land-based neighbors. Despite a common dialect and efforts by the Yongzheng emperor to allow them to be registered as ordinary citizens, the Cantonese continued to regard them as a separate and inferior ethnic group.

There was a marked contrast in both economy and society between the Pearl River delta and the rest of Lingnan. Paddy-rice agriculture, with double and even triple cropping, was practiced on the alluvial land and especially in the delta, and was well suited to nucleated villages and strong lineages. Where sericulture was extensive, settlements were dispersed and large lineages rare. On Hainan and along the coast, the competition was over fishing and trade, and water transport linked peoples over vast distances.

The culture of the mountains, oblivious to macroregional boundaries, resembled that in other highland peripheries, especially the adjacent Middle Yangtze. Here Hakkas and Zhuang competed for scarce valley land, and immigrants shared the mountains with Yao and Miao tribesmen. Miners from western Guangdong sojourned in adjacent Vietnam. Single males, attracted by work in mining and charcoal burning, lived together in barracklike structures and organized voluntary associations of their own. Other socially marginal men found their way into bandit gangs who were closed out of the rich delta lands where dominant lineages monopolized coercion and cooperated with better-organized secret societies. Without such regular incomes, the gangs in the mountains were more fluid in their composition and inherently unstable in membership.

The contrast between delta and mountains extended into family life. Only the delta soils could produce the wealth required for large families (although the silk industry gave unusual freedom to its productive women workers), while men engaged in marginal highland occupations were more likely to remain unmarried because they could not afford the price of a bride. Delta lands were associated with extended family units, the hills with voluntary associations that functioned as substitutes for the family. Hakka women had unbound feet, worked in the fields, and enjoyed the leverage that came with earning power. The relative egalitarianism of hill society contrasted sharply with the complex stratification found in the delta, where the lower levels of society included females sold as secondary wives, concubines, or prostitutes and girls sold as child brides and as servants for wealthy women. Males were also sold, most frequently as heirs for childless men. Male servitude, indeed chattel slavery, also existed in Guangdong during the early Qing. These slaves were owned hereditarily (although originally acquired by purchase) and seem to have been a form of conspicuous consumption among powerful rural families.

Lingnan's wealth was partially based on the production of goods for sale, and commerce and industry as well as agriculture were well developed. Canton's famous fruit, the lychee and the longan, were dried for sale in the markets of North China. The iron pots and pans made in Foshan (Fatshan), one of Lingnan's major industrial centers, had a wide market, and the iron industry here was in a peak period until the end of the eighteenth century. Salt flats along the sea supplied Guizhou as well as Lingnan. Fruits, sugar cane, tobacco, and indigo were replacing both rice, which could be more cheaply imported from Guangxi or Southeast Asia, and cotton, which was purchased from the Lower Yangtze and (at the end of the century) India.

A foreign entrepôt for centuries, Lingnan owed its fortunes in the middle Qing above all to the growing overseas trade. The small Portuguese settlement at Macao, downriver from Canton, had attracted Westerners since the sixteenth century, but Canton easily outstripped it in economic importance. Export sales to the West, increasing by nearly 500 percent during the century, stimulated domestic industries in the region as a whole and benefited the local licensed merchants (some of whom were actually

Fujianese). The region adapted well to changing consumer demand. The delta, which exported over three million pounds of sugar to Amsterdam and Nagasaki in 1637, sold sugar to India in the eighteenth century. Silk had been a traditional export to Southeast Asia, but the new demand from the British East India Company in the early Qing encouraged the growth of the silk textile industry, and sericulture became a specialty of Shunde, a delta county. Tea from the Bohea Hills of Fujian became a staple of the trade and displaced silk as the leading export in the latter part of the century; the tea trade provided employment for processers and packers in Canton as well as transport workers in the region. As a taste for Chinese porcelain grew in Europe, Chinese in Canton learned to paint foreign scenes on bowls and plates for export, though this demand receded in the next century when European porcelain making improved. The foreigners paid for these exports mostly with specie from the New World, and Mexican silver dollars poured into China through Canton, fueling investment and growth.

The emperor's representative in the foreign trade was the customs superintendent, called the Hoppo by Western traders. He was appointed from the ranks of the Imperial Household Department and was responsible for delivering an annual "surplus" quota of the customs revenue directly to the emperor's private purse. The merchants who were given a monopoly on this trade in 1720 (known as the Co-hong in English) reaped the profits on the spot. The throne further tapped their wealth by expecting (and receiving) substantial "donations" for defense and other public purposes similar to those made by Liang-Huai salt merchants. Toward the end of the century, the "Canton system" as it is known began to break down: private traders on both sides challenged the Chinese and British monopolies, opium began to displace silver as payment for silk and tea, and the coastal world became increasingly militarized.

The Cantonese were among the first to be exposed in a regular fashion to some aspects of Western culture, through occasional European tribute missions as well as the traders and seamen who were generally isolated outside the city (the British did not begin spending the winters in Canton until 1771) but placed orders for many Western-style objects (furniture, porcelain, knicknacks) with local shops. Although it was sojourners from the Southeast Coast who had previously established most emigrant Chinese communities in Southeast Asia, domestic disorder and the secession of Hong Kong island to the British in 1842 turned the Canton delta into a major source of overseas emigrants in the nineteenth century.

Growing imports of opium from India, resulting in a net outflow of silver by the 1820s, had very deleterious effects on the region and the empire but not necessarily on the merchants who handled the legal trade. Moreover, official exactions did not prevent the Canton delta from reaping the economic benefits of the huge expansion of legal trade that followed the abolition of the East India Company monopoly in 1833. By the close of the trading season in 1836–1837, for example, exports out of Canton had risen 181 percent and imports 164 percent over the last trading season under the monopoly five years before.[14]

All roads in Lingnan led to Canton, the region's largest city, market, and cultural center and the provincial capital of Guangdong, which in the eighteenth century had a population estimated at between six hundred thousand and eight hundred thousand. Foshan, located nearby, had a population of approximately two hundred thousand and like several other economic centers was an administrative anomaly in having only *zhen* (subcounty) status. The wealth from foreign trade permitted a luxurious life-style for the city's mercantile elite, and they built homes and gardens that dazzled Westerners. Their guilds in Peking, Hankou, and elsewhere exposed Cantonese businessmen and literati to the urban elite culture of other regions. Sojourning merchants attracted drama troupes from their native places to Canton: in a thriving year like 1791, forty-four traveling troupes played to Cantonese audiences. The prosperity of the eighteenth century had brought new vigor to the founding of academies, and they increased greatly in number. Although Lingnan as a whole made only a poor showing in *jinshi* production during the eighteenth century, Panyu and Nanhai, the two metropolitan counties of Canton, were among the academically outstanding localities of the Qing. Other educational facilities were clustered in towns on the major rivers. More backward Guangxi was allotted only a small number of *juren*, and quotas for minorities like those found on other frontiers rarely propelled local men into the ranks of national office. The founding of the Xuehaitang Academy in Canton by Ruan Yuan in 1820 marked the region's rise to importance and fostered the statecraft scholarship that was to flourish in the early nineteenth century.

Urban society was becoming laced with associations, including guilds and, at the end of the century, secret societies. In this as in everything else, the environment of the Canton delta in the eighteenth century saw competitive instincts for wealth and power brought to a high pitch of sophistication. By the early nineteenth century, the Triad societies that had originated in the Southeast Coast had organized the marginal elements in the foreign trade—the money changers, compradores, dock-hands, small shopowners, yamen runners, clerks, and the criminal underworld. Triads controlled prostitution, gambling, and protection. Power in Canton was thus shared by the state, merchants, and these societies.

The lucrative foreign trade and Guangdong's association with Ming loyalism brought government attention to the region. Canton was considered an important point in the Qing coastal defense line and housed a navy and a garrison of Manchu bannermen. By 1820, Guangdong province had one of the most expensive military establishments in the empire. In contrast to the armies of other border regions, Guangdong troops had not been called into action much in the eighteenth century. In 1788 the Qing sent an unsuccessful expedition into Annam (northern Vietnam) to try to unseat a rebel regime. Partially as a result of that failure but also because of the expansion of coastal trade that had made smuggling a way of life along the coast, Guangdong shippers faced increasing harassment from coastal pirates at the end of the century. Land-based protection rackets entrenched in the already fragmented society, profitable sales of salt and opium, and assistance from Vietnam permitted small bands to coalesce into large fleets that the inexperienced Qing navy had great difficulty eliminating. As on the Inner Asian frontier, upstart foreigners chafed at restrictions, and there was an easy transition between trading and taking. A resulting cycle of growing militarization not unlike that on other peripheries at this time also affected the coastal world. These difficulties were, of course, only small harbingers of the loss of control and battles with Western ships that would follow in the 1840s and affect not just Lingnan but the empire. By the 1840s, too, Cantonese merchants had moved into the British Straits Settlements and were investing in Malaysian tin mines and plantations and summoning workers from the homeland. Singapore, founded in 1819, became a major node in an overseas network of businessmen, laborers, guilds, and secret societies.

Far away at the other end of the empire, the Northwest macroregion was also closely involved in foreign trade, but the poverty of the Inner Asia frontier that contrasted markedly with the prosperity of Lingnan highlights the post-Columbian centrality of sea trade in forging the most active linkages within the growing world economy.

NORTHWEST CHINA

Northwest China had long been the major overland channel for foreign trade with Central Asia (and, in previous centuries, India and Europe), and its strategic location on the edge of the steppe made it inevitable that the region's fortunes were tied to trade, tribute, and warfare. In the late

Ming and early Qing, this sparsely populated, grain-poor region had spawned the rebel Li Zicheng and seen more than its share of military operations. During much of the eighteenth century, it was used as a staging ground for campaigns into Central Asia, and secure frontiers brought a new openness to the regions to the west, whence periodic tribute missions came en route to Peking. Uprisings by non-Han groups in and near the region occurred at regular intervals and continued (with increasing success) into the nineteenth century. Trade more than agriculture brought some prosperity, especially from 1760 to 1820, but this region probably benefited less than the rest of China from the peace and prosperity of the middle Qing.

The Northwest macroregion, comprised of west Shanxi, Shaanxi, Gansu and the oases of the Gansu corridor, encompassed the upper basin of the Yellow River, the region's major artery. The region was separated from the rest of the empire by mountains on the east and south. The narrow regional core, which had been the once prosperous home of earlier dynasties, was comprised of the Wei and Fen river valleys and stretched along the southeastern edge of the region between the cities of Xi'an and Taiyuan. Because the Yellow River was not navigable except for short stretches, expensive land transport restricted the trade opportunities of most localities. Commodities had to be carried by camel, cart, pack animal, or human carrier over roads that were deeply rutted or mud swamps during the spring and summer rains. Expensive transport and an inhospitable semiarid climate with frequent droughts during the growing season limited agricultural productivity and made the density of settlement in the Northwest one of the lowest in the empire. In fact, laborious communications isolated this region culturally and socially as well as economically.

Like the Qing empire as a whole, the population of this macroregion was ethnically, religiously, and linguistically very diverse, but the mix was very different from the regions so far considered. On the northern peripheries where the desert began, there were Mongols who were herdsmen and (increasingly since the sixteenth century) followers of Tibetan Lamaist Buddhism. Nomadic and agricultural Tibetans lived in the high grassy uplands and wooded valleys of southwest and south Gansu adjacent to Qinghai (Kokonor). Han Chinese populations were concentrated in the cities and in the river valleys of the east and south; among them were a small number of "musician households," classified until 1727 as mean. There was a large and more significant Chinese Muslim population in Shaanxi and Gansu, descended from Yuan and pre-Yuan migrants. Xi'an had seven mosques and thousands of Muslims in 1781, and even larger communities were to be found in the towns of Lanzhou and Hezhou. By the late nineteenth century Muslims constituted a third of the total population in Gansu. They revealed their accommodation to Chinese culture in their adoption of Chinese names, speech, and dress but lived in segregated villages and neighborhoods, followed their own religious leaders, and eschewed the consumption of pork. Muslim separatism was reinforced by occupational specialization: they concentrated on livestock farming, dominated the camel-, donkey-, and horse-transport services and were very active in the caravan trade with Central Asia. A subgroup, the Turkic-speaking Salar Muslims, virtually monopolized raft transport on the far reaches of the Yellow River.

It was Chinese, Muslims, Mongols, and Tibetans who mingled in this region and gave its society its distinctive character. Internal disunity, prompted by differences of dialect, customs, and, particularly, religious belief, allowed the Qing to play off one against the others; each group could and did side with the state against their neighbors. The Qing used the *tusi* system of hereditary chieftains among the tribes of Gansu, Qinghai, and Tibet. Manchu emperors interpreted the separation of ethnic groups as a sign of the success of their policy of disinterested benevolence toward all the peoples of the empire, and when Han officials in the eighteenth century urged severity toward Muslims, the Yongzheng and Qianlong emperors responded (in this as in other matters) with counsels of restraint and laissez-faire. A long-term process of sinicization, very apparent by the early twentieth century when Westerners visited the region, was punctuated here as elsewhere by outbreaks of feuding and violence.

Geography and the limits of available technology checked the advance of agriculture into the Inner Asian frontiers of the Northwest. As a result, this region did not experience the waves of new settlement occurring in other parts of China in the middle Qing. Agriculture was stimulated by government efforts in the 1720s and the 1730s to reconstruct and expand irrigation works in Shaanxi and on the Yellow River in Ningxia, but registered taxable lands in Shaanxi and Gansu did not increase during the eighteenth century. Some people actually left the region to seek better opportunities in the Han River area, in Manchuria, and even in Mongolia and Central Asia. Deficient in grain, the region did produce wool, leather, fur, cashmere, and livestock, but by the nineteenth century more horses were being raised on stud farms in Gansu than the throne could use. Cotton was grown in the Wei River valley, indigenously produced salt was marketed within and beyond the region, and wild rhubarb was much in demand by Russian traders. The liquor of Fenzhou in Shanxi and the tobacco of Gansu both had national reputations for quality.

The Northwest was best known for its export of human capital in the form of long-distance traders, the most important link between the region and the empire. The prominence of Shanxi merchants in the early Qing grew out of their participation in the official border trade during the Ming. They had entered the Liang-Huai salt market by supplying northern garrisons with grain in exchange for salt certificates that entitled them to market salt in designated districts. Building on this foundation in the Qing, Shanxi merchants built a huge trading network. They camped near monasteries and nomad encampments in Mongolia, then built trading posts and shops, becoming the object of local hostility as the trade imbalance created Mongol indebtedness. They were similarly active in the opening up of Manchuria and were the primary brokers in the trade at Kiakhta with Siberia and Russia. Dongans, Chinese Muslims who were also traders, moved westward out of the region, first into northern Xinjiang and subsequently into the oases of the Tarim Basin, the major entrepôts for trade with Kokand, Bukhara, the Pamirs, Afghanistan, and India. Here they were joined by other merchants from the Northwest (and the Lower Yangtze) who transported tea, silk, bullion, spices, and medicines for sale, returning to China with local silk, cattle, and (after the Imperial Household monopoly was abolished in 1773) the jade for which Yarkand was famous.

Merchants from the Northwest naturally dominated the long-distance trade in their own region, shipping wool, drugs, woods, and minerals from Lanzhou, Gansu's major urban center, down to Xi'an. They also expanded into the adjacent Han River valley as this area was being developed in the middle Qing and, using their niche in the salt monopoly, into Sichuan and the Southwest. Dominating as they soon did most of the interregional trade in northern China (and rivaled on a national level only by the merchants of Huizhou), the Shanxi-Shaanxi merchants were an important presence in Peking. Collections of stele inscriptions show that Shanxi merchants founded many of the early *huiguan* in the capital and constituted the largest single bloc of traders in the eighteenth century, specializing in dyestuffs, tobacco, tung oil, metals, paper, cloth, felt, and other goods. Most of the Shanxi bloc in Peking came from Pingyang prefecture along the lower reaches of the Fen River in the southern part of the province. Shanxi cloth merchants from the Taiyuan area farther upstream saw a need for remittance services for private traders and government in the early Qing and began concentrating on banking. By the nineteenth century Shanxi banks formed a national network that extended along established routes into Inner Mongolia, Manchuria, and Central Asia.

Administrators in the Northwest were preoccupied for much of the early and middle Qing with campaigns farther west and the attendant problems of communication and supply (Gansu had more post stations than any other province). A considerable military presence had to be managed and fed: there were large banner units in half a dozen cities, and very sizable Green Standard Army garrisons—almost one-fifth of the total force in 1685 was stationed in Shanxi, Shaanxi, and Gansu.

Provincial officials were further burdened with the administration of huge new territories in Central Asia. Campaigns in the late seventeenth and early eighteenth centuries under three emperors had culminated in the destruction of the Oirat (Kalmuk) empire based in Zungharia, and the vast ranges of Qinghai were brought within the empire in 1723. Other attempts to check Mongol power had led Chinese troops to Lhasa, seat of the Yellow sect of Lamaist Buddhism that was so influential among Mongols and Tibetans. Perhaps recognizing the limits of their power, the Qing were content to chastize but not conquer Tibet, and merely posted a resident official there. In Central Asia, by contrast, the Manchu state intervened to block a Muslim secessionist movement in mid-century and in 1759 annexed the land on both sides of the Tian mountains as far west as Lake Balkhash, naming it Xinjiang, their "new dominion."

To govern Xinjiang, the Qing began incorporating the local leadership into a loose bureaucratic structure. A resident imperial agent appointed Muslim governors in the oasis towns along the main routes of trade who were in turn responsible for their communities. In Kucha, Aksu, and Khotan, power thus resided in the hands of the native officials and religious leaders. The officials received a salary, supplemented with land grants and gifts of slaves; religious leaders received income from endowed land. Like Mongol banner leaders, local tribal chiefs in Hami and Turfan were granted Qing titles and were made part of the Qing nobility. Among the Muslim nomads, the Kazakhs and Kirghiz, transhuming in the steppe beyond the imperial frontier, a tributary system similar to that used across the northern frontier was employed; the Qing tried to limit their trading privileges and mobility, but without much success.

Loose political institutions were given backbone by the deployment of large armies. Garrisons totaling between ten thousand and twenty-three thousand men were stationed in Xinjiang, and separate citadels were built to house bannermen and officials in the oasis towns of the Tarim basin. In

哈密國

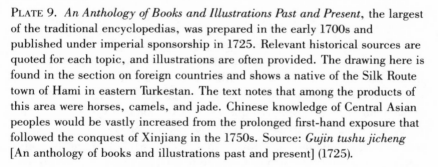

PLATE 9. *An Anthology of Books and Illustrations Past and Present*, the largest of the traditional encyclopedias, was prepared in the early 1700s and published under imperial sponsorship in 1725. Relevant historical sources are quoted for each topic, and illustrations are often provided. The drawing here is found in the section on foreign countries and shows a native of the Silk Route town of Hami in eastern Turkestan. The text notes that among the products of this area were horses, camels, and jade. Chinese knowledge of Central Asian peoples would be vastly increased from the prolonged first-hand exposure that followed the conquest of Xinjiang in the 1750s. Source: *Gujin tushu jicheng* [An anthology of books and illustrations past and present] (1725).

eastern Xinjiang these banner forces were supplemented by the Army of the Green Standard, staffed by Han Chinese from Shaanxi and Gansu. By making these soldiers permanent military colonists, the Qing reduced the burden of supporting such enormous armies and promoted the colonization of the new and not entirely hospitable frontier region.

The government also permitted Han Chinese and Uighurs from the Northwest to settle in north Xinjiang, Hami, and Turfan. Xinjiang became a favored place of exile for criminals from China proper who were awarded to local Muslim leaders or sent to work in mines that were supplying the state with needed metals. During the relative peace that resulted from the new order, trade was regularized, and the population and cultivated acreage increased. Urumchi, lying on the eastern end of Zungharia, was an administrative center as well as the site of an Imperial Household depot, established in 1757, that sold cloth produced in the imperial manufactories. At the western edge of the Tarim basin south of Zungharia, beyond the oasis and market town of Kashgar, lay Yarkand, a commercial center and a major market for jade. Farther west still, in the Ferghana valley, lay Kokand, a tributary to Kashgar, and the home of powerful merchants who came into the Tarim-basin towns for trade. Although Xinjiang developed significantly under Qing control, the number of registered taxpaying households was miniscule compared with the developing peripheries of China proper. Government expenditures in Xinjiang consistently exceeded revenues and required a substantial annual subsidy from Peking. The burden of management of the region's military forces fell on administrators in Shaanxi and Gansu.

The Northwest macroregion's distance from abundant grain markets and its need for reserves to ensure food supplies during the year as well as during droughts meant that maintenance of local granaries was a particularly important task of government. Yet even during the latter part of the century, when Qing mobilization of grain was at its most effective, the Northwest (and particularly Gansu) struggled to keep sufficient reserves. The efforts of the governor of Shanxi, Nomin, to resolve the province's regular deficits led the Yongzheng emperor to regularize the meltage fee and create the "nourish honesty" allowance nationwide in the 1720s, but the Northwest continued to require a regular subsidy. The best-known consequences of government efforts to tap the mercantile wealth of the region by selling licentiate-by-purchase degrees for grain was the fraud perpetrated by officials in Gansu and exposed in 1781; more than fifty officials were given the death sentence (later commuted) in a case that became a milestone in the advancing career of the imperial favorite, Heshen.

Ethnic and religious minorities in this region were given considerable independence by the state. Although quick to prevent the Dalai Lama or Panchen Lama from gaining undue political power among the Mongols, the Qing court encouraged the growth of Lamaist Buddhist monasteries such as Lambrang and Kumbum, both on the edge of Qinghai in Gansu (founded in 1709 and rebuilt in 1723, respectively), and thus contributed to urbanization and the decline of nomadism. Local organization among ethnic minorities was tolerated (how could it not be?) so long as these groups remained loyal and law-abiding. Chinese Muslims were consequently free to organize most of their community life around the mosque, under the direction of a religious leader who could exert considerable influence. The custom of making pilgrimages to saints' tombs, traveling Sufi teachers, and Muslim predominance in trade and transportation all served to create far-flung networks reaching into Central Asia and the major cities in China. During the eighteenth century, religious strife within Central Asia had led to conflict in the Ili region between rival saintly families, whose networks extended along the trade routes into the Middle East. Even the troublesome (from the perspective of the Qing) saintly Sufi families were able to perpetuate their authority and influence over many generations and across a wide area from Yarkand to Gansu. Religious movements spawned in Central Asia were transmitted rapidly into the Northwest macroregion, and gave rise, as we noted in chapter 4, to outbreaks of violence in the late eighteenth and nineteenth centuries.

The Northwest was not a region of strong lineages, although it had its occasional great descent line that produced officials and degree-winners generation after generation. The Fans of Jiexiu (Shanxi) for example, were border merchants who had been made official brokers for the Imperial Household during the Shunzhi reign. They reciprocated by providing military assistance from their own purses for some of the Kangxi emperor's campaigns and were rewarded in turn with rank, official posts, and access to lucrative commercial opportunities in salt, copper, timber, and foreign trade. Despite the vicissitudes of profit and indebtedness that came with imperial favor, the Fans held on to their position until the late eighteenth century. The closest Chinese counterpart to Muslim networks, however, was to be found in the Shanxi *huiguan* located in the major cities of the empire, organizations that brought together different merchants on the basis of native place, intermarriage, and the share partnership. Although the patron deity of these merchants, Guandi (the apotheosis of the third-century warrior Guan Yu who was a native of Xiezhou, Shanxi), was elevated to new heights by Qing emperors and incorporated into the imperial pantheon in 1725, the worship of this god extended far beyond the Shanxi merchants, and there were no organizational connections among the temples to Guandi that dotted the empire.

With the exception of Ningxia and the twin cities of Guihua and Suiyuan (modern Huhehot) located on the edge of the steppe, most cities of the macroregion were in the regional core and on the trade routes that

linked Central Asia with Xi'an and Peking. The higher population densities of the cities contrasted sharply with the isolated settlements so typical
of the region.

Xi'an, with a population of almost three hundred thousand by the
1840s, was the regional metropolis and, such as it was, cultural center.
Despite the city's past glories as an imperial capital and the former
prominence of the aristocratic families of this region, the elite of the
Northwest now played only a minor role in national literati culture. There
were few academies, and the region took a negligible part in the scholarly
projects so typical of the Qing period. Some merchants dabbled in literati
culture, many did not. Nor was the macroregion particularly outstanding
in producing degree-holders. Because of its mercantile wealth, Shanxi
managed to rank sixth in the empire in the number of *jinshi* degrees won in
the eighteenth century, but Shaanxi and Gansu did markedly worse. In
fact, until the provincial *jinshi* quotas were established in 1702, Gansu
had failed to produce a single Qing *jinshi*.

It was to Qing urban culture that the Northwest made more notable
contributions. The merchants of Pingyang prefecture, like those of other
areas, had encouraged the development of the dramatic tradition of their
native place, and as their trading network expanded, wider audiences
were exposed to their clapper opera. Xi'an became the center for this Qin
(an old name for the region) style in the eighteenth century; the city had
thirty-six opera companies in the 1770s (as many as Peking) and may have
pioneered the development of public theaters. These somewhat rowdy and
daring performances had already become popular in Hankou, and in 1779
the genre was introduced to the capital through the talents of a very
appealing female impersonator. In consequence, this regional opera form
enjoyed a great wave of popularity even among the snobbish officials and
scholars from the Lower Yangtze.

Life in the countryside was quite different, and presented a sequence
of contrasts between the nomadic and the settled way of life and among the
cultures of the different ethnic groups. Han Chinese who lived in the
loessic uplands grew winter wheat and millet as their main crops and lived
in caves carved out of the thick loess soil, an adaptation encouraged by the
scarcity of wood in this semi-arid climate. Although peasant caves tended
to be simple, those of landlords could be quite elaborate, with courtyards
and even free-standing buildings. Chinese Muslims lived in houses not
unlike Chinese ones, and their mosques were architecturally similar to
Chinese temples. Both the Muslim and the Chinese ways of life differed
strikingly from the pastoral economy, based on herds of sheep and goats,
pursued by Mongols and nomadic Tibetans who lived in tents and relied on

meat and dairy products as the mainstays of their diet. Agricultural Tibetans in southwest Gansu, where oats and barley were commonly grown, lived in their own distinctively styled wooden houses.

The ethnic composition of the Northwest was further reflected in its diversity of religious cults. Travelers to Shanxi noted the prevalence of a tree cult that doubtless underlay more systematized worship, each village honoring a certain tree and praying to it for relief from ill health or bad fortune. Several pilgrimage mountains important to Chinese were located in the region: Mount Heng in Shanxi (near Datong), Mount Hua in Shaanxi (near where the Yellow River broke through to the plain), and Mount Wutai, a mountain sacred to Tibetans, Mongols, and Manchus as well as Chinese. Located in the Taihang mountains just over the border in the North China region, Wutai helped integrate the two regions by drawing a regular traffic of varied pilgrims from all over the north.

The contact with Central Asian oasis kingdoms brought, as we have noted, new currents in Islam to China. The eighteenth century saw the introduction to the Muslim community of a reformist Sufi movement, a sect that caused major disturbances in the 1780s and was eventually an important stimulus in the Muslim rebellions of the Northwest in the nineteenth century. Ma Mingxin, the founder of this New Teaching, was a native of Gansu who returned from a visit to religious centers in the Middle East and Central Asia in 1761 and began criticizing the Chinese Muslim establishment. Ma's converts were concentrated especially among the Salars who lived in west Gansu in the town of Xuanhua. His doctrines directly challenged the entrenched religious leadership on points such as the vocal invocation of Allah and the power of the tomb congregations dominated by the landed Muslim elite. Tensions between the New Teaching and the Old Teaching Muslims increased and erupted into violence in 1781. The government intervened, of course, arrested Ma Mingxin, and eventually executed him when his followers attempted a jailbreak. Successful suppression of further violence lasted only until 1784, when another religious leader of the New Teaching rebelled in an attempt to avenge Ma's death. After the Qing succeeded in putting down this uprising, they banned the spread of the New Teaching and tried to curb the evangelical activities of Muslims generally, especially those from Central Asia. The Sufi sect went underground, to survive into the nineteenth century as a force that both inspired revolt and divided Muslims.

UPPER YANGTZE

The Upper Yangtze macroregion, encompassing the eastern two-thirds of Sichuan and portions of the adjacent mountains to the south in Guizhou and Yunnan and to the north in Gansu, was on the far-western edge of the empire yet was better integrated into the national economy than any other peripheral region. The Chengdu basin in the regional core was blessed with good climate and rich resources, and it had a long history of Chinese settlement. The southern portion of the regional core near Chongqing (Chungking) had developed more slowly but benefited from access to cheap transportation via the Yangtze River, which cut across the south-eastern two-thirds of Sichuan. Ecology limited Chinese expansion into the Tibetan plateau to the west, though there was a steady stream of military and commercial traffic to and from Tibet.

The seventeenth century found the Upper Yangtze in a trough in its regional cycle. The devastation of Sichuan by the late Ming rebel Zhang Xianzhong and the subsequent Wu Sangui rebellion were followed after 1680 by a period of recovery and growth, stimulated by government encouragement of resettlement of abandoned lands. First the regional core and then the peripheries received substantial numbers of new migrants; the economic boom that accompanied the eighteenth century continued into the next. The Upper Yangtze was the only macroregion unaffected by a major catastrophe in the mid-nineteenth century.

In order to reduce the power of the Tibetans, Mongols, and Lamaist church and to stabilize the Inner Asian frontier, the Manchus sent expeditions to Central Asia through the Upper Yangtze in the 1720s and again in the 1790s. Yongzheng's willingness to carve out tribal territories by force produced resistance largely on the region's borders with the Southwest. The Qianlong emperor, perhaps dazzled by visions of his other "great campaigns," took an aggressive attitude toward tribes on the western periphery and launched two prolonged and expensive operations against them in the 1740s and 1770s. The first of these Jinchuan ("gold river") campaigns alone used forty thousand soldiers and cost more than seventy million taels. In the 1790s, the need to suppress White Lotus rebels in the Han River area of the northeastern Upper Yangtze demanded not only soldiers but also mobilization of local militia. In all of these instances, the stimulus of government expenditures for military expeditions was probably more than offset by the informal exactions demanded of the populace. Each campaign advanced the militarization of society on the regional peripheries.

The tribes living along the western edge of the macroregion were mostly of Tibetan stock. The Khams, who resided along the far border of Sichuan province, were Lamaist Buddhist herders, farmers, and traders with a characteristically rigid social structure. Their diet was also typically Tibetan: milk and mutton, and tsamba (parched barley meal) mixed with salt, tea, and butter. Some of their territories were annexed to Sichuan as a result of the Tibetan expeditions of 1720 when several hundred new *tusi* were created. The Giarong tribes of the Jinchuan area northwest of Chengdu were finally subdued in the 1770s. Rather than confiscate their lands, as was usual, the court enrolled them as military colonists and militia and used them in Qing armies (they did the same in Taiwan). In general, Han penetration into the western frontier was impeded by the inhospitable terrain and the fierceness of these tribes.

The loss of life in the late Ming rebellions had been concentrated in the regional core. In the early Qing, the availability of good land and ease of access brought many immigrants here from many different regions. A poor man could work his way west as a tracker along the Yangtze, hauling the boats upriver along precarious paths carved into the cliffs. The first settlers came from nearby Huguang and Shaanxi, but the greatest number came from the Middle Yangtze, including Jiangxi and the overcrowded Hakka areas on the southeast periphery. By all accounts the largest number of settlers were from Hubei. Macheng county in east Hubei, whose merchants were interregional cotton traders, had already sent an extraordinary number of immigrants to Sichuan in previous centuries, and this chain migration continued at a slower pace in the eighteenth. Merchants came from all over the empire in search of a share of the extraregional trade: Jiangxi men to recover their control of trade in lacquer, hide, glue, and medicine; Shaanxi men to run the salt monopoly.

Upper Yangtze cities had a large Muslim population who had come from the Northwest and were here, as elsewhere, usually involved in trade. There were a small number of Manchus stationed in Chengdu, where a banner garrison was established in 1717 in a special enclave within the city. Some foreign Catholic priests lived secretly in the region and had converted perhaps a few thousand households; there was even a small Christian cemetery outside Chengdu. One of the principal attractions of the region for ordinary people was Mount Emei, southwest of Chengdu. Dedicated to Puxian (the bodhisattva Samantra-bhadra), who was said to have come from India on a white elephant, the three thousand three hundred meter high mountain had also incorporated a variety of ancient indigenous cults. Lavishly patronized in the late Ming, Emei was a pilgrimage site for Chinese, Tibetans, and tribal peoples from the west and southwest. Such a shared site may have helped promote regional identity.

The main products of the Upper Yangtze, "heaven's storehouse," were agricultural. The registered acreage increased dramatically in the first half of the eighteenth century; irrigation systems were built, terraces constructed, and cultivation extended in the Tuo and Yangtze river valleys. Wheat and especially rice were produced in such quantities that the macroregion could export grain to Tibet and to the rice-deficient Lower Yangtze. Maize and potatoes were grown in the northeast adjacent to the Han River basin in particular, and mountain industries (paper, timber, iron) were developed in those highlands. Continuing in-migration, which did not peak until the early nineteenth century, stimulated further commercialization of the agricultural economy. Silk, cotton, dyes, rape-seed oil, and sugarcane were produced, as well as tobacco in Chengdu and Daju liquor in Mianzhou.

As Paul Smith has demonstrated, the growth of trade along the Yangtze, encouraged by the opening up of Yunnan and Guizhou, promoted the development of the Tuo River and Chongqing portions of the regional core. Valuable Yunnanese copper was shipped northward to the Yangtze, and Luzhoufu in southeast Sichuan became a major transshipment center. The deep narrow brine wells in this same area produced salt in quantity and quality sufficient for export to both the Southwest and the Middle Yangtze. This salt monopoly, financed by Shanxi-Shaanxi merchants, employed hundreds of laborers and draft animals. Chongqing had come into its own, and the prosperity generated by trade and protected by agricultural growth was reflected in the city's surge past the rest of the province in the number of *jinshi* degrees won in this century.

In addition to selling rice to Yangtze merchants, the region exported silk and brocades, copper, timber, medicines, red safflower dye, and women, who were sold as servants and concubines. The brick tea of Yazhou prefecture on the western border of the macroregion was shipped almost entirely to Inner Asia. Tea production and distribution were handled by several hundred licensed merchants, and the bricks (made by steaming, pounding, and compressing the tea leaves) were carried by porters in enormous bundles over the high mountains. At Dajianlu in west Sichuan, stable relations with Tibet allowed a customs office to tax the trade on behalf of the Dalai Lama, and Kham merchants, part of a Lamaist monopoly, exhanged felt, wool, hides, and furs for tea.

For the first century of Qing rule, the administration of Sichuan at the highest bureaucratic levels was shifted in and out of the jurisdiction of a governor-general located in Shaanxi. Only in 1760 was the post of an independent governor-general made permanent. The absence of this crucial bureaucratic level probably meant a significant loss of effectiveness in provincial government and enhanced the possibilities for independent elite action. Local government was generally weak and had difficulty keeping up with the population expansion. Early in the century, large numbers of magistrates' and prefects' positions went unfilled, and government functions devolved on local organizations and the permanent yamen staff. Nevertheless, as a result of military campaigns, sprawling Yazhou prefecture was created in the Yongzheng reign to administer the vast mountain lands in the west, well beyond the limits of Ming territory.

It is thus no surprise that when the Yongzheng emperor tried to carry out a much-needed land survey during 1727–1730, the local elite (although themselves not nearly as powerful as their counterparts in the Lower Yangtze) organized large protests and successfully forced officials to compromise. Similarly, when a new governor arrived in Chengdu in 1755 and found a temple built by Huguang immigrants inauspiciously overshadowing his offices, he innocently ordered a portion torn down. Immediate public riots convinced him not only to change his mind but also to reimburse the temple for damages.

The large armies commanded by Manchu generals appointed personally by the throne and sent at frequent intervals during the century presented special opportunities for a more abusive relationship between government and populace. The precedents for exceedingly large expenditures in the interest of frontier security were established by mid-century, and they certainly did not diminish as Heshen and his faction, many of whom led armies sent to Sichuan, gained power at the close of the Qianlong reign.

Although the presence of many ethnic and subethnic minorities appears to have created a fragmented and ever more militarized society on the periphery of this region, as of others, there was a rather unusual lack of hostility among the migrants and sojourners of different subethnicities in the cities of the Upper Yangtze. The early cooperation among merchant groups illustrated by the establishment of the Eight Provinces Huiguan in Chongqing during the Kangxi reign reflects the emergence of an urban Sichuanese elite. In this region, perhaps uniquely, native-place organizations were located in rural as well as urban settings and founded by peasant immigrants as well as merchants. Present research does not tell us whether or not the many community temples founded by migrants in the early Qing were controlled by large corporate landowners then as they were in the nineteenth century. Perhaps the devastation wrought upon the regional core in the seventeenth century and the relative abundance of resources put most newcomers on a more equal footing.

Generous exam quotas helped ambitious scholars, but only into the middle ranks of the national elite; Sichuan ranked relatively low in the production of *jinshi*. If the writing of local histories is any indication, the payoff for eighteenth-century growth came later: between 1796 and 1850, Sichuan shot from eighth position in the nation in gazetteer writing to first. The numerous military campaigns may have made the army an equally promising route of upward mobility–, witness the career of Yang Yuchun, a 1779 military *juren* from Chongqing, who began as a noncommissioned officer, served under Fukang'an in many parts of the empire, rose to become a general, and was rewarded with hereditary rank as a marquis.

According to G. W. Skinner, the Upper Yangtze was one of the least urbanized regions of China in the mid-nineteenth century. The major cities at the time were Chengdu, the provincial capital and principal city of earlier eras, and Chongqing, the terminus for the Southwest and the Yangtze trade and a growing commercial center, with populations ranging only between one hundred thousand and three hundred thousand. Regional culture was heavily influenced by sojourning merchants, particularly those from Northwest China.

Newer forms of social organization appeared in the fast-growing and unstable society of the regional periphery where social conflict was increasingly common. Competition for land, mobility of the population, isolation imposed by the terrain, threat from armed tribesmen, distance from government authority, and presence of groups like the Hakkas who were accustomed to community feuding all contributed to the survival of subethnic differences, the perpetuation of closed communities, and the resolution of conflict by violence. As early as 1740, gangs known as the Guolufei (possibly Hakkas) became professional bandits, and growing numbers of wandering households contributed to salt smuggling, counterfeiting, and robbery. The government and local elites in the Upper Yangtze struggled unsuccessfully to maintain control. As we have already seen, in the 1770s and 1780s, millenarian prophecies and a flexible White Lotus sectarian structure spread from the Middle Yangtze into the Han River highlands on the eastern border and created networks capable of mobilizing large numbers of people; rebellion broke out at the end of the century. In the nineteenth century, Triad organizations expanded into the Upper Yangtze and led to the emergence of groups such as the Gelaohui, who played important roles in late Qing Sichuan.

Despite the Upper Yangtze's close economic ties with the regions downstream, it shared more with the developing parts of the empire than with the Lower Yangtze and North China. As we have noted, the extension of commerce in the Upper Yangtze was closely tied to the colonization of the territories directly to the south. It was in the Qing that a new macroregion emerged in the provinces of Yunnan and Guizhou in the southwestern corner of the empire, a region even less integrated into the high culture of the urban centers of the east.

SOUTHWEST CHINA

The Southwest macroregion (called Yun-Gui by Skinner) consisted of a "congeries of five small, fairly autonomous central place systems . . . only very tenuously related,"[15] including important river systems in Yunnan and Guizhou provinces and a piece of south Sichuan. The society of this region was strongly influenced by its topography and its proximity to Southeast Asia and Tibet. Its rivers were not generally navigable, and most transport was overland by foot or pack animal along steep, narrow paths. High mountains created small enclaves for tribal groups with different cultures and discouraged immigration. As in other frontier regions, foreign trade and defense played important roles in the local economy. Tributary missions passed on a regular basis through Yunnan from Laos and Burma, and there was a lucrative trade in tea and silk with Tibet and Southeast Asia. Military threats from Southeast Asia were rare, though Yunnan was occasionally a staging ground for campaigns into Burma and Tibet.

The Southwest had attracted settlers during the Ming and had doubled its scanty population to five million by 1600. The Qing takeover of the area was quite prolonged. Remnants of Ming rebel bands controlled territory through the 1650s and gave shelter to the last claimant to the throne. It was the Ming general Wu Sangui who took the Southwest for the Qing in 1657. His soldiers, most of whom were natives of Anhui and Huguang, settled here but were provisioned at considerable expense from Peking. Wu's revolt in 1673 made the Southwest a battleground during the Rebellion of the Three Feudatories. After the reestablishment of Qing authority in 1681, Yunnan and Guizhou were finally governed by bureaucrats subject to recall from Peking. During the subsequent peace that lasted into the 1720s, the region recovered from the disruptions of the transition and began a new cycle of growth. By 1700, the population had returned to its sixteenth-century level and grew through the eighteenth and early nineteenth centuries. The devastation of the Muslim rebellion of the 1850s marked the nadir of the Qing regional cycle.

It was government policy that propelled the Southwest into the orbit of China's national economy. The imperial interest in this region in the

1720s was stimulated by the need to keep the monetary system in balance by minting copper coins to keep pace with rising silver imports. Copper mines had already been developed by Wu Sangui and reorganized as a monopoly in 1705, but it was the 1723 halt in copper imports from Japan, upon which the Qing had relied heavily, that spurred the Yongzheng emperor to begin mining the rich deposits in the southwest on a new scale. Under a combination of government supervision and merchant capital and entrepreneurship, production of copper in the Southwest rose rapidly from less than one million catties a year in the early 1720s to average ten million catties annually for most of the eighteenth century. Between 1700 and 1850, Southwest copper output was approximately one-fifth of the world production. In addition to copper, the mining of silver, coal, iron, cinnabar, zinc, and lead also began, if on a smaller scale. After the 1760s, mineral deposits accessible with current technology began to be used up. Production slowly declined (Guizhou mines, although developed later, were exhausted more quickly than those in Yunnan) and by the early nineteenth century had returned to the level of the 1720s. The mining of copper was accompanied by local minting of copper cash, required for the prospering economy. The need to ship cash and ore out of the region stimulated the development of integrative interregional trading routes, particularly those leading from Kunming in Yunnan north into Sichuan, and thence down the Yangtze, and those from Guiyang to the Middle Yangtze or to Lingnan, where copper was exchanged for silver, which could be injected in turn into the economy of the Southwest.

Most important, however, was the effect mining development had on immigration. By James Lee's calculations, the four to five million people of 1700 had more than doubled to total eleven million by 1800 and had reached twenty million in 1850. Guizhou's population, which was initially larger, grew faster in the early eighteenth century, while it was not until about 1800 that Yunnan's growth reached its peak. This rapid population increase was concentrated in what was becoming the regional core. Because good land was scarce and employment opportunities were concentrated in or near towns, many migrants ended up living in urban areas. Cities such as Guiyang and Kunming achieved populations of one hundred thousand, and Dali was said to have had more than three hundred thousand people by 1750. Thus, an unusually large percentage of the population (perhaps 10 percent by 1830) lived in towns and cities. Urban culture, a blend of the traditions of different immigrant communities, became the foundation for a regional culture that would emerge in the nineteenth century. The cultural changes in the valleys and towns of the regional core spread slowly into adjacent but sparsely inhabited highlands.

Tribal peoples made up about half of the population of the Southwest and consisted of many different ethnic and subethnic groups who formed tightly closed, mutually hostile societies and seldom intermarried. Indigenous south China peoples, Tibetan tribes with cultural links to the west, and Tai peoples related by religion and culture to Southeast Asia, all combined to give the Southwest more fundamental cultural diversity than any other macroregion. For many of these ethnic groups the eighteenth century was a period of shock and forced adjustment to the Chinese presence.

Before the eighteenth century, the Lolo (also known as the Yi or Nosu) lived primarily at higher altitudes on the western, southern, and northern peripheries. Linguistically and culturally Tibetan, their society was marked by sharp class stratification. The dominant Black Lolo occupied fortified camps high in the mountains where they lived by hunting and herding. Their power was reinforced by hereditary appointments as *tusi* chiefs under the Ming and Qing. One ruling family in the Liangshan area on the border with the Upper Yangtze received tribute from some forty-eight other tribes. The subordinate, tribute-paying White Lolo, a group that actually included non-Lolo peoples as well, lived at lower altitudes and were primarily cultivators. Marriage between the two groups was forbidden, upward social mobility almost impossible, and domination by the Blacks supported by tradition as well as superior force. The basic social unit among the Lolo was the patrilineal group, each with its own settlement area and frequently engaging in feuds with other clans lasting for many generations. Both the Black and White Lolo owned slaves, some of whom were captured Chinese. Crude estimates suggest that the Blacks may have represented from 2 to 10 percent of the population, the Whites 50 to 90 percent, and the slaves anywhere from 1 to 50 percent.

The Qing development of mines and promotion of in-migration led to conflicts between the Han Chinese newcomers and indigenous tribal peoples of the sort we have seen in other regions. In the Shunzhi and Kangxi reigns, the government had concentrated on winning the allegiance of the minorities and restoring order, but the Yongzheng policy of "converting native rule into regular administration" brought rebellion as the tribal chieftains resisted the abolition of their hereditary posts. From 1726 to 1728, Governor-General Ortai put down a succession of uprisings by Miao and other tribes in the Southwest. Further tribal resistance in the 1730s was vigorously suppressed by Qing armies.

Government policies became far less interventionist under Qianlong, who preferred to give more latitude to the tribes still under the *tusi* system. Instead, provincial administrators ate away slowly at tribal spheres through increasingly complex regulations and incremental extensions of bureaucratic control. Toward the end of the century, a new rash of tribal uprisings broke out. There were Lolo and Shan risings in 1775 on the Yunnan-Sichuan border, and a large, festering Miao revolt in 1795 on the borders of the Middle Yangtze. These revolts were apparently provoked by the new encroachments of Han settlers into tribal lands at higher elevations, as the filling up of regional cores pushed settlers into the peripheries.

Minority areas and the peripheries in general were thus characterized by a high level of violence and a relatively closed posture toward the outside world. Because the government maintained and used tribal militias in campaigns outside the Southwest, the militarization of local society continued into the nineteenth century under official sponsorship. This frontier world came but slowly into contact with the urban, commercialized, somewhat cultured, and relatively open societies of the Southwest's developing core. It was not until after the rebellions and suppressions of the 1720s that some tribal groups gradually became more sinicized. The expanding commercial economy provided them with new opportunities for employment as transport workers, miners, and prostitutes; many also fell into indebtedness and poverty. Wild tribes remained hidden in the mountains, temporarily safe from the Han advance.

Geographic fragmentation and ethnic heterogeneity were also characteristic of Han communities, although city life was relatively open and cosmopolitan. The Chinese settlers came mostly from the three adjacent macroregions, the Upper Yangtze, Middle Yangtze, and Lingnan, some to work in the mines, others to settle the land. Community leadership came primarily from the sojourning merchants. Shanxi-Shaanxi merchants, as we mentioned earlier, controlled the salt trade between the Sichuan wells and the distribution network of the Southwest. Jiangxi merchants dominated the timber trade and the tea trade of south Yunnan and ran inns throughout the macroregion. Merchants from Huguang, Sichuan, Fujian, Canton, and Huizhou each had their regional specializations. Judging from the temples constructed, the most important immigrant communities in the eighteenth century were from Jiangxi and Hunan. There was also a sizable Muslim community in Yunnan that was active in trade with Central Asia. Tensions between Chinese and Muslims, reflective of the increased violence of the nineteenth century, began in the 1810s and erupted in 1855 in a rebellion that ravaged the region.

Development of agriculture was stimulated here as elsewhere by government policies that encouraged improvements in seeds and irrigation and promoted cash crops. The attractiveness of permanent tenancy on *tusi* lands, taxed lightly if at all, encouraged settlers to move into the peripheries, while local officials ignored the underregistration so long as existing tax quotas were filled. The new settlement is reflected in figures for taxable agricultural land, which increased from 959,000 *mu* in 1685 to 2,760,000 *mu* in 1812 in Guizhou, and from 6,480,000 *mu* to 9,310,000 *mu* during the same period in Yunnan. Actual acreage by the early nineteenth century, according to James Lee, was several times the registered totals, amounting to between forty million and sixty million *mu* for the region.

Trade and industry, even more important to the macroregional economy, were also promoted (and taxed) by government officials. Dali prefecture in west Yunnan was well known as the site of a fair to honor Guanyin that attracted traders from outside the region and abroad. Tea produced in Puer prefecture of south Yunnan was a government monopoly and an important export. A silk industry was begun in Zunyi prefecture in Guizhou in 1737 when an official introduced the technique of raising wild tussore silk from his native Shandong. Zunyi, typical of the most developed portions of the regional core, also had lead, cinnabar, and iron mines, a paper-making industry, and a timber-export business. In the nearby town of Maotai, on the overland route between Guiyang and Sichuan along which salt was shipped, Shanxi salt merchants encouraged development of the local liquor industry. Brewers from Fenzhou, where Shanxi's most famous liquor was made, collaborated with local brewers to produce a potent liquor that was famous by the end of the century and soon a sizable industry.[16]

The most important industry was of course mining. Mines varied widely in size, and spawned many subsidiary operations because of their demand for timber, draft animals, porters, and fuel as well as food, housing, and entertainment for miners. Although mining was financially risky and subject to cycles of boom and bust, many settlements became large enough to survive the decline of their mines. A miner's life was dangerous and unpleasant; collapsing tunnels, poisonous gases, and sudden fires were commonplace in the cramped, damp, dark, and airless tunnels. Yet a living could be made, and many made this a profession and traveled in gangs from mine to mine. Immigrant, single, and urban, the miner was a rather typical representative of the Han Chinese settler in the Southwest in this period.

To promote the sinification of tribal peoples, provincial officials set special quotas on the exams and sponsored the building of community and charitable schools. Chen Hongmou, a Qing official much concerned with raising the cultural level of the citizenry, is credited with having given special attention to the education of the Miao and with having founded more than 650 schools while financial commissioner of Yunnan in the 1730s. Local granaries were stocked for military supplies, disaster relief, and price stabilization, and the Southwest's record in meeting its quotas was rather good in the eighteenth century. Nevertheless, official morale was apparently low, and the region was notorious for the poor quality and inadequate supervision of its local officials. There were more than eighty thousand Green Standard soldiers in the region, very high for the small population. Many became pioneers, stationed in military colonies in remote areas on land seized from the tribes and marrying local women. The Southwest was unusual in having no Manchu garrisons anywhere.

The most important higher-level social organizations in the Southwest were those run by the government and by sojourning merchants, for it was some time before a local elite of any size emerged. The creation of schools and establishment of generous provincial quotas, intended to pass one in ten rather than the one in twenty prevailing in the Lower Yangtze, slowly produced an elite who could begin to bind the region together. The ratio of degree-holder families to population became rather high—two or three times that of North China or the Lower Yangtze—but in the critical *jinshi* exams the Southwest's record was very poor (it had the fewest degree-holders of any region between 1662 and 1796).

Prospects for upward mobility were good for families with enough land or a successful business, but even those winning high degrees found it difficult to enter the top levels of the national bureaucratic elite. The academies that were established in response to imperial order did not become centers for real intellectual life, and leading patrons of literati avoided postings to this barbaric place. The reaction of the scholar Hong Liangji (a native of the Lower Yangtze) when he came to Guizhou in the 1790s from the cosmopolitan east was probably typical: the average native could be identified, he said, by his straw raincoat and staff to drive off snakes.[17]

There were a few important monastery sites in the Southwest, many dating from the Ming or earlier, the most famous of which was probably Mount Jizu near Dali. Monasteries were in all likelihood among the earliest corporate landlords, but it is hard to judge their cultural influence. Buddhist monks had competition not only from Theravada Buddhists in the Shan areas, representing the Buddhist traditions of Southeast

Asia, and Tibetan lamas in the western regions but also from a variety of priests and shamans from among the tribal peoples, whose skills at expelling demons and curing illnesses may have seemed powerful even to Chinese immigrants.

The present state of research does not tell us much about family structure and life among Chinese in the Southwest beyond some of the features already mentioned: its settlements were small and its population was dominated by male sojourners. The presence of so many tribal groups with a variety of un-Chinese practices (the levirate, matrilineal descent, permissive attitudes on premarital sex, and so forth) probably contributed to a wider diversity in the society than in many other macroregions. A two-way traffic in human beings made some Chinese slaves in tribes like the Lolo and a good many more minority men and women slaves, servants, and sexual partners for Chinese in the towns.

The Southwest, although backward by comparison with more developed regions, was more populous and probably more wealthy than other frontier areas. In contrast with Yunnan and Guizhou's 11 million people circa 1800, the population of Manchuria was 2.5 million, of Taiwan about 1 million, and of Xinjiang no doubt even less. Having considered Xinjiang as part of the Northwest, let us turn to look next at the incipient regions of Manchuria and Taiwan.

MANCHURIA

Arguably no more than a developing periphery of the North China macroregion, Manchuria in the eighteenth century came to consist of the areas beyond the Great Wall, east and west of the Liao River, extending beyond the Willow Palisade to Jilin ("auspicious forest") and more remote Heilongjiang ("black-dragon river"). The Liao River basin, with access to water transport and fertile land, was already emerging as the populated core. The tip of the Liaodong peninsula was only a hundred kilometers from Shandong, and these fortunate sea connections tied the northeast to the entire China coast. Proximity to Korea, Russian territories to the north, and Mongol lands to the west made security a high government priority.

The northeast had been the homeland of the tribes who became the Manchus, and for much of the early seventeenth century the process of consolidation under Nurgaci, the founding ancestor of the Qing ruling house, had disrupted the area with politicking and fighting. Chinese residents of the Liao basin were crucial to Manchu success and by 1644 made up a majority of the Eight Banner population. After the conquest, many bannermen moved into China proper, but no attempts were made to restrict Chinese migration into Manchuria until 1668, and then as part of an emerging Qing policy of isolating the Manchus in order to preserve their culture and martial vigor. Thereafter, only in times of dearth in North China did the court permit migration from Zhili, Shandong, and Shanxi. But this ban failed to halt migration into Manchuria by sea, and in 1747 the restrictions on coastal trade were finally lifted altogether. There was in reality an irregular but significant growth of population and expansion of land under cultivation in the eighteenth century as a result of Han immigration.

These settlers proceeded up the rivers and out of the Liao basin. Han penetration promoted a moderate degree of urbanization and commercialization even among the hunting, fishing, and nomadic tribes of the far north. The multiplication of new administrative units followed the spread of the Chinese population. From 1600 on, the Russian advance across northern Asia brought them into contact with China, and their desire for trade was eventually regulated through a series of treaties, at Nerchinsk in 1689 and Kiakhta in 1728. The Qing experienced no further security threat from the northeast for more than a century. Manchuria's growth continued slowly until a complete end to immigration restrictions late in the nineteenth century led to dramatic increases in population and the transformation of the region into one of China's key industrial and agricultural areas, much coveted by Russia and Japan.

In the seventeenth century the majority of the northeast's inhabitants were either nomadic Mongols or the more sedentary Tungusic tribes out of whom the Manchus emerged. The Qing used the banner system to organize these peoples in the more developed areas and the *tusi* system to divide and control tribes in remote parts of Jilin and Heilongjiang. The Solun tribe of Heilongjiang, like others on the frontier, was liable for special corvée as a crack military unit. Seventeen percent of all banner troops were stationed in Manchuria in the eighteenth century. Society there was stratified as preconquest society had been: chiefs, ordinary soldiers and their families, and slaves. Among Manchus, descent was reckoned in terms of the patriline, and the patrilineal group survived as a marker of identity. Nevertheless, the most important group was probably the *niru*, or company, a banner administrative unit originally imposed by the Qing on kin groups that had come to be the locus for decisions about marriage, residence, work, and many aspects of daily life. Shamans, the religious professionals of tribal society, continued to be used for divination, exorcisms, and burials. Lamaist Buddhism had found converts in the northeast, particularly among the Mongols, and was patronized by the Qing court. Kangxi, brought up by his grandmother, who was a Mongol princess, was the first of the Qing rulers to display a personal religious interest in Lamaism. Here and along the borders with Inner Asia, the Qing subsidized the building of temples to Guandi as the tutelary deity of bannerman-officials, equating him with Geser Khan, a Tibetan-Mongolian folk hero.

The nonbanner population of the northeast in 1661 was only 5,577 *ding* (a fiscal corvée unit), the taxable land close to 61,000 *mu*. By 1820, the registered population had grown to almost 2.5 million people (70 percent in the Liao basin, 22 percent in Jilin, and 7 percent in Heilongjiang), and the registered acreage to 6.7 million *mu* (54 percent in the Liao basin, 23 percent in Jilin, and 22 percent in Heilongjiang). These increases are somewhat greater in absolute terms than the much less restricted growth of Chinese settlement in Taiwan, a fact that suggests both the limits of Qing controls on population movement and perhaps the greater pressures of population in North China. Immigrants to Manchuria came primarily from Shandong, secondarily from Zhili and Shanxi.

Many of Manchuria's natural resources became important commodities in Qing interregional trade. Some were precious luxury goods, bought and sold through the monopolies exercised by the Imperial Household: ginseng; sable, fox, ermine, and mink furs; pearls; and gold. But agricultural products also entered long-distance trade. By the mid-eighteenth century Manchuria was exporting wheat, soybean-cake fertilizer, and cotton to the Lower Yangtze. It appears that merchants from North China, especially the Penglai area of Shandong, were in control of this sea trade. Shanxi-Shaanxi merchants were predictably dominant in trade with the nomads and other tribes, making the usual exchange of tea and textiles for hides, furs, and forest products.

The great expansion in registered acreage in the northeast testifies to the growth of the agricultural economy. The climate was cold but the land was rich and needed no fertilizer; barley, soybeans, sorghum, millet, and wheat were the primary crops. There are numerous indications that the sorghum-liquor industry was particularly flourishing and contributed to the commercialization of the rural economy. Brewers were important sources of investment capital, and it was said that in 1725 there were one thousand liquor stores in Shengjing alone.

The society of the northeast was well known for its untamed frontier quality. Some of the settlers were criminals banished for life—there were one hundred thousand of them in 1735. Most immigrants were single men who traveled in small groups looking for supplemental income as ginseng diggers, pearl fishers, gold miners, hunters, and trappers. These migrants brought with them, among other things, gambling, prostitution, popular religion, and Chinese cuisine. Shengjing, seized by Nurgaci in 1618, became the primary city of the region and in the eighteenth century served as a summer retreat for bannermen who lived in China proper. By comparison with Peking, whose cultural influence could be felt, the cultural level was quite low in the northeast. Despite imperial pronouncements about the value of traditional ways, Manchu officials stationed in Shengjing could justly feel banished from civilization. Trading posts and forts on the rivers of the far north became nuclei for towns like Jinzhou in the corridor leading to Peking, Jilin and Ningguta in Jilin, Qiqihaer in Heilongjiang. These central places helped transmit the appeal of town life and Chinese culture to Manchu tribes.

For Manchus, the banner hierarchy was the primary ladder to fame, fortune, and escape from Manchuria. Although most never left the region, some traveled to China on military expeditions for which reserve units were needed, and a few used these opportunities to distinguish themselves. Eledengbao was a conscript from Jilin who demonstrated his abilities in the Burma and Sichuan campaigns of the 1760s and 1770s. He eventually became an imperial bodyguard, received many honorary titles, and had a successful career as a military commander without ever being able to read or write Chinese.

The elite of the northeast were probably the relatives of wealthy landowning bannermen (including the Liaodong Chinese) who were themselves living in Peking. The region produced only fifty-three *jinshi* in the period 1662–1796, much more than Gansu but one quarter the number from the next least successful province, Guizhou. This figure was far surpassed by almost any important metropolitan prefecture in the Lower Yangtze.

Like Manchuria, Taiwan was colonized in the Qing period by immigrants from an overcrowded area, was most closely integrated into that adjacent region, but did not emerge as a significant part of the empire until the twentieth century.

TAIWAN

Although separated from the mainland by ninety miles of rough ocean, Taiwan should be seen as the eastern frontier of the Southeast Coast region. High mountains in the center of the island, inhabited by head-hunting tribesmen, limited Han settlement in the eighteenth century, but the developing core along the west coast of the island was closely tied to Fujian by seaborne trade. Taiwan's position on the rim of East Asia opened the island to early and frequent contact with Japan to the north, the Philippines to the south, and the Western traders who appeared in these oceans in the sixteenth century.

In the seventeenth century, Dutch forces in south Taiwan had driven out the Spanish in the north, only to be themselves expelled by the forces of the Ming loyalist Zheng Chenggong (Koxinga). While the Zheng forces occupied Taiwan, they not only encouraged Chinese settlement but—more significantly—made the island part of their trading network with the mainland, Southeast Asia, and Japan. After 1683, initial imperial reluctance to incorporate Taiwan into the empire yielded to an appreciation of the importance of the island's rice production and trade with the Southeast Coast. By 1700, with Qing administration established, merchants from Amoy (in Fujian) further developed and marketed the island's resources. Immigration continued, even though it was formally forbidden until 1732 and ineffectually limited until the 1760s.

Maintenance of order in this remote frontier island was a persistent problem. The government was never strong, and there were countless small affrays, several major rebellions, and by the 1790s piracy and secret-society activity. Campaigns in the 1780s, when imperial armies actually sailed to the island, only drew Taiwan into the network of abuse by generals associated with Heshen. Taiwan's dependence on foreign trade and imported silver also made it particularly vulnerable to the economic contractions induced by the shift in the balance of payments that occurred in the 1820s with the explosive increase in opium imports. Central-government control appears to have been even more substantially reduced in the nineteenth century.

In 1683 Taiwan's aboriginal population consisted of about one hundred thousand people from about seventeen ethnolinguistic groups, all of Malayo-Polynesian stock. Those who lived in villages along the western plains grew some millet and rice and hunted the huge herds of wild deer, whose skins, antlers, and meat were already traded abroad. Fierce tribesmen lived in small settlements in the high mountains in the center of the island and were frequently at war with each other. Their headhunting and poisonous arrows discouraged intruders.

The Chinese population grew throughout the eighteenth century, from about one hundred thousand in 1683 to close to one million people a century later. Initially, the migrants were mostly single men, but by mid-century normal population increase supplemented in-migration. Judging from the twentieth century, about 45 percent of the settlers came from Quanzhou, 35 percent from Zhangzhou (both in Fujian), 16 percent (many of them Hakka) from the three northeastern Guangdong prefectures, and a few from north Fujian. The island was thus entirely settled by Chinese from the Southeast Coast.

Ready markets for deer products, rice, sugar, and lumber on the mainland brought merchants to Taiwan. Villages, markets, and cities developed. Taiwanfu (Tainan), with a population of less than fifty thousand, remained the largest city and foremost port during the century. Lugang and Mengjia (Taipei) ranked next but were not even walled until late in the century. As on other remote frontiers, urban high culture was almost nonexistent, degree-holding elites were slow to emerge, and merchants and officials (especially military men) were the dominant social actors. Cloth and tobacco were first used in barter trade with the tribesmen, but silver flowed in with foreign trade, and the economy was soon monetized. Despite the importance of the commercial sector, there was little government involvement with it.

The average immigrant came because of Taiwan's rich coastal plains. Though the earliest settlements were in the southwest, near Taiwanfu, by mid-century there was development in the northern end of the island. A wealthy individual or corporation would acquire title to a large land tract, then bring in tenants who would irrigate and reclaim the land in exchange for permanent-tenancy rights. These tenants in turn frequently sublet the land, so a system of multiple rights to land developed. As elsewhere, this multitiered "large rent, small rent" system facilitated development of new lands and benefited the tenant in periods of expansion. Tensions with minority groups were not as acute here as in southwest China, in part because extensive Han encroachment into the high mountains did not come until the nineteenth century.

As John Shepherd has shown, because the partially assimilated plains aborigines were assigned tax and corvée obligations by the Qing state, the government tried to protect this source of revenue and treated the aborigines with a benevolence not found in frontier regions where the court had reasons for more actively favoring Chinese in-migration. In policy debates in the eighteenth century, the conflicts caused by unrestricted Chinese expansion were weighed against the order achieved by isolating and protecting the tribesmen; in Taiwan (as in Manchuria), the latter arguments won out. By the 1760s, as the wild deer were killed off, settlers on tribal lands were made to pay a "large rent" to the aborigines in exchange for permanent-tenancy status. The aborigines became land-lords, rather like the bannermen. As problems of local control increased at the end of the century, more and more satisfied their corvée obligations by serving as local militia. Small tribal revolts took place periodically, but they did not match the violence of Chinese against Chinese.

In Taiwan, neither the initial land reclamation nor the later commu-nal violence was organized by powerful lineages, but by groups linked together by other ties, people who banded together for mutual aid in competition with neighbors. Native place, community temple, or common surname were the usual bases of organization—the latter was convenient in a society where 20 percent of the population were surnamed Chen or Lin. The simultaneous settlement of Taiwan by different subethnic groups from a region where such differences were already sharply defined resulted in frequent conflict. Two major rebellions erupted, both led by Zhangzhou men, the Quanzhou people having achieved dominance in the coastal cities and thus, perhaps, the upper hand.

The militarization of Taiwan society was given its first boost by the Zhu Yigui uprising of 1721, when migrant Hakka labor gangs (already used to violence) were transformed into a militia force of thirteen thousand men to fight for the government against Zhu, who claimed to be a descendant of the Ming imperial house and captured the island's capital. When peace was restored, a shrine dedicated to the slain militiamen became the focus of a confederation of Hakka communities that was periodically reactivated into the twentieth century. The Lin Shuangwen rebellion in the 1780s was sparked by the government's execution of a Zhangzhou gambler and murderer. Lin, a Zhangzhou native and leader of the Heaven and Earth (Triad) Society of north Taiwan, rose up in rebellion; Quanzhou natives sided once more with the government forces. The islandwide resistance led by Lin took more than a year (and soldiers from seven provinces) to suppress, and it left a worried government and militarized society in its wake.

Research on eighteenth-century Taiwan allows us to see its local religious institutions in greater detail than we can elsewhere. We know that temples were set up almost immediately by immigrants of all social classes, including officials, and that they became central to community life. In 1720 in Taiwanfu, there were eight Buddhist monasteries, one hundred temples to twenty-two different deities, a large but unspecified number of shrines to nameless unappeased spirits called *wangye* in the countryside, and earth-god shrines on each street. The five major gods included several whose adherents encompassed different subethnic groups: Guanyin, Mazu, and Guandi, as well as those associated with more limited followings, such as Baosheng dadi, patron of natives of Tongan county, Quanzhou. New shrines to these deities were created by dividing the incense of an existing temple, a process that produced a hierarchy of branch temples that related communities to one another and created networks for pilgrimage and military alliance.

REGION AND NATION

In the preceding sections, we have tried to describe the particular environments, physical as well as cultural, in which eighteenth-century society developed. We have tried to emphasize the pluralism and diversity of China and to show the different clusters of social organizations and social problems that characterized the empire's major macroregions. This kind of analysis underlines the varied historical and environmental contexts in which people lived, and emphasizes both differences and similarities. Comparing these regions more systematically to one another, however, can also be important to our understanding of the whole. We might begin with simple measures of relative size.

Table 3 shows the great variation in total area, population, and population densities of the macroregions on the threshold of the post–Opium War era (at the outer edge of the time boundary for our study). In population, the ratio of the most to the least densely populated region was 15 to 1. In size, the Lower Yangtze, the very smallest macroregion, was less than a third of the size of the largest macroregions, North and Northwest China, yet its population density was more than twice that of North China and more than nine times that of the Northwest. It was also the most highly urbanized region in the empire. Figures for regional output such as might be measured by GNP, if they were available, would surely show even greater disparities. It is important to remember that the seeming equality imposed by the division of the empire into eighteen provinces—and even our language of macroregional units—actually masks enormous inequalities in size and resources.

As Skinner's work has also shown, there were distinctive patterns of regional urbanization in China by the mid-nineteenth century. Some regions, particularly along the coast, were highly urban, both in economy and culture: the Lower Yangtze, Southeast Coast, and Lingnan. The newly developing frontier regions with ample agricultural land, the Upper Yangtze, Manchuria, and Taiwan, were the least urbanized. Some regions

TABLE 3: Chinese Macroregions: Area, Estimated Populations, and
Population Densities, 1843

Macroregion	Area (sq. km)	Population (millions)	Density (persons per sq. km)
North China	746,470	112	150
Lower Yangtze	192,740	67	348
Middle Yangtze	699,700	84	120
Southeast Coast	190,710	26	136
Lingnan*	424,900	29	68
Northwest China**	771,300	29	38
Upper Yangtze	423,950	47	111
Southwest China	470,570	11	23
Manchuria	1,230,000	3***	2
Taiwan	36,000	1	28
Total	5,186,340	409	79

Source: G. W. Skinner, "Regional Urbanization in Nineteenth-Century China," in
G. W. Skinner, ed., *The City in Late Imperial China* (Stanford: Stanford University
Press, 1977), p. 213. Manchurian population from table A.5, p. 212, in Dwight H.
Perkins, *Agricultural Development in China, 1368–1968* (Chicago: Aldine, 1969).
Area from Chiao-min Hsieh, *Atlas of China* (New York: McGraw-Hill, 1973), p. 261.
* Includes Hainan.
** Excludes Xinjiang.
*** 1851 population.

had many cities of comparable size and importance (Lower Yangtze,
Southeast Coast), others were dominated by single metropolises (Peking,
Canton, Shengjing). The presence of government, transportation technology, environmental endowments, and population densities all shaped
the size and location of cities, and, as we have seen, shifts of population
and of economic activity (domestic and foreign) left some towns in eclipse
and others in new ascendancy. Although the circulation of officials,
merchants, scholars, and peasants helped homogenize city life, the urban
experience of individuals nevertheless very much depended on the
macroregion within which they lived.

Similarly, although we have emphasized the common processes at
work on China's various frontiers in the early Qing, it might be well to
remember also how different these borderlands were. The most promising
frontiers (Taiwan, Manchuria) had open, easily worked, irrigable arable
lands; the most difficult (the Southwest, Xinjiang) had high mountains or
extensive deserts. Even with modern technology, Tibet and Xinjiang are

today being colonized only with great difficulty. Different ecological patterns and culturally divergent tribal peoples produced very different mixes of culture in the remote outposts of the empire.

These macroregional contrasts mask, however, similar or even greater disparities *within* macroregions. Each region had by definition a very uneven distribution of population and resources. The relatively low population density for Lingnan in table 3, for example, indicates how much of the macroregion lay outside the packed Canton delta: the ratio of the average to the highest densities in this region was 1 to 20. Similar but not quite so great disparities existed between the counties of the Chengdu plain and the Upper Yangtze peripheries (a ratio of 1 to 9).[18] It would, moreover, be an error to think of macroregions as units whose internal homogeneity was necessarily greater than the affinities that crossed macroregional boundaries. Those who lived on the peripheries usually had much more in common with people over the mountain range than those downriver in a distant city. On the borders, sharp contrasts and innate tensions based on ethnicity, class, and status coexisted with shared economic networks and common culture (including dialect).

Common ethnicity created its own national linkages. A map of Hakka settlement would cut across the macroregional boundaries of the Southeast Coast, Lingnan, the Middle Yangtze, and the Upper Yangtze. One could argue that continuing bonds among Hakka created important empirewide social networks. (Of course, *huiguan* and other native-place associations also created social networks that transcended regional boundaries.) Manchu bannermen stationed in the garrisons located in China's strategic cities clung to and even strengthened their sense of ethnicity in the eighteenth century, as they slowly became sinicized in many ways. It was only in this century that the Manchu shamanistic tradition and oral history were written down (and elaborated in the process) and formerly oral genealogies transformed into written documents. Similarly, Muslims were scattered in Chinese towns and cities throughout the empire. Their strong sense of ethnic and religious identity influenced virtually every aspect of their lives, from the daily routine to their choice of occupation and residence, and was continually reinforced by the movement of Muslim traders across China.

Differences within and among regions, cross-cut as they were by similar processes, were also reduced by a long-term trend toward the creation of a national economy, no longer simply in luxury goods such as jade or ginseng but in bulky products used by ordinary people. Grain, raw cotton, cotton cloth, raw silk, silk textiles, tea, and salt were perhaps the most important (in terms of the volumes traded) of the mass-market goods that crossed macroregional boundaries in large quantities. Some of these commodities, such as salt, had long histories as trade items; others, like rice, seem to have become major items of long-distance trade only with the post-sixteenth-century economic boom. Grains (rice and dryland grain such as wheat) were the single largest item traded in early Qing national markets.

Yeh-chien Wang has called our attention to the flow of goods and people performing services across macroregional boundaries and to the increasing convergence of price trends in major urban grain markets throughout the empire in the eighteenth century. The government frequently reallocated the surplus between regions by shifting tax revenues from developed to developing areas: the Southwest, Northwest and the Upper Yangtze were notable recipients of such government subsidies during the eighteenth century. Moreover, as we have noted repeatedly above, the eighteenth century was also a time of great physical mobility. In general, peasants moved out of the more developed and densely populated areas of the Lower Yangtze, Southeast Coast, North China, and parts of the Middle Yangtze and eastern Lingnan into the lands to the west and north: into the Han River drainage area, the Upper Yangtze, the Southwest, and the devastated areas in Hunan and Hubei, into Manchuria and eastward to Taiwan.

To government funds and migrants were added imports (if we may so designate shipments across macroregional boundaries) of goods from the Lower Yangtze and other developed regions, primarily cotton textiles. In exchange, the developing regions in the eighteenth century exported grain to the urban centers of the developed regions; soybeans as well as wheat were sent down from Manchuria to Tianjin and Shanghai. Copper and other precious metals were the Southwest's contribution to the national economy. Wang has summed up the exchange relationship this way: "While the developed area provided the developing area with manpower, capital, and technical know-how, the latter area in the course of development supplied the former with foodstuff and raw materials."[19] And he notes that, in the course of time, successful areas such as Manchuria and Sichuan began to contribute more and more to central-government tax revenues, shifting the balance among regions. These changes were paralleled in the rise to cultural and social prominence of new elites in the nineteenth and twentieth centuries.

Macroregional development in the eighteenth century was thus part of a broader context of exchange, conducted by the government as well as by merchants and peasant migrants. Although the national sector was not enormous, it seems to have been firmly in place in this period and, significantly, was crucial to the functioning of the component regional economies.

Merchant networks and patterns of exchange had, furthermore, reinforced the continuing process of cultural unification. Private and public action, trade, bureaucracy, and ritual all tied the macroregions to each other and to a larger entity, the Qing empire. Qing society was thus not simply a loose collection of different unrelated communities. The diffusion and standardization of culture traced in earlier chapters was spurred by economic exchange but also fostered by the policies of the government and the actions of a truly national elite. Because political units often cross-cut economic linkages, neither province nor macroregion developed as a strong rival of the state for the loyalty of its citizens. The likelihood that China might dissolve into its component regional units was progressively reduced by the multistranded ties that bound the empire together, a not insignificant heritage of the early and middle Qing.

6

The Eighteenth-Century Legacy

It has been generally accepted that the eighteenth century was the apogee of Qing power and that the social, economic, and political problems of the end of the century were the signals of the protracted dynastic collapse that culminated in 1911, when nationalist movements forced the tenth emperor of the ruling house to abdicate in favor of a republican form of government. Traditional Chinese historians, accustomed to viewing their past in terms of the rise and fall of ruling houses, have used the so-called dynastic cycle to explain the repeated progression from strength to weakness in this and previous dynasties. These cycles, which were characterized by similar factors at each phase, revolved around the activities of rulers: bold founding emperors produced a period of economic and political strength, and then weak leadership, excessive expenditures, and increasing taxes and corruption led to administrative breakdown and peasant revolt. In 1800 there already seemed to be abundant evidence of such dynastic decline in the century just past. The campaigns against the Miao and White Lotus rebels in the 1790s illustrated government weakness of the expected type: domination of the center by court favorites, waste and corruption, ineffective and oppressive local government, and military incompetence. Extravagance and irresponsibility among the rich seemed to parallel impoverishment among the poor. From this point on, the road to 1911 seemed clear.

Modern historians looking at the late Qianlong reign have echoed these views but, considering the state of the country as well as the dynasty, have pointed also to other problems that were not so narrowly political in origin: population increase, intellectual apathy, and foreign imperialism.

Mounting population growth seemed not only to increase the disaffection of the elite, strain administrative structures, and cause popular unrest, but more generally to exhaust the natural resources and available technology. According to one historian, this was "a system working near the limit of what was possible by pre-modern means."[1]

Concretely, some scholars have cited the land shortage, increased fiscal burden on citizens, transformation of farmers into agricultural laborers, and concentration of land into the hands of a few landowners, especially in the south, as important elements in the nineteenth-century decline. The scholasticism of eighteenth-century evidential scholarship, denounced in the early nineteenth century for its lack of moral commitment, was seen by modern historians as one of the many examples of the intellectual sterility that matched the technological stagnation of the period. Finally, the beginnings of the foreign threat, which would culminate in Chinese defeats at the hands of the British in the 1840s, were located in the eighteenth century when the system of Canton monopolies started to unravel and opium purchases fed (and fed off) popular alienation. This opium trade, which altered the net balance of payments against China, brought outflows of silver and depreciation of copper coinage, with harmful ramifications for the domestic economy. These various roots of nineteenth-century decline thus seemed securely located in the century before.

Rather than see the end of the imperial system in 1911 as the most important end product of Qing history and rather than measure events and conditions by their relationship to the strength of the dynasty (routinely presumed to be a good), it seems to us much more productive to assess the place of the eighteenth century in Chinese history simply by looking at the long-term developments that ran through this period. Few of these developments began in 1644 or stopped in 1911, and each had a complex of consequences not easily reduced to an indicator of dynastic strength or weakness. There is no denying that Qing emperors did become weaker, the treasury emptier, and the bureaucracy and army less effective, so we shall begin with government, where many traditional processes were indeed at work. But we shall then move on to consider broader social trends.

DYNASTIC DECLINE?

The imperial institution has long been the focus of students of dynastic decline, and there is some justification for claiming that Qing emperors began as tough founders and ended up as ineffective weaklings. From this perspective, the three eighteenth-century emperors displayed admirable leadership qualities, and the conventional view of Qianlong as the last of these great rulers seems well taken. If, however, we look at those individuals who actually wielded imperial power even if they did not reign, Qing beginnings are shakier, and the nineteenth-century decline is less precipitous and unidirectional. The revival of the regency at the end of the dynasty drew on earlier Manchu experience, and Prince Gong and Empress Dowager Cixi certainly displayed as much or more vigor as regents than had their immediate predecessors (Jiaqing, Daoguang, and Xianfeng) as emperors. Between the periods of Manchu dominance at the beginning and end of the dynasty, moreover, there was a long era (extending into the late Qing) of Manchu-Chinese cooperation in government. Chinese held significant power at court and in turn gave their allegiance to Qing rule; the dominant position of Lower Yangtze elites within the bureaucracy provided stability and continuity in this era and may have compensated for imperial inadequacies.

The financial strength of the Qing state does appear to follow the expected course from vigor to weakness. The eighteenth century was a period of surplus revenues for the Qing state: bulging treasuries and a fat Privy Purse, the product not only of peace and prosperity but also of the successful tightening of control over tax remittances from the provinces under Yongzheng. There is no doubt, however, that the tax structure, weakened by the generous freezing of corvée quotas in 1713, garnered less than 5 percent of the gross national product and was too narrowly based to finance either a large modern government or the transformations of industrialization.

The Qing coffers were probably at their peak during the Qianlong reign: the 1736 treasury surplus of twenty-four million taels had tripled by 1786. Surpluses enabled the government to grant tax remissions to famine-stricken areas, ignore arrears, and spend lavishly on military campaigns. The conversions of surplus to deficit took place in the last decades of the century. The conquest of Xinjiang, for example, cost twenty-three million taels; the campaigns against the Jinchuan rebels in Sichuan, three times that amount. By the time of the White Lotus rebellion in the 1790s, the court had to draw on its own reserves for financing domestic military operations and, for the first time since the conquest, there was not enough. The campaign is said to have cost one hundred million taels, about 30 percent more than a year's income for the central government. The fiscal weakness that continued to plague the government as it moved into the nineteenth century was exacerbated after 1840 when new burdens, including heavy foreign indemnities, were imposed in escalating amounts while the revenue base under the control of Peking stagnated. New transit taxes on trade (known as *likin*) brought new revenues into provincial treasuries but did not significantly alter the central government's fiscal weakness. By 1900, the Chinese government was actually obtaining less of the national product than in 1753. The end of the eighteenth century appears, in this perspective, to be a significant turning point.

Qing standing armies did tend to become less battle ready over time, but this deterioration should not be surprising, considering that they created a century-and-a-half of domestic peace. The problem was probably worse in the Chinese Green Standard Army than among the bannermen. Although historians have often claimed that the armies of the Manchu invaders atrophied early in the eighteenth century and were useless by 1800, in fact, they had fought regularly in border campaigns during this period and were not remarkably less able to handle the guerrilla fighting of the White Lotus rebellion than were Chinese armies.

But modes of warfare were changing. On the frontier, traditional nomadic enemies were becoming increasingly sedentary, while unexpected threats were coming by sea; inside China, foreign cannons and muskets were replacing archers mounted on horseback and infantry armed with lances. In part as a result of these changes, the once formidable Qing military monopoly had slowly broken down. By the early nineteenth century, more and more peasant bandits were armed—sometimes even with muskets—and mounted on horseback, and many communities were walled and protected by local militias. As armies became underfunded and poorly trained, the task of maintaining order over a growing and increasingly belligerent population intensified, and central-government control over the use of force receded further. By turning to the more effective militia forces and regional armies led by local elites and provincial bureaucrats, the dynasty was able to survive the empire-shaking challenges of mid-century rebels, but opened the door to the warlordism of the Republican era.

We can also see the beginnings of what looks like administrative breakdown in the course of the eighteenth century. The Qing state was, of course, plagued from the outset with responsibility for many intractable problems and huge maintenance costs, and administrative agencies did experience frequent cycles of collapse and partial reinvigoration in this period. But regular renewals were rarer after 1800, and few parts of the Qing government were operating as efficiently in 1850 as in 1750. It is difficult not to call this process a form of dynastic decline, and yet, to understand this failure, we must see its different components, for it was in part a breakdown, in part an inability to keep up with expanding responsibilities, and in part a deliberate shift of state functions onto private groups. The difficulties the Qing state had in keeping pace with a society and economy that were becoming increasingly large and complex must be understood with reference to a wider range of trends.

GROWTH AND COMPLEXITY

As we have frequently noted, the growth of the Qing economy in size and sophistication certainly increased the difficulty of Qing governance. The foundations for a well-developed commercial economy had been in place since the Song, and the early Qing witnessed a steady growth of commercialization in agriculture, regional and subregional specialization, extension of extraregional and foreign trade, and concomitant development of credit institutions.

This commercialization of the economy was accompanied by the increasing power of money and market relationships in society. We have noted in earlier sections some of the major dimensions of this cash nexus: the replacement of servile labor with contract tenancy, the growth of a labor market in rural and urban locales, the combining of bureaucratic and mercantile careers within elite families; the fluidity of movement between commercial and literati pursuits; the ease with which adoption of the appropriate life-style became itself a definition of high status; the dissonance between theoretical status hierarchies and the social reality. Qing literati and officials alike, in search of higher rates of return, made very untraditional investments in commerce, pawnshops, and urban real estate; endowments for schools and charitable enterprises likewise frequently drew on income from nonagricultural investments.

Monetary transactions also became central in government. In the early Qing, tax reforms continued the trend toward conversion of payments into silver that had been initiated in the late Ming. Except for tribute grain, which seems to have been collected largely in kind throughout the dynasty, Qing fiscal affairs were progressively monetized. Although the sale of degrees and posts can be used as evidence of dynastic decline, this practice also simply illustrates the considerable power of money in Qing society. Purchase of office and sales of degrees had the beneficial effect of enlarging the Qing elite without dramatically changing its character. The examination system and the orthodox curriculum on which it was based created common values and expectations among elites, and even if some of those values were being subtly undermined, the incorporation of new groups into the literati can be viewed as an enhancement of the process of social reproduction.

Although firm support for this statement is lacking, we hypothesize that the cash nexus may have influenced Qing behavior more generally: gifts, like relationships, were becoming more impersonal. Not only were taxes paid in cash, but money bribes and rake-offs were now commonplace at all levels of government, from the fees demanded by yamen gatemen to the system of fines on errant officials manipulated by Heshen. All these were part of what Kuhn and Jones have called the "commercialization of local administrative functions."[2]

Economic growth had had numerous positive consequences, and many of the social changes we have described throughout this book stemmed from the prosperity of the eighteenth century. Growth promoted cultural integration, as markets brought rural peasants into closer interaction with the world outside their village and contributed to the dissemination of norms from town to village. There was, however, another facet to increased participation in a larger economic system: commercialization also meant the loss of self-sufficiency; specialization in cash crops put the peasant at the mercy of market forces outside his control and increased his potential loss as well as gain.

Involvement in a monetary economy brought vulnerability to waves of inflation and depression. The eighteenth century was a period of moderate inflation lying between the depressions of the seventeenth century and the Daoguang period. Yeh-chien Wang's analysis of grain-price reports indicates a slow upward trend in the middle Qing with peaks in 1780, 1816–1817, and the early 1830s. Although price data for other commodities are not available in sufficient numbers to permit generalization, the current opinion is that this inflation, which produced a doubling of prices over the century, was absorbed fairly easily by the economy. Similarly, an increase in the price of copper relative to silver during the same period had generally beneficial effects: it reduced the cost of taxes, raised the sale price of grain for peasants, and created a climate that encouraged investment. What was true for the individual peasant was of course also true for localities and for the whole empire. Qing involvement in a world economy brought benefits in the eighteenth century.

The growth of the Qing economy also created very serious problems of control and prompted what William Rowe has called "the privatization of trade." Rowe is referring to the increasing inability of the government to manage even the commodities over which it had asserted monopolies, but the process had much wider ramifications. In mining and manufacturing, tea and salt production, domestic and foreign trade, the long-range trend was away from monopoly. The Qing state never reconciled the divergence between traditional notions of its proper economic function and its increasing impotence, nor did it evolve a new vision of its role in the economy. Until the last decade of its life, it preferred to try to preserve stability in the midst of change rather than to promote development.

As the economy grew, so did the population. Population increase is frequently identified as the root cause of nearly every ill that affected the Qing dynasty, even though the mechanisms by which pressure was exerted remain obscure. China's population was large, and it did increase steadily, but growth rates actually peaked around 1800 and generally tapered off thereafter, well before serious Malthusian natural disasters took their toll. Furthermore, here as in other matters, it is important to be impatient with national-level generalizations. Population growth occurred at different rates in different regions and was, moreover, due to natural increase in some areas and in-migration in others, with different consequences for social institutions. Out-migration was the common solution to overpopulation and, for most of the eighteenth century, an effective one. We certainly do not see uncontrolled social disorder in the Lower Yangtze, the most densely populated of China's regions, until rather late in the dynasty. Indeed, it was primarily the peripheries not the cores of macroregions that became unmanageable before 1800.

In fact, for much of the eighteenth century the increase in population was a reflection of—and a contributor to—prosperity. Population growth stimulated internal colonization, diffusion of technology, and maximization of yields, and made possible the remarkable territorial extension of the empire. It was the ineffectiveness of social institutions, government, and the economy in coping with this larger population that made more people a dangerous liability rather than a source of strength. And it was probably the sheer size of the citizenry that made the task of governance more and more difficult without a revolution in communications technology.

As this empire grew larger, more diverse, and more complex, the demands of administration mounted. Whatever their failures, the Qing responded to these demands not by giving up but by bettering, enlarging, and extending government. They made considerable improvements in the apparatus inherited from their Ming predecessors. In general terms, the power of the emperor—the image of the oriental despot notwithstanding—was probably reduced in the course of the Qing, not by personal incompetence at the top but by the expansion of government and the development of ever more effective bureaucratic institutions. The Grand Council, palace memorial system, and elaboration of government bureaus and clerks had the overall effect of checking the personal power of any single individual, even the emperor.

John Watt has called "the documentary character of Qing administration . . . perhaps its most outstanding bureaucratic feature,"[3] and the immensity of surviving archives (themselves a fraction of the original) testifies to the weight of paperwork and record keeping at all levels of government. A long-term process of bureaucratization, furthered by the spate of reforms under Yongzheng, extended into once highly personalized Manchu organizations and continued older trends toward the curtailment of special privilege in recruitment for office. This bureaucratization was made possible by improved communications that (given technological limits) tied together with growing effectiveness an ever-larger physical territory. For the Qing empire was not simply populous, it was also big. As newly conquered or colonized lands and their inhabitants were brought within the jurisdiction of centrally appointed civil officials, improved techniques of record keeping, dispute adjudication, licensing, and tax collection were introduced.

The size of the imperial Chinese administration had probably been expanding steadily since at least Song times and reflected the general strengthening of the state. The Qing continued and accelerated this trend. To the Ming administrative structure, the Manchus added the Court of Colonial Affairs, Eight Banners armies, Imperial Household Department, and the Yellow River, Grand Canal, and Grain Transport administrations. The metropolitan bureaucracy probably grew in size, especially in the number of clerks assigned to the boards and other central agencies. There were new units of provincial administration on the frontiers, only partially offset by consolidation in the cores. The latter process, which involved upgrading the administrative status of many units, also entailed increased staffing. The court even permitted some downward extension of government within counties through appointment of assistant and subdeputy magistrates (of whom there were about equal numbers by 1812) and constables (who were to provide a quasi-official link with villages). As provincial administration became more elaborate in the Qing, the positions of governor and especially governor-general grew in centrality and importance. Significantly before the mid-nineteenth-century shift of power to the provinces resulting from the suppression of the great rebellions, China's eight governors-general were already enormously powerful men.

Extrastatutory positions were created, furthermore, outside the civil service framework. Private secretaries and aides, clerks and runners proliferated in state offices in the eighteenth and nineteenth centuries as work became more complex and more specialized. In each government office, whether in Peking or in the provinces, degree-holding, bureaucratically appointed officials worked on a daily basis with employees who shared none of their education and training and who obtained posts through informal hereditary claims, patronage, and bribery. Qing armies and the military examination system had always relied much less on universalistic principles than their civil counterparts, and the new militias and armies of the nineteenth century also allowed new scope for the manipulation of private ties.

Like commercialization, the extension of bureaucratic norms threatened this deeply rooted particularism of Chinese society. Although bureaucratic mechanisms were supposed to constrain personal connections within government, for example, the tension between universalistic and particularistic considerations certainly did not disappear from official life. Indeed, there was a trend—paralleling the privatization of the economy—away from public and toward private responsibility. Perhaps reflecting these uneasy concerns, Qing intellectuals were very interested in rethinking and redefining the relationship between public and private obligations. Building on the work of their late Ming predecessors, they reaffirmed the value of human desires and so widened and strengthened the private sphere. It is noteworthy that the patriarchal Chinese family remained intensely particularistic and singularly invulnerable to the claims of outside authorities. In fact, Qing legal and bureaucratic requirements consistently and explicitly took second place to family claims.

Qing efforts to extend the formal bureaucracy somewhat into the world below the county seat notwithstanding, governance of towns and countryside still remained in the hands of eager local leaders, largely a private not public matter. Why didn't the Qing extend the state apparatus further? We cannot say for sure, of course, but many literati believed (especially in the nineteenth century when they drew on venerable precedents) that the public services provided privately by local elites were to be preferred to those of the state. A more realistic appraisal of the size and diversity of the empire suggests that this step would have required a further, enormous, expensive, and probably unmanageable expansion of government. Two crucial limitations were thus money and control.

To finance a larger bureaucracy, the Qing state would have had to increase revenues by taxing more heavily either the fast-growing commercial sector or the large amounts of unregistered agricultural lands. Uncertain of their power to invade these interwoven spheres of elite dominance, and perhaps fearful of the consequences even of trying, Qing rulers attempted neither. Moreover, even if they had had this new income, it is not clear that the available communications technology could have supported an even bigger and more effective government. In population and land mass, China in 1800 was about the size of the United States in 1980. This was, in short, a problem without an easy solution; indeed, some have asserted that nothing short of revolution could free the state from its symbiotic relationship with local elites, make possible a restructuring of the tax base to finance a modern government, and create new attitudes that would promote development.

Consideration of the national problems and processes we have been discussing so far should not blind us to the divergent experiences of specific areas. As the macroregional sections of chapter 5 demonstrated, generalizations about "China" are often misleading. The problems of dynastic decline, and of political, social, and economic control arose at different times and varied greatly with the environment.

Administrative inadequacy, social strife, and economic dislocation, problems of late Qing society that have been associated with decline, appeared in different regions at different times. In the eighteenth century, we see these problems primarily in the Middle Yangtze and Southeast Coast; other areas, such as the Lower Yangtze, were scarcely touched. More macroregions experienced such difficulties in the nineteenth century, and the conjunctions of the downward phases of a number of regional cycles did not really occur until that time.

It seems to us even more important to note that certain kinds of decline were actually associated first—and in the eighteenth century almost exclusively—with the peripheries of regions and not with the cores. It was in these peripheries, and especially those of the newly colonized highlands of south and central China, that we find disorder and rebellion, conditions caused not by a collapsing state but by the inability of government and elite institutions to incorporate new populations and new territory. The problems encountered by the state bureaucracy as it tried to cope with a growing population and an increasingly complex economy were quite different in the peripheries than in the cores. Not until the late Qing did breakdown and the devolution of power in the cores become a serious problem.

In the peripheries where in-migration brought rapid population growth, the quality of officials was generally lower than in more desirable posts and the beleaguered magistrate had few local allies. The chiefs of recently incorporated minority groups were often relied on to manage affairs among their own people, but, less thoroughly indoctrinated in the prevailing Han ideology, their loyalties to the state were weak and their potential for dissident leadership was considerable. Among new settlers, organizations of marginal orthodoxy and legality led by men untrained in the classics could become very powerful and fill the vacuum created by ineffective government. Armed lineages, bands of smugglers, and brotherhoods of migrant workers were the characteristic supplements to government on the peripheries. As the Qing state became unable to extend (or even maintain) its monopoly on military force—a situation already well advanced on the peripheries of some regions by 1800—subversion could and did turn into rebellion. The 1796–1804 White Lotus uprising, frequently cited as the turning point for the dynasty, occurred in a frontier society that had developed in relative freedom and resisted attempts by the government to increase its local administrative presence and to suppress unorthodox sectarian networks.

A survey of the disorders of the early nineteenth century serves to illustrate this point further, and indeed to underline the continuity between the eighteenth and nineteenth centuries. As table 4 shows, eight of the fifteen major domestic disturbances in the period 1795–1840 identified by one survey took place in ethnically diverse minority areas, and four more were located in frontier regions. Albeit symptoms of government failure, they must also be seen as the inevitable repercussions of the enormous expansion of the Qing empire through conquest and Han Chinese settlement. Only three of the rebellions in this table took place in the core of older settled regions and they were offshoots of White Lotus millenarian sects. We see no major unrest in the populous urbanized Yangtze delta or the Canton delta, areas where agricultural tenancy was very high and where traditional scenarios of class struggle might be expected.

Scrutiny of the distribution and pattern of uprisings in the early, or for that matter late, nineteenth century does not support the contention that the primary factors causing unrest were such classic elements as corrupt government, population pressure, or oppression of peasants by landlords. Those conditions were most aggravated not in the periphery but in the cores of the Lower Yangtze, Lingnan, and Southeast Coast. In fact, none of the great nineteenth-century rebellions was a typical "peasant uprising." The massive Taiping rebellion of the 1850s and 1860s drew first on the Hakka minority in the Guangxi hinterland and attracted smugglers and other marginal groups before it expanded as it moved out of Lingnan into

TABLE 4: Major Domestic Uprisings and Rebellions, 1795–1840

Participants	Date	Region	C or P
White Lotus sect	1796–1803	Han River highlands	P
Pirates (Cai Qian)	1800–1809	Southeast Coast, Lingnan	P
Eight Trigrams sect	1813	North China	C
Sancai timber workers	1813–1815	Northwest China	P
Lolo tribes	1817–1821	Southwest China	P
Muslims	1820–1828	Xinjiang	P
Tibetans and Mongols	1822	Qinghai	P
Tribal peoples	1822	Upper Yangtze	P
Blue Lotus Sect	1826	Southeast Coast (Taiwan)	P
Li tribes	1831	Lingnan	P
Yao tribes	1832	Lingnan	P
Heaven and Earth Society	1832–1833	Southeast Coast (Taiwan)	P
Great Way of Former Heaven sect	1835	Northwest China	C
Yao tribes	1836	Middle Yangtze	P
Lolo tribes	1837	Upper Yangtze	P

Source: Adapted and modified from "Appendix Table," in C. K. Yang, "Some Pre-liminary Statistical Patterns of Mass Actions in Nineteenth-Century China," in Frederic Wakeman, Jr., and Carolyn Grant, eds., *Conflict and Control in Late Imperial China* (Berkeley: University of California Press, 1975), pp. 209–210.
*C refers to *Core* and P to *Periphery*, terms used by G. W. Skinner to describe variation within macroregional units.

the Middle Yangtze and finally the Lower Yangtze core. Similarly, other mid-century rebellions were nurtured in unstable environments on mac-roregional frontiers and only subsequently invaded the more populous and better-policed cores. The particular problems of frontiers—areas where state and elites were weak and ethnic and religious minorities strong—were continuous during the Qing, albeit managed with greater and greater difficulty.

Declining though the dynasty may have been, it did succeed in putting down its domestic challengers throughout the nineteenth century. The reliance on local militias and methods of village pacification that had begun to be developed by the state at the turn of the eighteenth century in response to these problems of the periphery, copied and improved in the mid-nineteenth century, were crucial to the Qing government's ability to survive these challenges on the macroregional frontiers.

In densely populated core areas, by contrast, the challenges to government were different and were handled differently. The span of control had always been broad in regional cores and overworked officials gradually but more willingly delegated some government functions to local elites. Magistrates no longer oversaw local families in managing irrigation, dispute mediation, philanthropy, tax collection, schools, granaries, and militias, as they had in the early Qing, but yielded the initiative and responsibility to these elites. Just as important, merchants took charge more and more of public functions in commercial centers. Established elites welcomed these new tasks. This shift to private management, already visible at the end of the eighteenth century, gained rapid momentum in the nineteenth.

It was in the great cities of the regional cores, increasingly part of an integrated market hierarchy extending into their hinterlands, that peaceable but important challenges to Qing order arose. One challenge came from mercantile elites whose wealth and authority were essential to informal municipal governance, yet whose activities were less and less responsive to direct government control. Another came from the literati, who had to be encouraged to staff the bureaucracy and transform the marketplace values of the new monied classes yet could not be permitted to use arts and letters to question the orthodoxy or status quo. But whether one interprets it as encroachment on state power or an intelligent delegation of responsibility, local elites in the regional cores took on more and more government functions, and not until the twentieth century did they turn this power against the state.

The Qing state had to cope not only with the physical expansion of the empire but with the centrifugal forces of burgeoning diversity. The power of the government and the Confucian orthodoxy contributed, in concert with other forces, to what we can see in retrospect as a growing uniformity of culture.

Increasing bureaucratization characterized not just the Qing state but the society as well and was one way that standard practices were imposed on the empire. Within government, the number of statutes regulating official behavior swelled at least fivefold before 1800 and continued to proliferate for the rest of the dynasty. Codification of regulations and precedents was intensive in the eighteenth century and became an onerous burden on later generations. But here too rigidly legalistic prescriptions on behavior coexisted with expectations that circumstances varied, individual judgment was important, and exceptions to the rule could always be made. It seems very unlikely that Ming local officials tried as many cases or were as caught up in legal procedures as were their Qing successors, and it is probable that (as evidence of backlogs from the early nineteenth century seems to show) citizens' attempts to use the courts to resolve disputes grew faster than the government's ability to handle them. Pettifoggers who served as legal advisers were regularly singled out for criticism, testimony to the important role they played.

As written contracts became standard practice in daily life for formalizing agreements and reducing risks, red contracts that carried an official seal were outnumbered by the more inexpensive (but apparently equally enforceable) white ones that had no official authorization. Similarly, the middleman guarantor had probably become even more important as the need for establishing reliable connections and adjudicating disputes between strangers expanded. The idea of *bao*, a contract or guarantee of performance, was a pervasive nonbureaucratic but quasi-legal device that formed the foundation of personal and business relationships alike. Bureaucratic organizational devices like the rotating headship that allowed the orderly sharing of responsibility became widespread in businesses, temple communities, savings societies, irrigation associations, and other ad hoc groups. The spread of informal quasi-bureaucratic mechanisms outward and downward into the society contrasts with the increased recourse to armed force for resolving disputes in the nineteenth century, but the idea of an impartial authority not amenable to particularistic claims was not forgotten even then.

The eighteenth century was also marked by official and unofficial attempts to standardize local practices. Outside government, official and unofficial handbooks detailed with minute precision the rituals that were seen as the bedrock of social order and prescribed with enthusiasm standards for problematic groups such as women and lower degree-holders. A growing number of professional and informal specialists acted as middlemen who transmitted normative practices to the population at large. Local customs and non-Han traditions were corrected in the direction of national norms whenever possible. Manchu sinification typified the forced incorporation and voluntary acculturation of minority peoples to the dominant Han way of life that took place on Qing frontiers.

This trend further encouraged the suffusion (underway for centuries) of Chinese culture with bureaucratic language and ideals. The equation in popular religion between the hierarchy of the gods and that of government officials was more widely and permanently embedded in architecture, sculpture, ritual, and symbolism during the Qing. To receive aid from the deities, the average believer used many of the pragmatic techniques developed for dealing with bureaucrats and yamen employees. Religious values were expressed as merits and demerits, and rewards and punishments were central religious metaphors. Preoccupation with gifts and promises that much resembled bribes gave Qing popular religion a secular, transactional character that Christian missionaries later found appalling. Manipulation of the gods was a prime concern, while salvation was less clearly distinguished from this-worldly benefit. The devotional sects of the White Lotus tradition can be seen as one reaction against these developments; so can the revived concern with moral commitment by early nineteenth-century scholars and bureaucrats like Gong Zizhen and Wei Yuan.

As we have stressed in earlier sections, Qing society was also much influenced and made more homogeneous by the extension of national urban culture. We have enlarged on the vital role played in China by improved functional literacy and described the existence of large-scale printing for commercial as well as scholarly ends, producing everything from collections of winning examination essays, route books, religious pamphlets and scripture, short stories, jokebooks, and almanacs. Such works circulated broadly and crossed macroregional boundaries with ease, thanks to the increased geographical mobility produced with market integration and the commercial boom. They contributed to the formation and enhancement of an increasingly uncensorable national culture. Sojourning merchants in particular, but also geographically mobile peasants, literati, and officials, contributed to this process.

The vigor and dynamism of eighteenth-century urban culture bore many similarities to Tokugawa urban culture. Chinese historians have not called it bourgeois because of the lack of any barriers to mobility between merchant and literati and the degree to which wealth became an important criterion of status in and of itself; yet popular urban performance and fiction were certainly not elitest in their presentation of entertainment. Emphasis on the domestic drama, love story, and morality play and the depiction of historical heroes writ larger than life were appropriate for ordinary people as well. Popular culture reflected the complex crosscurrents of this society. It promoted the spread of the bureaucratic values described earlier but also perpetuated other ideas that the government tried to eliminate as immoral and heterodox. Subtler still, fiction intended for fairly educated audiences whose well-being depended on the status quo depicted a corrupt officialdom with convincing realism and expressed substantial alienation. The government tried to ban the most offensive dramatic performances, prohibited publication of "lascivious" novels, and outlawed heterodox sectarian practices, but it could not control culture much better than it could the economy. Challenges to the accepted orthodoxy had to be tolerated, but they could also be kept muted and explicit confrontations minimized.

The political timidity of intellectual life in the eighteenth century has often been seen as a reflection of the supposed decline in government and society. But the major contributions of the high Qing to China's intellectual heritage are unmistakable and increasingly recognized. Although the intellectual and artistic ferment and the creativity of this period may not have matched the levels achieved in the seventeenth and twentieth centuries, recent scholarship suggests that the repression of the so-called literary inquisition has been overstated and that late Ming and early Qing evidential scholarship contributed greatly to modern scholarly fields from history to musicology. Equally important, it was in the context of these philological endeavors that radically new approaches to the classics and to government developed. Traditions of Song learning were reinvigorated by members of the New Text school in Changzhou (Jiangsu) and in the early nineteenth century were expressed in new commitments to reform and political activism. In culture as in other areas, the eighteenth century experienced forces of growth and diversity that strengthened the Qing empire and drew it together as much as they weakened it.

THE OPIUM WAR

The long-standing view that the Opium War was the crucial marker of China's involvement in the wider world and 1840 the start of China's modern history has more recently been modified by the work of Ramon Myers and others, who have called our attention to the crucial impact of the world economy on China in the 1820s and 1830s. In those decades, the outflow of silver from China caused by the opium trade led to widespread price deflation and then depression, with catastrophic results.

But this catastrophe itself testifies to the Chinese dependence on a favorable balance of payments that for almost two centuries had fueled growth with imports of American silver. Like Europe and India, China was a beneficiary of the Spanish and Portuguese discovery of immense mines of silver and gold in Central and South America. China, whose silks, porcelain, and tea found insatiable buyers all over the globe, imported only some luxury goods and Indian cotton textiles, finding most of the products offered in payment less desirable than the Spanish silver dollars that quickly became the dominant money in world trade.

Some nine hundred million dollars was imported into China between the sixteenth century and 1826, at least half during the Qing, tripling the silver supply and directly feeding the process of commercialization. From the sixteenth century, China's economic rhythms had begun to be affected directly by and intermeshed with those of the rest of the world. In the middle of the seventeenth century and again in the 1820s, this interdependency was harmful to China, but for fully a century-and-a-half foreign trade contributed to the prosperity and growth of the high Qing. The entire Qing dynastic cycle, therefore, is inseparable from the currents of world history. Early modern China began with the Qing even before the late imperial era had ended.

By borrowing Chinese technologies, Europeans and others had begun to produce porcelain, silk, and tea for themselves in order to shift the balance of trade in their favor. The abrupt reversal of China's former foreign-trade surplus in the 1830s and 1840s, however, was caused by increasing Chinese imports of a new commodity, opium. The story of how the East India Company established a monopoly over opium cultivation in Bengal (in 1773), encouraged cultivation of the poppy crop, and exported the extracted opium to China to help pay for purchases of Chinese goods, has been told by many specialists. The prohibition of opium in 1800 drove the trade underground where it flourished despite official attempts to block imports in 1809, 1821, 1828, and almost continuously in the late 1830s. Opium found a growing market in China: average imports into the empire increased from about four thousand chests a year (1800–1810) to reach a peak of more than forty thousand chests in the 1838–1839 trading season. It was opium that dominated the private, or "country," trade that by 1828 constituted 55 percent of British imports into China, providing not only the wherewithal to pay for the tea exported but—a crucial change—a surplus that was taken out in silver.

Reduced growth, unemployment, urban unrest (another of the clusters of problems associated with dynastic decline) are directly attributable not to any of the dominant trends of the eighteenth century but to the sudden impact of this dramatic and disastrous shift in the balance of payments. This shock was felt initially and primarily in the most commercialized centers. Future histories of the early nineteenth century will have to sort out the different effects of this sudden shortage of capital on different regions and on the terms of trade of the urban and rural sectors. Here we can simply survey the leading features of this crisis.

The consequences of the growing importation of opium were keenly felt by officials. Opium addiction in early nineteenth-century China touched all social classes and most regions, alarming the emperor and court since it even penetrated into the Forbidden City and was taken up by eunuchs and imperial relatives. Addiction among soldiers became recognized as a serious problem in 1832, when the failure of a campaign to put down Yao rebels in northern Guangdong was blamed on addicted troops assigned to the campaign. But Qing officials recognized that addiction could have serious consequences not only for the dynasty's fighting strength but, more fundamentally, for the vigor of its civilian population.

Reports of widespread opium use among officials, merchants, and the common people, fed not only by foreign but later also by domestically grown opium (which was cheaper and consumed by the lower classes), led to repeated if ineffective prohibitions of poppy cultivation in the 1830s, coupled with attempts to break the complex illegal marketing networks that distributed the drug. Because many groups benefited (suppliers, dealers, and financial backers), this profitable commerce probably only increased corruption in government. Attempts to ban opium were to continue (with the same lack of success) through the rest of the dynasty and the Republican era, long after foreign supplies had been replaced by domestic ones. With what successes can Qing failures to control this drug traffic be fairly compared?

Imperial and official perceptions about the opium problem were quite clear and consensual. When we turn to the monetary problems arising from the shift in the balance of trade, we find, by contrast, some misunderstandings about the nature of the relationships between copper cash, Spanish dollars, and sycee silver, as well as severe constraints on the dynasty's ability to deal with the consequences of the silver outflow.

After 1828 the net balance of trade shifted against China, and silver began to flow out in large and increasing quantities. One estimate puts the net export of silver in the two decades between 1827 and 1849 at perhaps half the total amount of Spanish dollars that had flowed into China in the preceding 125 years. In sharp contrast with the eighteenth century, which had seen an expansion in the supply of money, this era witnessed a contraction of the money supply and sudden deflation.

The impact of rapid, large exports of silver was most obvious in the exchange rates of copper cash and silver. In the period 1835–1850, the rate of exchange rose from 1,420 to 2,230 copper cash per silver tael in the area near Peking; scattered reports from southern provinces confirmed the same trend. And yet the impact of the silver outflow on the domestic economy was being cushioned somewhat by changes in the supply of copper cash and private notes that were taking place at the same time. The second quarter of the nineteenth century saw many provincial mints closing down or sharply reducing their annual production of coins, so that the volume of both silver and copper cash in circulation was shrinking in the late 1820s and 1830s. A rise in counterfeiting and the issuing of debased coins by mints still in operation had a countervailing inflationary effect and helped keep the price of commodities that were sold in copper cash fairly stable during the second half of the nineteenth century.

Neither a depreciated copper cash nor a private-note issue whose stability declined with the silver reserve could arrest the negative impact of the large-scale flow of silver out of China. Northern China was not as badly affected as the more commercialized south, which was hard hit by the shrinkage in the silver supply and the instability of private notes issued with insufficient silver reserves. The deflation brought a sharp decline in prices for grain, raised the real cost of land taxes that were paid in silver, and produced a contraction of business activity that lasted through most of the 1840s.

Was the government of the Daoguang emperor aware of the monetary problem, its causes, and hence its potential solutions? A survey of the official documents suggests that alarm at the repercussions of a silver drain existed before this drain was linked to the growing opium trade, and that for a long time official discussion failed to connect the different markets in silver dollars and bullion with the overall silver problem. In short, through the early 1830s government policy operated on mistaken assumptions, and the solutions proffered were impossible for the government to enforce, because attempts to stop free movement of the money metal had immediate negative repercussions on market activity.

It was not until 1836 that a consensus emerged that the outflow of silver was caused by opium purchases and that the solution of both the silver drain and opium addiction rested on termination of the opium imports. The events that followed this consensus are well known: the appointment of Lin Zexu to the post of governor-general of Guangdong and Guangxi, his initial success at forcing Western traders to hand over their opium stores, the traders' anger and demands for compensation, and the resulting Opium War and disadvantageous treaty settlement, the first of many.

The Qing policy discussions concerning the silver drain illustrate the complexity of the monetary economy and the close relationship between domestic and foreign trade and highlight the constraints on government action. Both the confusion and the impotence reflect the reality, which was that eighteenth-century developments had created a very complex system that was scarcely amenable to government control except in the most marginal sense. The silver question hit at the heart of the economy: it affected everyone in the society, but it did so through indirect market mechanisms. Government attempts to resolve the problems of the silver drain without creating even worse crises illustrate dilemmas that are very modern and familiar.

And yet, despite defeat at the hands of the English and the massive mid-century rebellions, the Qing dynasty did not in fact collapse from any of the social and political problems of the late eighteenth century. It would be a gross distortion of historical reality to ignore the continuing competence of the central government by focusing solely on its failures; important government reforms, such as Tao Zhu's restructuring of the salt monopoly, were being successfully implemented during the reign of the Daoguang emperor. Major campaigns, such as the 1810–1811 famine-relief effort in Gansu and the suppression of the Eight Trigram rebels in 1813, both supervised by Governor-General Nayancheng, could still be mounted despite the gloomy state of government finances. Modern Chinese historians, pointing to the late Qing reforms, have indeed argued that the government was capable of enacting significant changes even into the last decade of its existence. It is anachronistic to see inexorable decline in Qing government power from 1800, or indeed from any date in the nineteenth century.

The eighteenth-century legacy is thus a complex one. In brief, it is possible to see certain changes taking place around 1800: the weakening of government institutions through age and underfinancing, the increasing loss of control on the peripheries, the gradual elite encroachment on government functions in the cores, the end to prosperity resulting from foreign trade, and the call for a renewed commitment by scholar-officials to political reform. But these developments must be seen in the context of the numerous long-term secular trends suggested in this book that began in the late Ming and extended without significant interruption into the late Qing. In addition to an involvement in the world economy that was continuous but increasingly problematic, there was, as we have seen, the commercialization of the economy on a broad scale and the creation of financial institutions able to survive depression; a steady and intensive internal colonization that incorporated Yunnan, Xinjiang, Taiwan, and Manchuria and many minority groups into the Chinese world; the proliferation of a variety of social institutions that structured growth and maintained some degree of social order; and the transformation of literati culture into a national culture with a broad urban base. Contemporary China owes much to its early modern past.

Notes

CHAPTER 1: GOVERNMENT POLICIES

1. Jonathan Spence, *Ts'ao Yin and the K'ang-hsi Emperor, Bondservant and Master* (New Haven: Yale University Press, 1966), p. 189.

2. *Qinding xuezheng quanshu* [Complete imperial regulations on education] (1812).

3. Zhao Quancheng, *Qingdai dili yange biao* [A chart of the changes in provincial administrative units in the Qing] (1940: repr. ed. Taipei: Wenhai, 1979).

4. Zhang Yuexiang, "Qingdai jinshi zhi dili di fenbu" [The geographic distribution of *jinshi* in the Qing], *Xinli* 4.1:1–12 (1926).

5. *Daqing shizong xian huangdi shilu* [Veritable records of the Yongzheng reign], juan 87, quoted by Raymond W. Chu and William G. Saywell, *Career Patterns in the Ch'ing Dynasty: The Office of Governor-General* (Ann Arbor: University of Michigan, Center for Chinese Studies, 1985), p. 54.

6. In the interest of historical accuracy, and with no pejorative intent, we have here and throughout the text used the terms for aboriginal peoples and ethnic minorities that are found in Qing documents, even though some of these designations have now been rejected by the peoples concerned.

7. Ping-ti Ho, *Studies on the Population of China, 1368–1953* (Cambridge: Harvard University Press, 1959), p. 210; Yeh-chien Wang, *Land Taxation in Imperial China, 1750–1911* (Cambridge: Harvard University Press, 1973), table 4.2, p. 72. See Wang for details on the Qing tax system.

8. Yeh-chien Wang, *Land Taxation*, pp. 23–25. Guo Songyi, "Qingchu fengjian guojia kenhuang zhengce fenxi" [Analysis of the Qing feudal state policy on vacant lands], *Qingshi luncong* 2:111–38 (1980); Jiang Taixin, "Qingchu kenhuang zhengce ji diquan fenpei qingkuang di kaocha" [Investigation of early Qing reclamation policy and conditions of land right distribution], *Lishi yanjiu* 5: 167–82 (1982).

9. Yeh-chien Wang, *Land Taxation*, table 1.1, p. 7; for reasons explained by

Ping-ti-Ho, *Studies on the Population of China*, part 1, official population and acreage totals cannot be accepted without qualification. Studies by historians in the People's Republic of China continue to use official totals: compare figures presented in Sun Yutang and Zhang Qijian, "Qingdai di kentian yu dingkou di jilu" [Records of Qing cultivated land and population], *Qingshi luncong* 1:112–13, 117–20 (1979) with P. T. Ho's table 21, p. 102, appendix I, pp. 281-82.

10. Quoted by Helen Dunstan, Document 36, in her *An Anthology of Chinese Economic Statecraft* (London and Hong Kong: School of Oriental and African Studies, University of London, and the Chinese University of Hong Kong Press, forthcoming).

CHAPTER 2: SOCIAL RELATIONS

1. *The Study of Chinese Society: Essays by Maurice Freedman*, ed. G. W. Skinner (Stanford: Stanford University Press, 1979), p. 262.

CHAPTER 3: CULTURAL LIFE

1. G. W. Skinner, "Marketing and Social Structure in Rural China," part 1, *Journal of Asian Studies* 24.1:5 (1964).

2. James T. C. Liu, "Integrative Factors Through Chinese History: Their Interaction," in *Traditional China*, ed. James T. C. Liu and Wei-ming Tu (Englewood Cliffs, N.J.: Prentice-Hall, 1970), p. 14.

3. Cited in Ye Xian'en, *Ming Qing Huizhou nongcun shehui yu dianpu zhi* (Anhui: Renmin chubanshe, 1983), p. 283.

4. Colin Mackerras, *The Rise of Peking Opera, 1770–1870: Social Aspects of the Theater in Manchu China* (New York: Oxford University Press, 1972), p. 42.

5. *Daqing gaozong chun huangdi shilu* [Veritable records of the Qianlong reign] (1938; repr. ed. Taipei: Huawen, 1964), 1143.29–31.

6. Mark Elvin, *The Pattern of the Chinese Past* (Stanford: Stanford University Press, 1973), p. 235.

7. Lynn Struve, "The Hsü Brothers and Semiofficial Patronage of Scholars in the K'ang-hsi Period," *Harvard Journal of Asiatic Studies* 42.1:231-66 (1982).

8. Pei-yi Wu, "Self-Examination and Confession of Sins in Traditional China," *Harvard Journal of Asiatic Studies* 39.1:5–38 (1979).

9. Wu Ching-tzu [Wu Jingzi], *The Scholars* [Rulin waishi], trans. Gladys and Hsien-yi Yang (Peking: Foreign Languages Press, 1957).

10. Nelson Wu, *Chinese and Indian Architecture* (New York: Braziller, 1963), chap. 3.

11. Maurice Freedman, *Lineage Organization in Southeastern China* (New York: Humanities Press, 1958), p. 42.

12. Dwight C. Baker, *T'ai Shan: An Account of the Sacred Eastern Peak of China* (Shanghai: Commercial Press, 1925), p. 8.

13. Robert Weller, *Unities and Diversities in Chinese Religion* (New York: Macmillan, 1987), chap. 3.

14. Robert Oxnam, *Ruling from Horseback: Manchu Politics in the Oboi Regency, 1661–1669* (Chicago: University of Chicago Press, 1975), p. 41; C. K. Yang, *Religion in Chinese Society* (Berkeley: University of California Press, 1961), p. 128.

15. See N. J. Girardot, *Myth and Meaning in Early Taoism: The Theme of Chaos (Hun-tun)* (Berkeley: University of California Press, 1983), pp. 176–79.

CHAPTER 4: SOCIAL CHANGE

1. Arthur Wolf, "Domestic Organization," in *The Anthropology of Taiwanese Society*, ed. Emily M. Ahern and Hill Gates (Stanford: Stanford University Press, 1981), p. 354; Yang Guozhen, "Shilun Qingdai Minbei minjian di tudi maimai— Qingdai Minbei tudi maimai wenshu pouxi" [Land transactions in northern Fujian in the Qing—analysis of land transaction documents], *Zhongguoshi yanjiu* 1:29–42 (1981): Chou Yuanlian, "Qingdai qianqi di tudi maimai" [Land transactions in the early Qing], *Shehui kexue jikan* 6:89–99 (1984).

2. Robert P. Gardella, "Fukien's Tea Industry and Trade in Ch'ing and Republican China: The Developmental Consequences of a Traditional Commodity Export," Ph.D. diss., University of Washington, 1976, p. 72.

3. This estimate is based on figures for marketed tea produced by Wu Chengming, "Lun Qingdai qianqi woguo guonei shichang" [Domestic markets in early Qing], *Lishi yanjiu* 1:99 (1983).

4. Robert Y. Eng, *Economic Imperialism in China: Silk Production and Exports 1861–1932* (Berkeley: University of California, Institute of East Asian Studies, 1986), p. 23.

5. Ping-ti Ho, *Studies on the Population of China, 1368–1953* (Cambridge: Harvard University Press, 1959), p. 206.

6. We rely on James Lee and Robert Y. Eng, "Population and Family History in Eighteenth-Century Manchuria: Preliminary Results from Daoyi 1774–1798," *Ch'ing-shih wen-t'i* 5.1:1–55 (1984); data from the 1930s give higher mortality rates. For the imperial lineage: Qu Liusheng, "Qingdai yudie" [The Qing imperial genealogy] *Lishi dang'an* 1:87 (1984).

7. See Richard E. Barrett, "Historical Demography and the Study of Chinese Family and Kinship," paper prepared for the conference on family and kinship in Chinese history, Asilomar, Calif., 1983.

8. Liu Ts'ui-jung's study of Ming and Qing genealogies from the Middle and Lower Yangtze indicates that fewer than 5 percent of these males never married: "Ming Qing renkou zhi cengzhi yu qianyi—Changjiang zhong xiayou diqu zupu ziliao zhi fenxi" [Population growth and migration in Ming and Qing—analysis of genealogical materials from the Middle and Lower Yangtze], *Dierqu Zhongguo shehui jingjishi yanjiuhui lunwenji* [Papers from the second seminar on Chinese social and economic history], ed. Hsu Cho-yun, Mao Han-kuang, Liu Ts'ui-jung (Taipei: Chinese Research Materials and Service Center, 1983), p. 288, table 2.

9. Arthur Wolf, "Chinese Family Size: A Myth Revitalized," unpub. paper (1984), pp. 30, 22.

10. Stevan Harrell, "The Rich Get Children: Segmentation, Stratification, and Population in Three Chekiang Lineages, 1550–1850," in *Family and Population in East Asian History*, ed. Susan B. Hanley and Arthur P. Wolf (Stanford: Stanford University Press, 1985), pp. 81–109.

11. We have enlarged Chung-li Chang's estimate of total gentry size because recent demographic studies indicate that he used an average household size (five) that is too low for this wealthy group. Given our additional uncertainty about the size of the total population, precise measurements are specious.

12. Ye Xian'en, *Ming Qing Huizhou nongcun shehui yu dianpu zhi* [Agricultural society and the servile tenancy system in Ming and Qing Huizhou] (Anhui: Renmin chubanshe, 1983), p. 235.

13. Quoted in Wang Gung-wu, "The Chinese Urge to Civilize: Reflections on China," *Journal of Asian History* 18.1:17 (1984).

14. Laurence G. Thompson, "Formosan Aborigines in the Early Eighteenth Century: Huang Shuch'ing's *Fan-su liu-k'ao*," *Monumenta Serica* 28:41–147 (1969).

CHAPTER 5: REGIONAL SOCIETIES

1. G. W. Skinner, "Presidential Address: The Structure of Chinese History," *Journal of Asian Studies* 44.2:288 (1985).

2. G. W. Skinner, "Regional Urbanization in Nineteenth Century China," in *The City in Late Imperial China*, ed. G. W. Skinner (Stanford: Stanford University Press, 1977), p. 216.

3. An Shuangcheng, "Shun Kang Yong sanchao baqi dinge jianzhe" [A preliminary analysis of the number of registered males in the Eight Banners during the Shunzhi, Kangxi, and Yongzheng reigns], *Lishi dang'an* 2:100–03 (1983), citing a report written in Manchu held by the No. 1 Historical Archives, Peking.

4. *Gongzhongdang* [Palace Memorial Archive], National Palace Museum, Taipei, Yongzheng #21533. The prefecture is Xuanhua.

5. Richard Strassberg, *The World of K'ung Shang-jen, A Man of Letters in Early Ch'ing China* (New York: Columbia University Press, 1983), pp. 131–32.

6. Quoted by Stephen C. Averill, "Revolution in the Highlands: The Rise of the Communist Movement in Jiangxi Province," Ph.D. diss., Cornell University, 1982, p. 11.

7. This and further discussion of Hankou draws on William T. Rowe, *Hankow: Commerce and Society in a Chinese City, 1796–1889* (Stanford: Stanford University Press, 1984), p. 23.

8. Liu Yongcheng, "Lun Qingdai guyong laodong" [Wage labor in the Qing], *Lishi yanjiu* 4:110 (1962).

9. Fu Lo-shu, *A Documentary Chronicle of Sino-Western Relations (1644–1820)* (Tucson: University of Arizona Press, 1966), p. 193.

10. Quoted in Chin-keong Ng, *Trade and Society: The Amoy Network on the China Coast 1683–1735* (Singapore: Singapore University Press, 1983), p. 61.

11. Peter Y. L. Ng, *New Peace County: A Chinese Gazetteer of the Hong Kong Region* (Hong Kong: Hong Kong University Press, 1983), p. 74.

12. Andrew Boyd, *Chinese Architecture and Town Planning, 1500 B.C.–A.D. 1911* (Chicago: University of Chicago Press, 1962), p. 103.

13. Harold Wiens, *China's March Toward the Tropics* (Hamden, Conn.: Shoe String Press, 1954), p. 269.

14. Hosea B. Morse, *The International Relations of the Chinese Empire* (1910; repr. ed. Taipei: Book World Co., 1966), I, 168.

15. G. W. Skinner, "Regional Urbanization in Nineteenth Century China," p. 241.

16. Guizhou sheng gongshangye lianhehui, ed., "Guizhou maotaijiu shi" [A history of Guizhou maotai liquor], *Gongshang shiliao* 1:98–117 (1980).

17. Susan Mann Jones, "Hung Liang-chi (1764–1809): The Perception and Articulation of Political Problems in Late Eighteenth-Century China," Ph.D. diss., Stanford University, 1972, p. 105.

18. George B. Cressey, *China's Geographic Foundations: A Survey of the Land and Its People* (New York: McGraw-Hill, 1934), pp. 362, 317.

19. Yeh-chien Wang, *Land Taxation in Imperial China, 1750–1911* (Cambridge, Mass.: Harvard University Press, 1973), p. 89.

CHAPTER 6: THE EIGHTEENTH-CENTURY LEGACY

1. Mark Elvin, *The Pattern of the Chinese Past: A Social and Economic Interpretation* (Stanford: Stanford University Press, 1973), p. 309.

2. Susan M. Jones and Philip A. Kuhn, "Dynastic Decline and the Roots of Rebellion," in *The Cambridge History of China*, 10.1, ed. J. K. Fairbank (Cambridge: Cambridge University Press, 1978), p. 113.

3. John Watt, "The Yamen and Urban Administration," in *The City in Late Imperial China*, ed. G. W. Skinner, p. 377.

Selected Readings

Note. A number of systems exist for using the Western alphabet to represent Chinese sounds. The two most common systems are called Wade-Giles, which was named for two nineteenth-century English scholars and was used in most American and English scholarship until the 1970s, and Pinyin, the system developed in the People's Republic of China and increasingly adopted around the world. This book employs Pinyin, but many of the books and articles to which we refer used Wade-Giles.

In order to enable our readers to find a book or article in a Western language, we have kept the romanization used by the author—whatever it was—for the title, author's name, and journal title. On the other hand, all works in Chinese, regardless of when or where they were published, have been rendered in Pinyin; we hope that readers who know Chinese also know how to convert to the system used by their libraries.

We apologize to the reader for the resulting confusion.

PREFACE

1.1. For a brief introduction to the *Annales* school's tenets, see Fernand Braudel, "History and the Social Sciences: The *Longue Durée*," in his *On History*, trans. S. Matthews (Chicago: University of Chicago Press, 1980), pp. 25–54, and Emmanuel LeRoy Ladurie, "History That Stands Still," in his *The Mind and Method of the Historian*, trans. B. and S. Reynolds (Chicago: University of Chicago Press, 1981), pp. 1–27. For recent sharp criticism of the apolitical orientation of social history, see Theda Skocpol, "Bringing the State Back In: Strategies of Analysis in Current Research," in Peter B. Evans, Dietrich Rueschemeyer, and Theda Skocpol, eds., *Bringing the State Back In* (Cambridge: Cambridge University Press, 1985), pp. 3–37.

1.2. For an excellent introduction to the historiography of Qing (and Republican) social history, see William T. Rowe, "Approaches to Modern Chinese Social History," in Olivier Zunz, ed., *Reliving the Past: The Worlds of Social History* (Chapel Hill: University of North Carolina Press, 1985), pp. 236–96.

1.3. Some recent works that have surveyed Chinese society in the middle Qing include: Frederic Wakeman, Jr., *The Fall of Imperial China* (New York: Free Press, 1975); Albert Feuerwerker, *State and Society in Eighteenth Century China* (Ann Arbor: University of Michigan, Center for Chinese Studies, 1976); Gilbert Rozman, "Social Integration," in Gilbert Rozman, ed. *Modernization of China* (New York: Free Press, 1981), pp. 141–82; and Richard J. Smith, *China's Cultural Heritage: The Ch'ing Dynasty, 1644–1911* (Boulder: Westview Press, 1983). For a survey of the extensive scholarship in Japanese, see *State and Society in China: Japanese Perspectives on Ming-Qing Social and Economic History*, ed. Linda Grove and Christian Daniels (Tokyo: University of Tokyo Press, 1984).

CHAPTER 1: GOVERNMENT POLICIES

1.4. For information on the Ming-Qing transition, particularly the Ming loyalist movements, see Lynn Struve, *The Southern Ming, 1644–1662* (New Haven: Yale University Press, 1984). The Manchu side of the story is presented in Frederic Wakeman, Jr., *The Great Enterprise: The Manchu Reconstruction of Imperial Order in Seventeenth-Century China*, 2 vols. (Berkeley: University of California Press, 1985). For background on the Manchu factions in the Shunzhi and Kangxi reigns, see Robert B. Oxnam, *Ruling From Horseback: Manchu Politics in the Oboi Regency, 1661–1669* (Chicago: University of Chicago Press, 1970) and Lawrence D. Kessler, *K'ang-hsi and the Consolidation of Ch'ing Rule, 1661–1684* (Chicago: University of Chicago Press, 1976). Important aspects of Qing rule are treated in David Farquhar, "Mongolian vs. Chinese Elements in the Early Manchu State," *Ch'ing-shih wen-t'i* 2.6:11–23 (1971); Jonathan Spence, *Ts'ao Yin and the K'ang-hsi Emperor* (New Haven: Yale University Press, 1966); and Silas H. L. Wu, *Communication and Imperial Control in China: Evolution of the Palace Memorial System, 1693–1735* (Cambridge: Harvard University Press, 1970).

Political structures. 1.5. On government organizations see: Beatrice S. Bartlett, "The Vermilion Brush: The Grand Council Communication System and Central Government Decision Making," Ph.D. diss., Yale University, 1980; Preston M. Torbert, *The Ch'ing Imperial Household Department: A Study of Its Organization and Principal Functions, 1662–1796* (Cambridge : Harvard University, Council on East Asian Studies, 1977); Thomas A. Metzger, *The Internal Organization of Ch'ing Bureaucracy: Legal, Normative, and Communication Aspects* (Cambridge: Harvard University Press, 1973); Adam Yuen-chung Lui, *The Hanlin Academy: Training Ground for the Ambitious, 1644–1850* (Hamden, Conn.: Archon Books, 1981); John R. Watt, *The District Magistrate in Late Imperial China* (New York: Columbia University Press, 1972); Kung-chuan Hsiao, *Rural China: Imperial Control in the Nineteenth Century* (Seattle: University of Washington Press, 1960).

1.6. On the examination system the still-standard works are Chung-li

Chang, *The Chinese Gentry: Studies On Their Role in Nineteenth-Century Chinese Society* (Seattle: University of Washington Press, 1955) and Ping-ti Ho, *The Ladder of Success in Imperial China* (New York: Columbia University Press, 1962). On the staffing of the important post of governor-general through the Qing, see Raymond W. Chu and William G. Saywell, *Career Patterns in the Ch'ing Dynasty: The Office of Governor-general* (Ann Arbor: University of Michigan, Center for Chinese Studies, 1984).

Social policies. 1.7. The classic source for information on members of the Qing elite (including emperors) and their careers is Arthur W. Hummel, ed., *Eminent Chinese of the Ch'ing Period (1644–1911)*, 2 vols. (Washington, D.C.: U.S. Government Printing Office, 1943–44). See also the works of Chung-li Chang and Ping-ti Ho in 1.6 above and Robert Kent Guy, "The Scholars and the State: The Politics of the *Ssu-k'u ch'üan-shu* Project," Ph.D. diss., Harvard University, 1981. A somewhat anachronistic glimpse of the lifestyle of the quintessential elite family has recently been published: see Demao Kong and Lan Ke, *In the Mansion of Confucius' Descendants* (Peking: New World Press, 1984).

Economic rehabilitation. 1.8. On the reclamation policies of the Qing during the late seventeenth and early eighteenth centuries, see Guo Sung yi, "Qingchu fengjian guojia kenhuang zhengce fenxi" [Analysis of the Qing feudal state policy toward vacant lands], *Qingshi luncong* 2:111–38 (1980). The Grand Canal has been the subject of many articles and books by Hoshi Ayao; a recent work is *Daiunga hatten shi* [History of the development of the Grand Canal] (Tokyo: Heibunsha, 1982). The best work on water control remains Morita Akira, *Shindai suirishi kenkyū* [Research on Qing water management] (Tokyo: Aki shobō, 1974). For tax policies see: Yeh-chien Wang, *Land Taxation in Imperial China, 1750–1911* (Cambridge: Harvard University Press, 1973); Ping-ti Ho, *Studies on the Population of China, 1368–1953* (Cambridge: Harvard University Press, 1959); and Madeleine Zelin, *The Magistrate's Tael: Rationalizing Fiscal Reform in Eighteenth-Century Ch'ing China* (Berkeley: University of California Press, 1984).

1.9. For government action in famine relief, see Pierre-Etienne Will, *Bureaucratie et famine en Chine au 18e siècle* (Paris: Mouton, 1980) and the excellent review of this book, which provides additional information and analysis on famine relief, R. Bin Wong and Peter C. Perdue, "Famine's Foes in Ch'ing China," *Harvard Journal of Asiatic Studies* 43.1:291–332 (1983). On Qing price reporting, see Endymion Wilkinson, "Studies in Chinese Price History," Ph.D. diss., Princeton University, 1970. Qing granaries are analyzed in W. Plow (R. Bin Wong, Pierre-Etienne Will, et al.), "Nourish the People: The State Civilian Granary System in China, 1650–1850," unpub. MS, 1986.

Foreign relations. 1.10. For historical perspective, see Morris Rossabi, ed., *China Among Equals: The Middle Kingdom and Its Neighbors, 10th–11th Cen-*

turies (Berkeley: University of California Press, 1983). For excerpts from Chinese records, see Fu Lo-shu, *A Documentary Chronicle of Sino-Western Relations (1644–1820)* (Tucson: University of Arizona Press, 1966). For the view from Japan, see Kazui Tashiro, "Foreign Relations During the Edo Period: *Sakoku* Reconsidered," *The Journal of Japanese Studies* 8.2:283–306 (1982) and Ronald P. Toby, *State and Diplomacy in Early Modern Japan: Asia in the Development of the Tokugawa Bakufu* (Princeton: Princeton University Press, 1984). Essays in John K. Fairbank, ed., *The Chinese World Order: Traditional China's Foreign Relations* (Cambridge: Harvard University Press, 1968), are also useful, particularly David Farquhar, "The Origins of the Manchus' Mongolian Policy," pp. 198–205, Mark Mancall, "The Ch'ing Tribute System: An Interpretive Essay," pp. 63–89, and Joseph Fletcher, "China and Central Asia, 1368–1884," pp. 206–24. See also David M. Farquhar, "Emperor As Bodhisattva in the Governance of the Ch'ing Empire," *Harvard Journal of Asiatic Studies* 38.1:5-34 (1978).

CHAPTER 2: SOCIAL RELATIONS

2.1. A useful review of analyses concerning variants in family organization is provided in Arthur Wolf, "Domestic Organization," in Emily M. Ahern and Hill Gates, eds., *The Anthropology of Taiwanese Society* (Stanford: Stanford University Press, 1981), pp. 341–60. This article can be paired with Myron Cohen, "Developmental Process in the Chinese Domestic Group," in Maurice Freedman, ed., *Family and Kinship in Chinese Society* (Stanford: Stanford University Press, 1970). Both authors move beyond pioneering work done on these topics by Maurice Freedman, collected in *The Study of Chinese Society: Essays by Maurice Freedman*, selected and introduced by G. W. Skinner (Stanford: Stanford University Press, 1979).

Kinship. 2.2. A similar review of lineage organization is provided in James L. Watson, "Chinese Kinship Reconsidered: Anthropological Perspectives on Historical Research," *The China Quarterly* 92:589–622 (1982), and Patricia Ebrey, "Types of Lineages in Ch'ing China: A Re-examination of the Chang Lineage of T'ung-ch'eng," *Ch'ing-shih wen-t'i* 4.9:1–20 (1983). The particular characteristics of the dominant lineage are presented in Maurice Freedman's works, notably *Chinese Lineage and Society: Fukien and Kwangtung* (New York: Humanities Press, 1966) (see also 2.1). Regional and historical variations in kinship structures are also treated in the essays included in *Kinship Organization in Late Imperial China*, ed. Patricia Ebrey and James L. Watson (Berkeley: University of California Press, 1986). Also see P. Steven Sangren, "Traditional Chinese Corporations: Beyond Kinship," *Journal of Asian Studies* 43.5:391–415 (1984).

Residence and Community. 2.3. The basic and pioneering work on market communities is G. W. Skinner, "Marketing and Social Structure in Rural China (Part I)," *Journal of Asian Studies* 24.1:3–43 (1964). C. K. Yang, *Religion in Chinese Society* (Berkeley: University of California Press, 1967) is still a useful source for information on temple associations. Also see Kristofer M. Schipper, "Neighborhood Cult Associations in Traditional Tainan," in G. W. Skinner, ed., *The City in Late Imperial China* (Stanford: Stanford University Press, 1977), pp. 651–76; James L. Watson, "Standardizing the Gods: The Promotion of T'ien Hou ('Empress of Heaven') Along the South China Coast, 960–1960," in David Johnson, Andrew J. Nathan, and Evelyn S. Rawski, eds., *Popular Culture in Late Imperial China* (Berkeley: University of California Press, 1985), pp. 292–324; and Steven Sangren, "Female Gender in Chinese Religious Symbols: Kuan Yin, Ma Tsu, and the 'Eternal Mother,' " *Signs* 9.1:4–25 (1983).

Economic organizations. 2.4. See William T. Rowe, *Hankow: Commerce and Society in a Chinese City, 1796–1889* (Stanford: Stanford University Press, 1984); Peter J. Golas, "Early Ch'ing Guilds," in *The City in Late Imperial China* (see 2.3 above), pp. 555–80. Institutional attempts to control urban populations are studied in William T. Rowe, "Urban Control in Late Imperial China: The *Pao-chia* System in Hankow," in Joshua A. Fogel and William T. Rowe, eds., *Perspectives on a Changing China* (Boulder: Westview Press, 1979), pp. 89–112. *Huiguan* are studied in He Bingdi (Ping-ti Ho), *Zhongguo huiguanshi lun* [A historical survey of *Landsmannschaften* in China] (Taipei: Xuesheng, 1966); see also Lü Zuoxie, "Ming Qing shiqi di huiguan bing fei gongshangye hanghui" [The huiguan of Ming and Qing were not guilds], *Zhongguo shi yanjiu* 2:66–79 (1982). Urban riots are analyzed by Tsing Yuan, "Urban Riots and Disturbances," in Jonathan D. Spence and John E. Wills, Jr., eds., *From Ming to Ch'ing: Conquest, Region, and Continuity in Seventeeth-Century China* (New Haven: Yale University Press, 1979), pp. 277–320. For the ways in which communities exported sojourner specialists, see G. W. Skinner, "Mobility Strategies in Late Imperial China: A Regional Systems Analysis," in *Regional Analysis*, ed. Carole A. Smith (New York: Academic Press, 1976), Vol. 1, pp. 327–64.

2.5. On philanthropy, see Liang Qizi (Angela K. Leung), "Shiqi shiba shiji Changjiang xiayou zhi yuyingtang" [Orphanages in the Yangtze delta in the seventeenth and eighteenth centuries], in *Zhongguo haiyang fazhan shi lunwenji* [Essays on the history of China's maritime development], compiled by Zhongyang yanjiuyuan Sanmin zhuyi yanjiusuo (Taipei: Zhongyang yanjiuyuan, 1984), pp. 97–130; her "Mingmo Qingchu minjian cishan huodong di xingqi—yi Jiang Zhe diqu wei li" [The rise of popular philanthropy in late Ming and early Qing— examples from Jiangsu and Zhejiang], *Shihuo yuekan* n.s. 15.7–8:304–31 (1986); and David E. Kelley, "Buddhist-Inspired Social Welfare Activities: Shelter Temples in the Late Ming and Early Qing: A Preliminary Essay," presented at the Association for Asian Studies, March 1984.

Patronage. 2.6. H. Lyman Miller, "Factional Conflict and the Integration of Ch'ing Politics, 1661–1689," Ph.D. diss., George Washington University, 1974; James Polachek, *The Inner Opium War* (Cambridge: Harvard University, Council on East Asian Studies, forthcoming); Jerry Dennerline, *The Chia-ting*

Loyalists: Confucian Leadership and Social Change in Seventeenth-Century China (New Haven: Yale University Press, 1981). For a good-guys and bad-guys picture of court factionalism, see Silas H. L. Wu, *Passage to Power: K'ang-hsi and His Heir Apparent, 1661–1722* (Cambridge: Harvard University Press, 1979).

CHAPTER 3: CULTURAL LIFE

City Life. 3.1. The best-known fiction of the early and middle Qing provides important insights into the life of the times. Translations include: Wu Ching-tzu, *The Scholars* [Rulin waishi], trans. Gladys and Hsien-yi Yang (Peking: Foreign Languages Press, 1957); Cao Xueqin (Ts'ao Hsueh-ch'in), *Story of the Stone* [Honglou meng] , trans. David Hawkes, 4 vols. (New York: Penguin, 1973–82), also translated under the titles *Dream of Red Mansions* and *Dream of the Red Chamber*; Pu Songling, *Strange Stories from a Chinese Studio* [Liaozhai zhiyi], trans. Herbert A. Giles, 4th ed. rev. (Shanghai: Kelly and Walsh, 1926).

3.2. On drama, see Colin P. Mackerras, *The Rise of Peking Opera, 1770–1870* (London: Oxford University Press, 1972); William Dolby, *A History of Chinese Drama* (New York: Harper and Row, 1975); and Tanaka Issei, *Chūgoku saishi engeki kenkyū* [Research on Chinese ritual drama] (Tokyo: Tōyō bunka kenkyujō, 1981). For cities generally, see the essays in the pathbreaking volume, *The City in Late Imperial China* (above 2.3).

Literati culture. 3.3. The first phase of accommodation to conquest is treated by Lynn Struve, "The Hsü Brothers and Semiofficial Patronage of Scholars in the K'ang-hsi Period," *Harvard Journal of Asiatic Studies* 42.1:231–66 (1982), and by John D. Langlois, Jr., "Chinese Culturalism and the Yuan Analogy: Seventeenth-Century Perspectives," *Harvard Journal of Asiatic Studies* 40.2:355–98 (1980). For the eighteenth century, see Benjamin Elman, *From Philosophy to Philology: Intellectual and Social Aspects of Change in Late Imperial China* (Cambridge: Harvard University, Council on East Asian Studies, 1984); Robert Kent Guy's thesis, "The Scholars and the State," cited above 1.7; Pei-yi Wu, "Self-Examination and Confession of Sins in Traditional China," *Harvard Journal of Asiatic Studies* 39.1:5–38 (1979); and Paul S. Ropp, *Dissent in Early Modern China: Ju-lin wai-shih and Ch'ing Social Criticism* (Ann Arbor: University of Michigan Press, 1981).

3.4. A fine introduction to the painting of this period is Ju-hsi Chou and Claudia Brown, eds., *The Elegant Brush: Chinese Painting Under the Qianlong Emperor, 1735–95,* (Phoenix: Phoenix Art Museum, 1985), particularly the essays by Harold Kahn and Howard Rogers. See also James Cahill, "The Orthodox Movement in Early Ch'ing Painting," in Christian F. Murck, ed., *Artists and Traditions: Uses of the Past in Chinese Culture* (Princeton: Princeton University Press, 1976), pp. 169–81. For poetry, see Arthur Waley, *Yuan Mei: Eighteenth Century Poet* (1956; repr. Stanford: Stanford University Press, 1970). Popular art, in particular the new-year woodcuts, is discussed by Mary H. Fong, "The

Iconography of the Popular Gods of Happiness, Emolument, and Longevity (Fu Lu Shou)," *Artibus Asiae* 44.2–3:155–99 (1983).

Material culture. 3.5. This is a relatively unexplored topic. Perhaps the most comprehensive analysis of domestic architecture is Liu Dunzhen, *Zhongguo zhuzhai gaishuo* [A study of Chinese domestic architecture] (Peking: Zhongguo jianzhugongye chubanshe, 1957). See also Ronald G. Knapp, *China's Traditional Rural Architecture: A Cultural Geography of the Common House* (Honolulu: University of Hawaii Press, 1986). Public structures and town planning are discussed by Liu Dunzhen, *Zhongguo gudai jianzhushi* [History of China's ancient architecture] (Peking: Jianzhu gongye chubanshe, 1984) (the reader should note that despite the title there are long chapters on Qing buildings), and Andrew Boyd, *Chinese Architecture and Town Planning, 1500 B.C.–A.D. 1911* (Chicago: University of Chicago Press, 1962). On Chinese gardens, see Maggie Keswick, *The Chinese Garden: History, Art, and Architecture* (New York: Rizzoli, 1978). On clothing, Schuyler Cammann, "The Development of the Mandarin Square," *Harvard Journal of Asiatic Studies* 8:71–130 (1943), and John Vollmer, *In the Presence of the Dragon Throne* (Toronto: Royal Ontario Museum, 1977), discuss Manchu influence on official garb. For porcelain, see R. L. Hobson, *Chinese Pottery and Porcelain*, vol. 2 (London: Cassell, 1915). On Qing eating habits, see Jonathan D. Spence, "Ch'ing," in Kwang-chih Chang, ed., *Food in Chinese Culture* (New Haven: Yale University Press, 1977), pp. 261–94. For technology generally, see Sung Ying-hsing, *T'ien-kung k'ai-wu: Chinese Technology in the Seventeenth Century*, trans. E-tu Zen Sun and Shiou-chuan Sun (University Park: Pennsylvania State University Press, 1966).

Life-cycle rituals. 3.6. Stephan Feuchtwang, "School-Temple and City God," in *The City in Late Imperial China* (see 2.3), pp. 581–608; Laurence Thompson, "Orthodox Official Religion and Orthodox Popular Religion in Early Ch'ing Taiwan," unpub. paper, 1981; Maurice Freedman, "Rites and Duties, or Chinese Marriage," in *The Study of Chinese Society: Essays of Maurice Freedman* (see 2.1), pp. 255–72; and the essays in James L. Watson and Evelyn S. Rawski, eds., *Death Ritual in Late Imperial and Modern China* (Berkeley, University of California Press, 1987).

Annual festivals. 3.7. The religious landscape is surveyed by Arthur P. Wolf, "Gods, Ghosts, and Ancestors," in Arthur P. Wolf, ed., *Religion and Ritual in Chinese Society* (Stanford: Stanford University Press, 1974), pp. 131–82. Robert P. Weller, *Unities and Diversities in Chinese Religion* (New York: Macmillan, 1987), chap. 3, considers the dynamics of change in popular festivals. The following sources provide good descriptions of customs current in the late nineteenth and early twentieth centuries: J. J. M. de Groot, *The Religious System of China*, 6 vols. (Leiden: Brill, 1892–1910), which presents a detailed ethnography of funeral practices in the Amoy region; Annie Cormack, *Chinese Birthday,*

Wedding, Funeral, and Other Customs (Shanghai: Kelly & Walsh, 1927); Justus Doolittle, *The Social Life of the Chinese*, 2 vols. (New York: Harper & Bros., 1865), which is based on his observations of Foochow customs; H. Y. Lowe, *The Adventures of Wu: The Life Cycle of a Peking Man* (1940–41; repr. Princeton: Princeton University Press, 1983), which is a lively description of life cycle and annual Peking festivals; and Ida Pruitt, *A Daughter of Han: The Autobiography of a Chinese Working-Woman* (New Haven: Yale University Press, 1945; repr. Stanford: Stanford University Press, 1967).

State ritual. 3.8. See E. T. Williams, "The State Religion of China during the Manchu Dynasty," *Journal of the North China Branch, Royal Asiatic Society* 44:11–45 (1913); Angela Rose Zito, "Re-Presenting Sacrifice: Cosmology and the Editing of Texts," *Ch'ing-shih wen-t'i* 5.2:47–78 (1984); Stephan Feuchtwang, "School-Temple and City God," in *The City in Late Imperial China* (see 2.3), pp. 581–608.

Chinese values. 3.9. See a recent analysis, based on peasant proverbs from North and Northwest China, by R. David Arkush, "If Man Works Hard the Land Will Not Be Lazy," *Modern China* 10.4:461–79 (1984), and the essays in *Death Ritual in Late Imperial and Modern China* (see 3.6).

CHAPTER 4: SOCIAL CHANGE

Economic diversity and growth. 4.1. An excellent broad survey of Chinese agriculture is Joseph Needham and Francesca Bray, *Science and Civilisation in China* 6.2: *Agriculture* (Cambridge: Cambridge University Press, 1984). On the changes in cropping, see Ping-ti Ho, *Studies on the Population of China, 1368–1953* (see 1.8), chap. 8.

4.2. The secondary literature on sprouts of capitalism is very extensive and still growing. A good survey of this discussion in English is William T. Rowe, "Approaches to Modern Chinese Social History" (above 1.2). The most substantive study of this topic in Chinese is Liu Yongcheng, *Qingdai qianqi nongye ziben zhuyi mengya chutan* [Preliminary discussions on the sprouts of capitalism in early Qing agriculture] (Fuzhou: Renmin, 1982). See also the collected articles in *Ming Qing shidai di nongye ziben zhuyi mengya wenti* [The issue of sprouts of capitalism in agriculture in the Ming and Qing], compiled by Zhongguo shehui kexue yuan, Jingji yanjiusuo (Peking: Zhongguo shehui kexue yuan, 1984).

4.3. For commerce and industry, see Wu Chengming, "Lun Qingdai qianqi woguo guonei shichang" [Domestic markets in the early Qing], *Lishi yanjiu* 1:96–106 (1983). For urbanization, see Gilbert Rozman, *Urban Networks in Ch'ing China and Tokugawa Japan* (Princeton: Princeton University Press, 1973), and the essays by G. W. Skinner in *The City in Late Imperial China*, see 2.3). The best overall survey of handicraft development is Peng Zeyi, "Qingdai qianqi shougongye di fazhan" [Development of handicrafts in early Qing], *Zhongguoshi yanjiu* 1:43–60 (1981). For the salt monopoly, see Thomas A. Metzger, "The Organizational Capabilities of the Ch'ing State in the Field of Commerce: The Liang-Huai Salt Monopoly, 1740–1840," in W. E. Willmott, ed., *Economic Organization in Chinese Society* (Stanford: Stanford University Press, 1972), pp. 9–45. On the tax-brokerage system, see Susan Mann, *Local Merchants and the Chinese Bureaucracy, 1750–1950* (Stanford: Stanford University Press, 1987).

4.4. For customary law, see Fu-mei Chang Chen and Ramon Myers, "Customary Law and the Economic Growth of China during the Ch'ing Period," *Ch'ing-shih wen-t'i* 3.5:1–32 (1976), 3.10:4–48 (1978); Rosser H. Brockman, "Commercial Contract Law in Late Nineteenth-Century Taiwan," in Jerome A. Cohen, R. Randle Edwards, and Fu-mei C. Chen, eds., *Essays on China's Legal Tradition* (Princeton: Princeton University Press, 1980), pp. 76–136; and Zhou Yuanlian, "Qingdai qianqi di tudi maimai" [Land transactions in the early Qing], *Shehui kexue jikan* 6:89–99 (1984).

4.5. On the trade with Southeast Asia, see Yu Siwei, "Qingdai qianqi Guangzhou yu Dongnanya di maoyi guanxi" [Early Qing trading relations between Canton and Southeast Asia], *Zhongshan daxue xuebao* 2:73–83 (1983). Louis Dermigny, *La Chine et l'occident: le commerce à Canton au XVIIIe siècle, 1719–1833*, 4 vols. (Paris: S.E.V.P.E.N., 1964), collects figures for the trade at Canton. Philip D. Curtin, *Cross-Cultural Trade in World History* (New York: Cambridge University Press, 1984), provides the world trade context in which Chinese overseas trade operated: see his chaps. 7, 8. On specific sectors, see Robert P. Gardella, "Fukien's Tea Industry and Trade in Ch'ing and Republican China: The Developmental Consequences of a Traditional Commodity Export," Ph.D. diss., University of Washington, 1976; and Robert Y. Eng, *Economic Imperialism in China: Silk Production and Exports 1861–1932* (Berkeley: University of California, Institute of East Asian Studies, 1986). John K. Fairbank, *Trade and Diplomacy on the China Coast: The Opening of the Treaty Ports, 1842–1854* (Cambridge: Harvard University Press, 1953), presents the context of the late Canton system and the tensions that led to the Opium War.

4.6. For bimetallic systems and Qing currency, see Yeh-chien Wang, "Evolution of the Chinese Monetary System, 1644–1850," in Chi-ming Hou and Tzong-shian Yu, eds., *Modern Chinese Economic History: Proceedings of the Conference on Modern Chinese Economic History, Academia Sinica, Taipei, Taiwan, Republic of China, August 26–28, 1977* (Taipei: Zhongyang yanjiuyuan, Jingji yanjiusuo, 1979), pp. 425–52; Wang Yejian, *Zhongguo jindai huobi yu yinhang di yanjiu (1644–1937)* [Research on China's modern currency and banks, 1644–1937] (Taipei: Zhongyang yanjiuyuan, Jingji yanjiusuo, 1981). On the Kangxi depression, see Mio Kishimoto-Nakayama, "The Kangxi Depression and Early Qing Local Markets," *Modern China* 10.2:227–56 (1984).

Demographic trends. 4.7. Ping-ti Ho, *Studies on the Population of China, 1368–1953* (see 1.8) remains the basic introduction to the evaluation of official population records. Michel Cartier, "La croissance démographique chinoise du 18e siècle et l'enregistrement des baojia," *Annales de démographie historique*, 1979:9–28 discusses another aspect of the government registration. To supplement these records, many scholars have used John Lossing Buck, ed., *Land Utilization in China*, 3 vols. (Chicago: University of Chicago Press, for the University of Nanking, 1937), the classic 1929–1931 survey of nearly fifty thousand farm families all over China. An important recent reevaluation of the Buck data is George W. Barclay, Ansley J. Coale, et al., "A Reassessment of the Demography of Traditional Rural China," *Population Index* 42.4:606–35 (1976). Attempts to use genealogies for demographic analysis have only just begun: an example is Stevan Harrell, "The Rich Get Children: Segmentation, Stratification, and Population in Three Chekiang Lineages, 1550–1850," in Susan B. Hanley and Arthur P. Wolf, eds., *Family and Population in East Asian History* (Stanford: Stanford University Press, 1985), pp. 81–109.

4.8. Archival sources for demographic analysis is another burgeoning field: two recent articles are James Lee and Robert Y. Eng, "Population and Family History in Eighteenth Century Manchuria: Preliminary Results from Daoyi, 1774–1798," *Ch'ing-shih wen-t'i* 5.1:1-55 (1984), using archival registers of Manchuized Chinese bannermen, and Qu Liusheng, "Qingdai yudie" [The Qing imperial genealogy], *Lishi dang'an* 1:83–87 (1984), introducing archival genealogical records for the ruling house.

4.9. Taiwan household registers compiled during the period of Japanese rule comprise another body of demographic sources for study of a Chinese population. The most substantial analysis of this material is Arthur P. Wolf and Chieh-shan Huang, *Marriage and Adoption in China, 1845–1945* (Stanford: Stanford University Press, 1980). Arthur P. Wolf, "Chinese Family Size: A Myth Revitalized" (unpub. paper, 1984), reconsiders traditional household size using Taiwan household registers. See also Richard Barrett, "Short-Term Trends in Bastardy in Taiwan," *Journal of Family History* 5.3:293–312 (1980).

4.10. On the medical literature concerning conception and childbirth, see Angela K. Leung, "Autour de la naissance: la mère et l'enfant en Chine aux XVIe et XVIIe siècles," *Cahiers internationaux de sociologie* 76:51–69 (1984), and Charlotte Furth, "Concepts of Pregnancy, Childbirth, and Infancy in Ch'ing Dynasty China," *Journal of Asian Studies* 46.1:7–35 (1987). For an anthropologist's analysis based on contemporary observation, see Margery Wolf, "Child Training and the Chinese Family," in *Family and Kinship in Chinese Society*, pp. 37–62. For gender difference and Chinese attitudes toward sex, see Angela K. Leung, "Sexualité et sociabilité dans le Jin Ping Mei, roman érotique chinois de la fin du XVIème siècle," *Information sur les sciences sociales* 23.4–5:653–76 (1984). On the Qing government's policies encouraging widow chastity, see Mark Elvin, "Female Virtue and the State in China," *Past and Present* 104:111–52 (1984) and Susan Mann, "Widows in the Kinship, Class, and

Community Structures of Late Qing Dynasty China," *Journal of Asian Studies* 46.1:37–56 (1987).

4.11. For European and Japanese comparisons, see the Wolf and Hanley volume mentioned in 4.7; Susan Cotts Watkins, "Spinsters," *Journal of Family History* 9.4:310–25 (1985); and John Hajnal, "Two Kinds of Preindustrial Household Formation System," *Population and Development Review* 8.3:449–94 (1982).

Hereditary statuses. 4.12. There is a large and growing literature on servitude in traditional times. On the legal aspects of hereditary status, see Jing Junjian, "Shilun Qingdai dengji zhidu" [On the Qing status system], *Zhongguo shehui kexue* 6:149–71 (1980). There is also Wei Qingyuan, Wu Qiyan, and Lu Su, *Qingdai nubi zhidu* [On Qing bondservants] (Peking: Renmin daxue, 1982). The most detailed study of servile tenancy is Ye Xian'en, *Ming Qing Huizhou nongcun shehui yu dianpu zhi* [The agricultural society of Ming and Qing Huizhou and the servile tenancy system] (Anhui: Renmin chubanshe, 1983).

Social mobility. 4.13. Ping-ti Ho, *The Ladder of Success in Imperial China* and Chung-li Chang, *The Chinese Gentry* (both cited in 1.6), are classic works. Defining the kinship network more widely than Ho did leads to different results: see Odoric Y. K. Wou, "The Political Kin Unit and the Family Origin of Ch'ing Local Officials," in *Perspectives on a Changing China* (see 2.4), pp. 69–87.

4.14. The mercantile elite are treated in Ping-ti Ho, "The Salt Merchants of Yangchow," *Harvard Journal of Asiatic Studies* 17:130–68 (1954). The bottom end of the social ladder was studied in James L. Watson, "Transactions in People: The Chinese Market in Slaves, Servants, and Heirs," in J. L. Watson, ed., *Asian and African Systems of Slavery* (Oxford: Blackwell, 1980), pp. 223–50. For an overall appraisal, see *The Modernization of China* (cited in 1.3).

Assimilation of minorities. 4.15. John Shepherd, "Plains Aborigines and Chinese Settlers on the Taiwan Frontier in the Seventeenth and Eighteenth Centuries," Ph.D. diss., Stanford University, 1981. For the north and west, there are Joseph Fletcher's essays "Ch'ing Inner Asia c. 1800" and "The Heyday of the Ch'ing Order in Mongolia, Sinkiang and Tibet," in *The Cambridge History of China*, vol. 10, part 1, ed. Denis Twitchett and John K. Fairbank (Cambridge: Cambridge University Press, 1978), pp. 35–106, 351–408, and Charles R. Bawden, *The Modern History of Mongolia* (New York: Praeger, 1968). For southwestern minorities, see Claudine Lombard-Salmon, *Un exemple d'acculturation chinoise: la province du Gui Zhou au XVIIIe siècle* (Paris: Ecole Française d'Extrême-Orient, 1972); Robert H. G. Lee, "Frontier Politics in the Southwestern Sino-Tibetan Borderlands During the Ch'ing Dynasty," in *Perspectives on a Changing China* (see 2.4), pp. 35–68; and Kent Smith, "Ch'ing Policy and the Development of Southwest China: Aspects of Ortai's Governor-Generalship, 1726–1731," Ph.D. diss., Yale University, 1970. Hyman Kublin, ed., *Studies of the Chinese Jews: Selections from Journals East and West* (New York: Paragon, 1971) pulls together information on Jews in China.

Frontier society. 4.16. For ethnicity, see S. T. Leong, "The P'eng-min: The Ch'ing Administration and Internal Migration," unpub. paper (1984), and Myron Cohen, "The Hakka or Guest People: Dialect as a Sociocultural Variable in Southeast China," *Ethnohistory* 15.3:237–92 (1968). The Fletcher articles cited in 4.15 also provide valuable information on ethnicity.

New associations. 4.17. For sectarian associations, see Susan Naquin, "The Transmission of White Lotus Sectarianism in Late Imperial China," in *Popular Culture in Late Imperial China* (see 2.3), pp. 255–91, and David E. Kelley, "Temples and Tribute Fleets: The Luo Sect and Boatmen's Associations in the Eighteenth Century," *Modern China* 8.3:361–91 (1982). On Triads, see Tai Hsuan-chih, "The Origin of the Heaven and Earth Society," trans. Ronald Suleski, *Modern Asian Studies* 11.3:405–25 (1977).

CHAPTER 5: REGIONAL SOCIETIES

General reading. 5.1. Basic comparative figures on degrees, population, government expenses, local histories, etc., have been taken from the following works: Zhu Shijia, *Zhongguo difangzhi zonglu* [A complete list of Chinese local histories] (1953; repr. Taipei: Xinwenfeng, 1975); Zhao Quancheng, *Qingdai dili yange biao* [A chart of the changes in provincial administrative units in the Qing] (1940, repr. Taipei: Wenhai, 1979); Luo Ergang, *Lüying bingzhi* [Treatise on the Green Standard Army] (Chongqing: Shangwu, 1945); Liang Fangzhong, *Zhongguo lidai hukou tiandi tianfu tongji* [Statistics on population, land, and taxes in Chinese history] (Shanghai: Renmin, 1980); Dwight Perkins, *Agricultural Development in China, 1368–1968* (Chicago: Aldine, 1969); He Bingdi, *Zhongguo huiguan shilun* [A historical survey of Chinese *Landsmannschaften* in China] (see 2.4); and Li Hua, ed., *Ming Qing yilai Beijing gongshang huiguan beike xuanbian* [Selected stele inscriptions from commercial and handicraft guilds in Peking in the Ming and Qing] (Peking: Wen-wu, 1980).

5.2. For elites, see Shang Yanliu, *Qingdai keju kaoshi shulu* [An account of the examination system in the Qing period] (Peking: Shenghuo dushu xinzhi, 1958); Ping-ti Ho, *The Ladder of Success in Imperial China* (see 1.6); Zhang Yuexiang, "Qingdai jinshi zhi dili di fenbu" [The geographical distribution of holders of the metropolitan degree in the Qing dynasty], *Xinli* 4.1:1–12 (1926); Evelyn S. Rawski, *Education and Popular Literacy in Ch'ing China* (Ann Arbor: University of Michigan Press, 1979); Qian Shifu, ed., *Qingdai zhiguan nianbiao* [A chronological chart of Qing office holders], 4 vols. (Peking: Zhonghua, 1980); and Arthur W. Hummel, ed., *Eminent Chinese of the Ch'ing Period* (see 1.7).

5.3. For the macroregions, see the works of G. W. Skinner, especially his articles in *The City in Late Imperial China* (see 2.3), as well as "Chinese Peasants and the Closed Community: An Open and Shut Case," *Comparative Studies in Society and History* 13.3:270–81 (1971). Also, for earlier periods, Robert M.

Hartwell, "Demographic, Political, and Social Transformations of China, 750–1550," *Harvard Journal of Asiatic Studies* 42.2:365–442 (1982).

North China. 5.4. Liu Chia-chü, "The Creation of the Chinese Banners in the Early Ch'ing," *Chinese Studies in History* 14.4:47–75 (1981); Muramatsu Yuji, "Banner Estates and Banner Lands in Eighteenth Century China—Evidence from Two New Sources," *Hitotsubashi Journal of Economics* 12.2:1–13 (1972).

5.5. Gilbert Rozman, *Urban Networks in Ch'ing China and Tokugawa Japan* (4.3 above); Alison Dray-Novey, "Policing Imperial Peking: The Ch'ing Gendarmerie 1650–1850," Ph.D. diss., Harvard University, 1981. *Ming Qing yilai Beijing gongshang huiguan beike xuanbian* edited by Li Hua (see 5.1) should be supplemented with Niida Noboru, *Pekin kōshō girudo shiryōshū* [Resource materials on industrial and commercial guilds in Peking], compiled by Saeki Yūichi and Tanaka Issei, 6 vols. (Tokyo: Tōyō bunka kenkyūjo, Tōyōbunken senta, 1975–1983). The latest attempt to count up *huiguan* in Peking is to be found in Lü Zuoxie, "Ming Qing shiqi di huiguan bing fei gongshangye hanghui," cited in 2.4. The figure in our text is Lü's. A much higher total of 598 *huiguan* for the city is cited by G. W. Skinner, "Mobility Strategies in Late Imperial China: A Regional Systems Analysis" (see 2.4), p. 338n10.

5.6. Four rather different studies investigate rural Shandong in the Qing: I Songgyu, "Shantung in the Shun-chih Reign: The Establishment of Local Control and the Gentry Response," trans. Joshua Fogel, *Ch'ing-shih wen-t'i* 4.4:1–34 (1980), 4.5:1–31 (1981); Jing Su and Luo Lun's *Landlord and Labor in Late Imperial China: Case Studies from Shandong*, trans. Endymion Wilkinson (Cambridge: Harvard University, Council on East Asian Studies, 1978), originally published in Chinese in 1957; Jonathan D. Spence, *The Death of Woman Wang* (New York: Viking, 1978); and Susan Naquin, *Shantung Rebellion: The Wang Lun Uprising of 1774* (New Haven: Yale University Press, 1981). The early Qing patronage of the Kong lineage is treated in Richard E. Strassberg, *The World of K'ung Shang-jen: A Man of Letters in Early Ch'ing China* (New York: Columbia University Press, 1983). For relief of a Zhili famine, see Pierre-Etienne Will, *Bureaucratie et famine dans la Chine du XVIIIe siècle* (see 1.9). Various studies of the Kaifeng Jews are included in Hyman Kublin, ed., *Studies of the Chinese Jews* (4.15 above).

Lower Yangtze. 5.7. The Lower Yangtze is the best-documented region of China, and there are many studies of its economy and major industries. See Liu Shih-chi, "Some Reflections on Urbanization and the Historical Development of Market Towns in the Lower Yangtze Region, ca. 1500–1900," *The American Asian Review* 2.1:1–27 (1984), and Chin James Shih, "Peasant Economy and Rural Society in the Lake T'ai Area, 1368–1840," Ph.D. diss., University of California at Berkeley, 1981.

5.8. The city of Suzhou has attracted a great deal of scholarly attention: one useful study of industrial organization there is Liu Yongcheng's "Shilun Qingdai Suzhou shougongye hanghui" [Handicraft guilds in Suzhou during the Qing dynasty], *Lishi yanjiu* 11:21–46 (1959), translated in *Chinese Studies in History* 15.1–2:113–67 (1981–1982), and Lü Zuoxie, "Ming Qing shiqi Suzhou di huiguan he gongsuo" [Huiguan and gongsuo in Suzhou in the Ming and Qing], *Zhongguo shehui jingji shi yanjiu* 2:10–24 (1984). Also E-tu Zen Sun, "Sericulture and Silk Textile Production in Ch'ing China," in W. E. Willmott, ed., *Economic Organization in Chinese Society* (see 4.3), pp. 79–108. Ping-ti Ho, "The Salt Merchants of Yangchow" (see 4.14) provides an overview of the salt monopoly and the role of Huizhou merchants that can be compared to Ye Xian'en, *Ming Qing Huizhou nongcun shehui yu dianpu zhi* (see 4.12).

5.9. Regional development is treated in Yoshinobu Shiba, "Ningpo and Its Hinterland," in *The City in Late Imperial China*, pp. 391–439; Mark Elvin, "Market Towns and Waterways: The County of Shanghai from 1480 to 1910," pp. 441–73 in the same volume (see 2.3); and Antonia Finnane, "Prosperity and Decline Under the Qing: Yangzhou and Its Hinterland," Ph.D. diss., Australian National University, 1985.

5.10. Jerry Dennerline, *The Chia-ting Loyalists* (see 2.6 above) provides a textured glimpse of local society in part of the delta on the eve of the Qing conquest. James H. Cole, *Shaohsing* (Tucson: University of Arizona Press, 1986), and Hilary J. Beattie, *Land and Lineage in China: A Study of T'ung-ch'eng County, Anhwei, in the Ming and Ch'ing Dynasties* (Cambridge: Cambridge University Press, 1979), present local studies of elites with national connections in two rather different settings. James H. Cole, "The Shaoxing Connection: A Vertical Administrative Clique in Qing China," *Modern China* 6.3:317–26 (1980), examines the national network created on the basis of native-place ties by one locality.

5.11. Benjamin Elman, *From Philosophy to Philology: Intellectual and Social Aspects of Change in Late Imperial China* (see 3.3), describes the community of *kaozheng* scholars based in this region in the eighteenth century. Shen Fu, *Six Chapters of a Floating Life*, trans. Leonard Pratt and Chiang Su-hui (Harmondsworth: Penguin, 1983), describes life, mostly in the Suzhou area, at the end of the eighteenth century. For Huizhou artists, see James Cahill, ed., *The Shadows of Mount Huang: Chinese Painting and Printing of the Anhwei School* (Berkeley: University Art Museum, 1981).

Middle Yangtze. 5.12. Industry is treated in Robert Tichane, *Ching-te-chen: Views of a Porcelain City* (Painted Post, N.Y.: New York State Institute for Glaze Research, 1983), and *Jingdezhen taoci shi kao* [Draft history of the Jingdezhen porcelain industry], compiled by Jiangxisheng qinggongye ting taoci yanjiusuo (Peking: Sanlian, 1959).

5.13. The hydraulic cycle has been described by several scholars, notably Pierre-Etienne Will, "Un cycle hydraulique en Chine: la province du Hubei du

XVIe au XIXe siècles," Ecole Française d'Extrême-Orient, *Bulletin* 68:261–87 (1980). Regional economic development is studied in Shigeta Atsushi, "Shinsho ni okeru Konan komeshijō no ichi kōsatsu" [An investigation of early Qing rice markets in Hunan], *Tōyōbunka kenkyūjo kiyō* 10:427–98 (1956), and R. Bin Wong, "The Political Economy of Food Supplies in Qing China." Ph.D. diss., Harvard University, 1983, chaps. 5–8 of which deal with Hunan in the eighteenth century, as does Evelyn S. Rawski, *Agricultural Change and the Peasant Economy of South China* (Cambridge: Harvard University Press, 1972), chap. 5 of which is on Hunan. Also Peter C. Perdue, "Population Growth, Agricultural Development, and Social Conflict in Hunan, 1500–1850." Ph.D. diss., Harvard University, 1981.

5.14. Eighteenth-century trends are mentioned in Ts'ui-jung Liu, *Trade on the Han River and Its Impact on Economic Development* (Taipei: Zhongyang yanjiuyuan, Jingji yanjiusuo, 1980). The growing importance of Hankou in the development of this region over several centuries is ably covered in William T. Rowe, *Hankow: Commerce and Society in a Chinese City, 1796–1889* (see 2.4). See Suzuki Chūsei, *Shinchō chūkishi kenkyū* [History of the mid-Qing period] (Tōyōhashi: Aichi daigaku Kokusai mondai kenkyūjo, 1952) for an analysis of the effect of Han River highlands settlement on China.

5.15. Here and in the other macroregional sections, our discussion of Hakka movements relies heavily on S. T. Leong, "Ethnicity and Migrations of the Hakka Chinese: A Regional Systems Approach," (unpub. MS, 1983), and "The P'eng-min: The Ch'ing Administration and Internal Migration" (see 4.16). Other studies bearing on the Hakka-*pengmin* movements include Liu Min, "Lun Qingdai pengmin di huji wenti" [The question of household registers for Qing pengmin], *Zhongguo shehui jingjishi yanjiu* 1:17–29 (1983), and Stephen Averill, "The Shed People and the Opening of the Yangzi Highlands," *Modern China* 9.1:84–126 (1983).

5.16. Anachronistic, but nonetheless valuable for giving a close description of the social milieu of the assimilated Miao region in western Hunan, is Shen Congwen's *Recollections of West Hunan*, trans. Gladys Yang (Peking: China Publications, 1982). E. G. Bridgman, "Sketches of the Miao-tsze," *Journal of the Royal Asiatic Society, North China Branch* 3:1–26 (1859) translates a Chinese description.

Southeast Coast. 5.17. John E. Wills, "Maritime China from Wang Chih to Shih Lang: Themes in Peripheral History," in *From Ming to Ch'ing* (see 2.4), pp. 201–38, looks at trade in its heyday. On overseas trade and emigration see Wen Guangyi, "Fujian huaqiao chuguo di lishi he yuanyin fenxi" [History and causes of Fujianese emigration], *Zhongguo shehui jingjishi yanjiu* 2:75–89 (1984). For selected aspects of economic development, see Fu Yiling, *Ming Qing nongcun shehui jingji* [Rural society and economy in the Ming and Qing] (Peking: Sanlian, 1961), Maeda Shōtarō, "Min Shin no Fukken ni okeru nōka fukugyō" [On subsidiary industries of Fujian peasant households in the Ming and Qing], in *Suzuki Shun kyōju kanreki kinen Tōyōshi ronsō* [Collected articles on Far Eastern history commemorating Professor Suzuki Shun's sixty-first birthday] (Tokyo: Sanyōsha, 1964), pp. 569–86, and Dai Yifeng, "Jindai Minjiang shangyou shanqu chuji shichang shitan" [On lower-level markets in the mountainous upper reaches of the Min River in modern times], *Zhongguo shehui jingjishi yanjiu* 3:93–104 (1985). See also the dissertation of Robert P. Gardella, Jr., "Fukien's Tea Industry and Trade in Ch'ing and Republican China," cited above 4.5; Margaret Medley, *The Chinese Potter* (New York: Scribner's, 1976), chap. 10 of which is on the Dehua kilns; and Evelyn S. Rawski, *Agricultural Change and the Peasant Economy of South China* (see 5.13), chap. 4 of which is on Ming Fujian.

    5.18 Trade is studied by Chin-keong Ng, *Trade and Society: The Amoy Network on the China Coast 1683–1735* (Singapore: Singapore University Press, 1983); Jennifer Cushman, "Fields from the Sea, Chinese Junk Trade with Siam During the Late Eighteenth and Early Nineteenth Century," Ph.D. diss., Cornell University, 1975; and Sarasin Viraphol, *Tribute and Profit: Sino-Siamese Trade, 1652–1853* (Cambridge: Harvard University, Council on East Asian Studies, 1977). On related legal developments, see Rosser H. Brockman, "Commercial Contract Law in Late Nineteenth-Century Taiwan" (see 4.4), and Fu Yiling, "Fujian nongcun di gengchu zudian qiyue ji qi maimai wenshu" [Contracts for renting, buying, and selling draft animals in Fujian], *Zhongguo shehui jingji shi yanjiu* 4:1–4 (1983).

    5.19. Dialect problems are discussed in Katayama Hyōe, "Shindai Min-Etsu chihō no seion kyōiku ni tsuite—Yōseichō o chūshin ni" [The Qing movement for orthodox language education in Fujian and Guangdong, focusing on the Yongzheng reign], *Ajiashi kenkyū* 2:51–73 (1978). On religion, see Xia Qi, "Mazu xinyang de dili fenbu" [The geographical distribution of the Mazu cult], *Youshi xuezhi* 1.4:1–32 (1962).

    5.20 In this and the section on Lingnan, our discussions of dominant lineages draw upon Maurice Freedman, *Chinese Lineage and Society: Fukien and Kwangtung* (see 2.2). See also Myron Cohen, "The Hakka or Guest People: Dialect as a Socio-Cultural Variable in Southeast China" (4.16 above), and Lü Xisheng, "Ming Qing shiqi Shezu dui Zhenan shanqu di kaifa" [The She people and the development of the mountains of southern Zhejiang in Ming and Qing], *Zhongyang minzu xueyuan xuebao* 2:90–91 (1982). Harry J. Lamley, "*Hsieh-tou*: The Pathology of Violence in Southeastern China," *Ch'ing-shih wen-t'i* 3.7:1–39 (1977), takes up ethnic tensions. Tai Hsuan-chih, "The Origin of the Heaven and Earth Society" (see 4.17) describes the emergence of this organization.

Lingnan. 5.21. Studies that explore the theme of land reclamation and lineage development include Rubie Watson, "The Creation of a Chinese Lineage: The Teng of Ha Tsuen, 1669–1751," *Modern Asian Studies* 16.1:69–100 (1982); James L. Watson, "Hereditary Tenancy and Corporate Landlordism in Traditional

China: A Case Study," *Modern Asian Studies* 11.2:161–82 (1977); and Sasaki Masaya, "Juntoku ken kyōshin to Tōkai jūrokusa" [The gentry of Shunde county and the Donghai delta], *Kindai Chūgoku kenkyū* 3:161–232 (1959). The relationship of urban networks to education is clarified in Tilemann Grimm, "Academies and Urban Systems in Kwangtung," in *The City in Late Imperial China* (see 2.3), pp. 475–98. Illicit networks are studied in Frederic Wakeman, Jr., "The Secret Societies of Kwangtung, 1800–1856," in Jean Chesneaux, ed., *Popular Movements and Secret Societies in China* (Stanford: Stanford University Press, 1972), pp. 29–47. On Hakka tensions, see Philip A. Kuhn, "Origins of the Taiping Vision: Cross-Cultural Dimensions of a Chinese Rebellion," *Comparative Studies in Society and History* 19.3:350–66 (1977).

5.22. For foreign trade, see Earl H. Pritchard, *The Crucial Years of Early Anglo-Chinese Relations, 1750–1800* (Pullman, Washington: Research Studies of the State College of Washington, 4:3–4, 1936); Hosea B. Morse, *The International Relations of the Chinese Empire*, 3 vols. (1910–1918; repr. Taipei: Book World Co., 1966). On local industry at Foshan, see Luo Hongxing, "Ming zhi Qing qianqi Foshan yetieye chutan" [The iron-smelting industry at Foshan from Ming to early Qing], *Zhongguo shehui jingjishi yanjiu* 4:44–54 (1983). On sugar, a thriving export crop in the eighteenth century, see Sucheta Mazumdar, "A History of the Sugar Industry in China: The Political Economy of a Cash Crop in Guangdong 1644–1834," Ph.D. diss., University of California, Los Angeles, 1984.

5.23. For the area that later became part of Hong Kong: James Hayes, "Rural Society and Economy in Late Ch'ing: A Case Study of the New Territories of Hong Kong (Kwangtung)," *Ch'ing-shih wen-t'i* 3.5:33–71 (1976), and Peter Y. L. Ng, *New Peace County: A Chinese Gazetteer of the Hong Kong Region* (Hong Kong: Hong Kong University Press, 1983). Dian Murray, "Sea Bandits: A Study of Piracy in Early Nineteenth-Century China," Ph.D. diss., Cornell University, 1979, describes the piracy along the coast at the end of the century.

Northwest China. 5.24. Few local studies have been done of this macroregion. Joseph Fletcher's two essays, "Ch'ing Inner Asia c. 1800" and "The Heyday of the Ch'ing Order in Mongolia, Sinkiang and Tibet," cited in 4.15, are the most useful single sources for information on this region's interaction with Inner Asia. A recent study of early commercial relations between China and Zungaria is Cai Jiayi, "Shiba shiji zhongye Jungeer tong zhongyuan diqu di maoyi wanglai lueshu" [Commercial relations between Zungaria and China in the mid-eighteenth century], *Qingshi luncong* 4:241–55 (1982).

5.25. For information on Shanxi merchants, about whom a good deal has been written in Japanese and Chinese, see Saeki Tomi, "Shinchō no kōki to Sansei shōnin" [Shanxi merchants and the rise of the Qing], *Shakai bunka shigaku* 1:11–42 (1966), and Chen Qitian, *Shanxi piaozhuang kaolue* [A study of Shanxi banks] (1936; repr. Taipei: Hua-shi, 1978).

5.26. Muslim sectarian tensions in the eighteenth century are best described by Fletcher (see 4.15); see also Jonathan Lipman, "The Border World of Gansu," Ph.D. diss., Stanford University, 1981.

Upper Yangtze. 5.27. The study of this region is also in its infancy. General regional descriptions appear in E. Colborne Baber, *Travels and Researches in Western China* (London: Murray, 1882), and Virgil C. Hart, *Western China: A Journey to the Great Buddhist Centre of Mount Omei* (Boston: Ticknor, 1888). The frontier phase is the subject of Robert E. Entenmann, "Migration and Settlement in Sichuan, 1644–1796," Ph.D. diss., Harvard University, 1982. Qing policies to resettle the province of Sichuan are discussed in Peng Yuxin, "Sichuan Qingchu zhaolai renkou he qingfu zhengce" [The policy to settle people and lighten taxes in early Qing Sichuan], *Zhongguo shehui jingjishi yanjiu* 2:1–9 (1984). Land utilization is analyzed by Han-sheng Ch'en, *Frontier Land Systems in South-ernmost China* (New York: Institute of Pacific Relations, 1949). On tenancy practices, see Madeleine Zelin, "The Rights of Tenants in Mid-Qing Sichuan: A Study of Land-related Lawsuits in the Baxian Archives," *Journal of Asian Studies* 45.3:499–526 (1986). Contemporary information is found in Henry Serruys, "Andrew Li, Chinese Priest, 1692–1774," *Nouvelle revue de science missionaire* 32:39–144 (1976). For the long-term development, see Paul Smith, "Commerce, Agriculture, and Core Formation in the Upper Yangtze, A.D. 2 to 1948," paper presented at the Conference on Spatial and Temporal Trends and Cycles in Chinese Economic History, 980–1980, August 1984.

5.28. For the tribes along the periphery, see Robert H. G. Lee's essay, "Frontier Politics in the Southwestern Sino-Tibetan Borderlands during the Ch'ing Dynasty" in 4.15 above. For Tibet, see Melvyn Goldstein, "Serfdom and Mobility: An Example of the 'Human Lease' in Traditional Tibetan Society," *Journal of Asian Studies* 30.3:521–34 (1971).

Southwest China. 5.29. Readers should consult several works by James Lee: "China's Southwestern Frontier: State Policy and Economic Development from 1250 to 1850," Ph.D. diss., University of Chicago, 1982; "Food Supply and Population Growth in Southwest China, 1250–1600," *Journal of Asian Studies* 41.4:711–46 (1982); "The Legacy of Immigration in Southwest China, 1250–1850," *Annales de démographie historique*, 1982:279–304. Another very good study of this macroregion is Claudine Lombard-Salmon, *Un exemple d'acculturation chinoise: la province du Gui Zhou au XVIIIe siècle* (see 4.15).

5.30 The ethnic groups in the region are treated in a number of works: see You Zhong, *Yunnan minzushi* [An ethnic history of Yunnan], 2 vols. (Kunming: Yunnan daxue lishixi, 1980); Inez de Beauclair, *Tribal Cultures of Southwest China* (Taipei: Orient Cultural Service, 1970); Feng Han-i and J. R. Shyrock, "The Historical Origins of the Lolo," *Harvard Journal of Asiatic Studies* 3:103–27 (1938); Emile Rocher, "Histoire des princes du Yunnan et leurs relations avec la Chine d'après des documents historiques chinois," *T'oung Pao* 10:1–32, 115–54,

337–68, 437–56 (1899); and Yoshirō Shiratori, "Ethnic Configurations in Southern China," in Toichi Mabuchi and Yoshirō Shiratori, eds., *Folk Cultures of Japan and East Asia* (Tokyo: Sophia University Press, 1966), pp. 147–63.

5.31. On Qing policy, see Robert H. G. Lee, "Frontier Politics in the Southwestern Sino-Tibetan Borderlands during the Ch'ing Dynasty," and Kent Smith, "Ch'ing Policy and the Development of Southwest China: Aspects of Ortai's Governor-Generalship, 1726–1731" (both in 4.15).

5.32. On mining, see James Lee, "State-Regulated Industry in Qing China, The Yunnan Mining Industry: A Regional Economic Cycle 1700–1850," presented at the 1984 Conference on Spatial and Temporal Trends and Cycles in Chinese Economic History, 980–1980. On brewing, see Guizhousheng gongshangye lianhehui, ed., "Guizhou maotaijiu shi" [The history of Guizhou maotai], in *Gongshang shiliao* [Historical materials on industry and commerce] 1:98–117 (1980).

Manchuria. 5.33. In addition to Joseph Fletcher's "Ch'ing Inner Asia" (see 4.15), a useful study is Robert H. G. Lee, *The Manchurian Frontier in Ch'ing History* (Cambridge: Harvard University Press, 1970). For background, see Morris Rossabi, *China and Inner Asia from 1368 to the Present* (London: Thames and Hudson, 1975); Pamela Crossley, "The Tong in Two Worlds: Cultural Identities in Liaodong and Nurgan during the 13th–17th Centuries," *Ch'ing-shih wen-t'i* 4.9:21–46 (1983); and Wu Wei-ping, "The Development and Decline of the Eight Banners," Ph.D. diss., University of Pennsylvania, 1969. On subsequent economic administration of resources, see Van Jay Symonds, *Ch'ing Ginseng Management: Ch'ing Monopolies in Microcosm* (Tempe: Arizona State University, Center for Asian Studies, 1981), and Preston M. Torbert, *The Ch'ing Imperial Household Department* (see 1.5). For newly studied population records, see James Lee and Robert Y. Eng, "Population and Family History in Eighteenth Century Manchuria" (see 4.8).

Taiwan. 5.34. John Shepherd's Ph.D. thesis, "Plains Aborigines and Chinese Settlers on the Taiwan Frontier in the 17th and 18th Centuries" (see 4.15), and Johanna Menzel Meskill, *A Chinese Pioneer Family: The Lins of Wu-feng, Taiwan, 1729–1895* (Princeton: Princeton University Press, 1979), provide valuable information on the settlement phase. Several useful essays are included in Ronald G. Knapp, ed., *China's Island Frontier: Studies in the Historical Geography of Taiwan* (Honolulu: University of Hawaii Press, 1980). See also Harry J. Lamley, "Subethnic Rivalry in the Ch'ing Period," in *The Anthropology of Taiwanese Society* (see 2.1), pp. 282–318, and Ramon Myers, "Taiwan under Ch'ing Imperial Rule, 1684–1895: The Traditional Economy," *Journal of the Institute of Chinese Studies of the Chinese University of Hong Kong* 5.2:373–409 (1972). Ties with Amoy are analyzed in Chin-keong Ng, *Trade and Society: The Amoy Network on the China Coast 1683–1735* (see 5.18).

5.35. On religion, see Laurence G. Thompson, "Orthodox Official Religion and Orthodox Popular Religion in Early Ch'ing Taiwan" (see 3.6) and Kristofer M. Schipper, "Neighborhood Cult Associations in Traditional Tainan," in *The City in Late Imperial China* (see 2.3), pp. 651–76.

CHAPTER 6: THE EIGHTEENTH-CENTURY LEGACY

Dynastic decline? 6.1. David S. Nivison, "Ho-shen and His Accusers: Ideology and Political Behavior in the Eighteenth Century," in Nivison and Arthur F. Wright, eds., *Confucianism in Action* (Stanford: Stanford University Press, 1959), pp. 209–43, describes the traditional view of late Qianlong politics. See also Harold L. Kahn, *Monarchy in the Emperor's Eyes: Image and Reality in the Ch'ien-lung Reign* (Cambridge: Harvard University Press, 1971), and Judith Whitbeck, "Kung Tzu-chen and the Redirection of Literati Commitment in Early Nineteenth Century China," *Ch'ing-shih wen-t'i* 4.10:1–32 (1983). For a more recent characterization of Qing decline, see Susan Mann Jones and Philip A. Kuhn, "Dynastic Decline and the Roots of Rebellion," in *The Cambridge History of China*, vol. 10, part 1 (see 4.15), pp. 107–62.

6.2. The White Lotus rebellion is best analyzed by Suzuki Chūsei, *Shinchō chūkishi kenkyū* [History of the mid-Qing period] (see 5.14). The 1774 and 1813 uprisings are analyzed in Susan Naquin, *Millenarian Rebellion in China: The Eight Trigrams Uprising of 1813* (New Haven: Yale University Press, 1976), and *Shantung Rebellion: The Wang Lun Uprising of 1774* (see 5.6). See Elizabeth Perry, *Rebels and Revolutionaries in North China, 1845–1945* (Stanford: Stanford University Press, 1980), for a close look at the Huaibei environment in which the Nian were born, and Frederic Wakeman, Jr., *Strangers at the Gate: Social Disorders in South China, 1839–1861* (Berkeley: University of California Press, 1966), for disturbances in Lingnan.

6.3. Other rebellions are described in Arthur Hummel, ed., *Eminent Chinese of the Ch'ing Period* (see 1.7), and in Xiao Yishan, *Qingdai tongshi* [A general history of the Qing] (Taipei: Shangwu, 1962). An overview of the mid-nineteenth-century rebellions is provided in Albert Feuerwerker, *Rebellion in Nineteenth-Century China* (Ann Arbor: University of Michigan, Center for Chinese Studies, 1975). For the significance of these rebellions on the distribution of power, see Philip A. Kuhn, *Rebellion and Its Enemies in Late Imperial China: Militarization and Social Structure, 1796–1864* (Cambridge: Harvard University Press, 1970).

The Opium War. 6.4. On the increasing opium problem and its history, see Jonathan Spence, "Opium Smoking in Ch'ing China," in Frederic Wakeman and Carolyn Grant, eds., *Conflict and Control in Late Imperial China* (Berkeley: University of California Press, 1975), pp. 143–73; and Frederic Wakeman, "The Canton Trade and the Opium War," in *The Cambridge History of China*, vol. 10, part 1 (see 4.15), pp. 163–212. The monetary problems arising from the net outflow of silver are treated in Ramon Myers and Yeh-chien Wang, "Economic Developments: 1644–1800," draft chapter for the *Cambridge History of China*, vol. 9, part 2, ed. D. Twitchett and F. Wakeman. See also William Atwell, "Notes on Silver, Foreign Trade, and the Late Ming Economy," *Ch'ing-shih wen-t'i* 3.8:1–33 (1977).

Index

Academies: and networks, 51, 53; in regions, 165, 173, 183; Ming, 16; policy on, 152

Administrative structures: and economy, 222–23; in Suzhou, 150; in Upper Yangtze, 196–97; limits to, 225–26; trends, 220–21, 223–24

Adoption, 39

Agriculture. *See* Cropping patterns

Aisin Gioro, 26, 29, 116, 147

Amateur/professional distinctions, 69, 122

Amoy (Xiamen), Fujian, 171

Ancestor worship, 89. *See also* Filial piety

Arable land (statistics), 25, 203, 207

Architecture, 77–79, 174, 192

Army of the Green Standard, 11

Banking, 101, 187–88. *See also* Credit

Bannermen, 9, 128, 141. *See also* Eight Banners

Baojia, 16–17

Births, 80, 110. *See also* Fertility

Board of Rites, 28

Bondservants, 7, 10, 118, 119, 141

Brewing industry, 143, 187, 207

Buddhism, 20, 42, 45, 112, 156, 176, 204, 211

Bureaucracy. *See* Factions

Bureaucratization: a trend, 10; in world view, 92–93; of behavior, 229; of religion, 90, 230–31; of values, 225

Calendar, 28, 83–84, 88

Canton, Guangdong, 102, 181–82, 183

Cao Yin, 10

Cash nexus, 53–54. *See also* Commercialization

Celibacy, 110

Central Asia, 29, 187, 190. *See also* Mongols; Muslims; Xinjiang

Central government, 7–8, 10–11. *See also* Administrative structures

Changsha, Hunan, 164

Chen Hongmou, 19, 204

Chinese identity, 90–91, 127–28

Christianity, 112

Christians, 20, 142, 195

Cixi, Empress Dowager, 53

Clothing, 75–76, 82, 127

Co-hong, 102, 171

Commercialization, 56, 63–64, 100, 101, 221–22

Commutation Act, 103

Complete Library of the Four Treasuries (*Siku quanshu*), 51, 66–67

Concubines, 111-12. *See also* Family; Marriage; Women

Confucian: concept of order, 92; confessions, 67; critique, 63; philanthropy, 45; pursuits, 126; support for family, 113

Confucianism: in Fujian, 173; statecraft, 165, 183; Tongcheng school, 155. *See also* Evidential scholarship

Conquest: ban on coastal trade, 105, 167; coastal evacuation, 148, 167, 176; resistance to, 15, 148, 167–68, 176

265

Contracts. *See* Law
Copper: 31, 105, 200. *See also* Money
Cores (of macroregions), 56–57, 112, 139, 181, 228–29
Cotton, 75, 101, 143, 154
Court of Colonial Affairs, 29
Credit, 101, 171
Cropping patterns: changes in, 23; compared with Europe, 98; in periphery, 159; New World crops, 130; regional, 73, 98, 99, 169–70, 177, 196, 207
Cycles (macroregional): Lingnan, 176; Lower Yangtze, 148, 157; Middle Yangtze, 159; North China, 140; Northwest, 185; Southeast Coast, 168, 169; Southwest, 199; Upper Yangtze, 194

Dai Zhen, 66
Dalai Lama, 29
Death ritual, 81, 83. *See also* Mortality
Deflation, 105, 157, 235
Demography. *See* Fertility; Mortality; Population
Depressions, 105, 222
Dialects, regional, 142, 152, 158, 169, 173
Dietary patterns, 73–74
Disease, 108, 113
Dizang (Kshitigarbha), 157
Domestic trade, policies on, 26–27. *See also* Commercialization; Marketing; Markets
Double burial, 172, 179
Drama, 60–62, 63, 122, 147, 183, 192
Dream of Red Mansions (The Story of the Stone), 34, 35, 68, 75, 79, 120

East India Company, 103, 104, 183
Eight Banners, 4, 5, 116, 141, 206, 220
Eight Great Families, 116
Elite: careers, 124–25, 126; definitions of, 114–15; life-style, 125; persons, 124
Erotica, 109
Ethnicity, 134–35, 214. *See also* Non-Han minorities
Europe: comparisons with, 107, 109, 111, 114; influenced scholarship, 65
Evidential (*kaozheng*) scholarship, 65–67, 125
Examination system: and cities, 59; and

factions, 52; bars outcasts, 118; competition, 123–24; curriculum, 9–10; quotas, 12, 122, 123, 124, 155; restored, 12–13; sale of degrees, 13; Shuntian prefecture, 146; structure, 9; successful regions, 9, 13; Yangzhou riots, 57; *yin* privilege, 123. *See also* *Jinshi, Juren*

Factions, 13, 51–52, 53
Family (*jia*); authority, 113; defined, 33–34; domestic cycle, 82, 110–11; internal dynamics, 34–35, 120; model for state, 92–93; policy on, 113; size of, 110–11, 112; strategies, 35, 57, 110, 124; types of, 34, 111
Famine relief, 25, 236
Fang Shishu, 69, 70
Farm types, 130
Feng-shui (geomancy), 172, 179
Fertility, 108–09
Festivals, 84–85, 86–87, 88
Fiction, 59, 62, 67–68
Field administration, 8, 224
Filial piety, 81, 92
Flowers in the Mirror, 68
Footbinding, 76, 80
Foreign trade: and money supply, 104, 105, 232–33; at Canton, 102, 103, 176, 181–82; exports, 77, 103, 170, 182; Fujianese in, 104, 171; importance of, 31–32; in Middle Yangtze, 162; shifts in, 102, 233; volume of, 103; with Europe, 102–03; with Southeast Asia, 102, 168; with Tibet, 196
Foshan, Guangdong, 183
Frontier, 194, 213–14. *See also* Peripheries
Frontier society: and the state, 226–27; crops, 130; demographics, 131, 132; in Lingnan, 180–81; in Manchuria, 207–08; in Middle Yangtze, 166–67; in Taiwan, 210; voluntary associations, 133
Fuca, 144
Funeral allowances, 83

Gambling, 62
Gardens, 78–79
Garrisons, 150, 164, 171, 184, 188, 189, 204
Gentry, 114–15. *See also* Elite

Geomancy. See *Feng-shui*
Ginseng, 7, 207
Government monopolies, 26, 143, 196
Granaries, 25–26
Grand Canal, 24, 50, 140
Grand Council, 8
Guandi, 191, 207
Guanxi. See Networks
Guanyin, 85, 156
Guilds (*gongsuo*), 49, 61, 151

Hairstyles, 82
Hakka, 78, 134–35, 160, 169, 180, 211
Han River highlands, 166–67
Hankou, Hubei, 161, 162–64
Hanlin Academy, 12, 53
Hengyang, Hunan, 37
Heshen, 52–53, 54, 137
Homosexuality, 63, 110
Hongren, 60
Hong Shen, 61
Hongtaiji, 4
Hoppo, 104, 182
Huaibei, 24
Huang Shuqing, 128
Huiguan (native-place association), 46,
   48–50, 143, 151, 163, 170, 197
Huizhou, Anhui: and painting, 60;
   houses, 78; merchants, 48–49, 60,
   146, 149, 151; servile statuses, 119, 121

Imperial Household Department, 7, 119,
   144
Imperial Textile Manufactories, 150
Infanticide, 108, 110
Inflation, 105, 222
Integration, cultural, 231
Islam, 20, 135, 191, 193. *See also*
   Muslims

Jade, 76
Japan, 31, 107, 109, 111
Jesuits, 68, 77, 142. *See also* Christians
Jews, 129, 142
Jiangnan Tax Case, 15
Jiansheng (degree), 13
Jin Nong, 60
Jingdezhen, Jiangxi, 77, 164
Jinshi (degree): defined, 9; expansion of,
   12; in evidential scholarship, 66;

regional production of, 146, 149, 165,
   173, 183, 192, 198, 204, 208
Jiuhua, Anhui, 156–57
Journey to the West, 59, 62
Juren (degree), 9, 66–67

Kangxi emperor, 6, 10, 19, 83, 107, 147,
   150, 207
Kiakhta, 31
Kong lineage, 146–47
Kong Shangjen, 61, 147, 152
Koxinga (Zheng Chenggong), 209
Kunqu style, 61. *See also* Drama

Labor: agricultural wage, 99–100,
   120–21; industrial, 49–50, 164, 203;
   servile, 100
Lamaist Buddhism: imperial patronage of,
   18, 19–20, 29, 142, 207; monasteries,
   142, 190; Qing control, 129
Land: multiple rights to, 100; national
   acreage, 25; resettlement, 22–23;
   transactions, 100–01
Landlords, 99, 146, 156, 173, 211
Law, 102, 119, 171, 230
Li Yu, 122
Liang Qichao, *x*
Liang-Huai Salt Administration, 150, 162
Lineages: genealogies, 107; higher-order,
   179; imperial, 116; in Lingnan,
   178–79; in Lower Yangtze, 151; in
   Southeast Coast, 172; Manchu, 144;
   policies on, 39; types of, 35–38
Literacy, 58–59. *See also* Schools
Literati: alienation of, 67–68, 155. *See
   also* Elite
Livestock economy, 192–93
Local elites: and state, 15; as managers,
   126; in peripheries, 132, 133; in Upper
   Yangtze, 197; resist taxes, 57
Lolo, 117. *See also* Non-Han minorities

Macheng, Hubei, 162, 195
Macroregions, 139. *See also* Cores;
   Peripheries
Manchus, 4, 11, 18–19, 128, 141, 206,
   208
Manjusri (bodhisattva of wisdom), 29, 145
Marketing: and assimilation, 129;
   networks, 161–62, 181, 186–88, 190,
   196, 203, 207; of tea, 104; trends, 99,
   214–15
Markets: in people, 121; in Yangtze delta,

Markets (*continued*): 149; long-distance, 101; periodic, 40–41
Marriage: age at, 108; allowances, 83; brideprice, 39; customs, 80–81, 110; dowry, 38; forms of, 38–39, 82, 109, 172; ritual, 82
Marxist models, *x*, 99–100, 115, 157
Mazu (Tianhou), 175, 179, 212
Men: life expectancy, 107; sales of, 118, 119; servile, 181
Miao, 158, 160, 178. *See also* Non-Han minorities
Migration: ban on, 206, Hakka, 160, 178; intraregional, 156; overseas, 168, 182; patterns, 215; policy on, 22–23; sojourning, 111; to frontiers, 130; to Middle Yangtze, 159; to Southeast Asia, 184; to Southwest, 202; to Taiwan, 210; to Upper Yangtze, 195; to Xinjiang, 189–90
Military. *See* Eight Banners; Garrisons
Ming: academies, 16, 152; Buddhism, 156; factions, 16; loyalists, 15, 209; monetization, 100; morality books, 64; Neo-Confucianism, 66; paper notes, 105; Religion of the Three Teachings, 176; Six Maxims, 19; tenancy, 100, 120
Ming History project, 65
Mining, 200, 203
Money, 100, 101, 104–05, 124, 234–35
Mongols, 5, 29, 117, 185
Morality books, 64
Mortality, 107–08, 111
Mount Emei, Sichuan, 195
Mount Huang, Anhui, 157
Mount Wudang, Hubei, 166
Mount Wutai, Shanxi, 145
Music, 122
Muslims: in Nanjing, 148; in Northwest, 185-86, 191; in posts, 17, 188; occupational specialization, 142; rebellions, 135, 193; restaurants, 74
Mustard Seed Garden Manual of Painting, 70

Nanchang, Jiangxi, 164
Nanjing, Jiangsu, 56
Native-place associations, 47–48. See also *Huiguan*
Networks, 50–54, 144
New World crops, 23, 143, 170
Ningbo, Zhejiang, 47, 152

Non-Han minorities: assimilation of, 127–28, 129; in Lingnan, 177; in Southwest, 201–02; in Taiwan, 209; marriage customs, 112; policies on, 17–18, 128–29, 204, 210–11; registration of, 107; vs. Han, 201, 202
Nurgaci, 4, 6

Occupations: hereditary, 121–22; Muslim, 142, 186; outcast, 117–18
Opera. *See* Drama
Opium, 74, 168–69, 170, 182–83, 233–34, 235
Outcasts (*jian min*), 117–18, 148, 185

Painting, 60, 68, 69, 70, 122
Panchen Lama, 29
Peking, 47, 61, 71, 78, 146, 187
Penghu islands, 74
Peripheries: and rebellions, 227–28; and the state, 132, 226–27; defined, 139; in Lingnan, 180–81; in Lower Yangtze, 154; local elites, 133. *See also* Frontier society
Philanthropy, 45–46, 113
Pilgrimages: in North China, 145; Muslim, 191; to Jiuhua, 156–57; to Mount Emei, 195, to Mount Huang, 157; to Mount Wudang, 166; to Mount Wutai, 145; to Putuoshan, 85, 156; to Taishan, 85–86
Piracy, 174, 184
Poetry, 70–72
Pollution, 109
Popular religion: and officials, 43, 175; and salvation, 92; ban on sectarians, 20; community religion, 40, 41–43; earth gods, 42; in Fujian, 176; in Northwest, 193; in Taiwan, 211–12; pilgrimage sites, 20, 29; shamanism, 206–07. *See also* Buddhism; Pilgrimages; Taoism
Population: data on, 107; densities, 98, 213–14; growth, 24–25, 107, 223; Manchurian, 207; per county, 8; policies, 113; registration, 106–07; Southwest, 200; Taiwan, 209–10
Porcelain, 77, 162
Precious Mirror for Gazing at "Flowers," 63
Prices, 25–26, 105. *See also* Deflation; Inflation

Prince Yu, 144
Princes, 6, 52
Provincial administration. *See* Field
    administration
Publishing, 20, 59, 70, 170
Puer tea, 74
Putuoshan, Zhejiang, 85, 156

Qianlong emperor, 18, 19, 26, 54,
    68–69, 81, 113, 150, 194
Qinqiang style, 61, 192. *See also* Drama
Quanzhou, Fujian, 40, 210, 211, 212

Rebellion of the Three Feudatories, 5
Rebellions, 5, 227–28
Rehe, 142
Religion, state, 89–90. *See also* Popular
    religion
Religion of the Three Teachings, 176
Revenues, 219. *See also* Taxation
Ritual, 84, 86, 88–90, 91
Romance of the Three Kingdoms, 59, 62
Russia, 30–31, 129, 206

Sacred Edict, 19
Salt. *See* Government monopolies
Scholars, The, 51, 67–68, 71
Schools, 128, 204
Sects. *See* Islam; White Lotus sect
Servants, 119–20, 121
Servitude, 118, 119, 181
Settlement types, 146, 155, 174
Shanghai, Jiangsu, 101, 152
Shanxi/Shaanxi merchants, 61, 142, 143,
    187, 191
Shaoxing, Zhejiang, 74, 144
Share partnership, 47
She aborigines, 169
Shed people, 117, 174
Shengjing (Mukden), 5, 208
Shengyuan, 9, 19
Shuntian prefecture (Peking), 13
Shunzhi emperor, 19, 83
Silk, 27, 75, 103, 104, 153–54, 182
Silver, 104, 105, 232–33, 234. *See also*
    Money
Slaves, 119. *See also* Bondservants;
    Servitude
Social conflict: ethnic, 158, 160, 161,
    180; in Taiwan, 211; on frontier, 132;
    strikes, 50, 164; urban, 40, 64, 173,
    xiedou, 157, 174

Social mobility, 57, 64, 115–16, 122,
    126–27, 208
Sojourning, 46, 111, 156. See also
    Huiguan
Southeast Asia, 49, 74, 102, 168, 170,
    184
Spinsterhood, 109
Standardization, of ritual, 230
State religion, 89–90. *See also*
    Pilgrimages; Popular religion
Status, social, 116, 122, 124, 125, 126
Strange Stories from an Eccentric's Studio,
    68
Sugar, 182
Suzhou, Jiangsu, 27, 40, 50, 87, 151,
    152, 154, 157

Tai people, 177. *See also* Non-Han
    minorities
Taiping rebellion, 53, 134–35, 157
Taishan, Shandong, 85–86
Taiwan aborigines, 127–28. *See also* Non-
    Han minorities
Tanka, 169, 178, 180
Taoism, 145, 165–66
Taxation, 21–22, 150, 162, 215, 219,
    220, 221
Tea, 74, 103, 104, 162, 170, 196, 203
Temples, 41–44, 211
Tenancy, 98, 99, 100, 119, 120, 156,
    173–74, 210
Theaters, 61
Tianhou. *See* Mazu
Tibet, 112, 188. *See also* Lamaist
    Buddhism
Tibetans, 185, 194–95, 201. *See also*
    Non-Han minorities
Timber, 162
Tobacco, 74, 187
Tongcheng, Anhui, 36–37, 155
Transport, 98-99, 102, 140, 185
Travel, 43, 72
Triads, 50, 137, 166, 172, 183–84
Tributary system, 27–28, 142
Trigrams, 136
Tusi, 17, 186

Urban: culture, 56–64, 231;
    philanthropy, 46
Urbanization, 27, 56, 149, 198, 200,
    212–13

Values, 92, 93, 225
Villages: leaders, 41; single-surname, 40;
    types of, 40
Voluntary associations: *bang*, 50;
    Guolufei, 198; irrigation, 45; on
    frontiers, 133; policy toward, 16,
    Taiwan, 211; Triads, 198

Wang Fuzhi, 127
Water control, 23–24, 43–45, 151, 154,
    161, 167
Water Margin, 59
Wells, 24
Wet nurses, 109
White Lotus sect, 135–37, 145, 166–67
Wine, 74
Women: dowry, 38; education, 19, 59;
    elite, 38; infanticide, 110; life course,
    80, 110; marriage, 108–09, 110; poor,
    39; sales of, 118–19; spinsterhood, 109;
    widows, 113, 173. *See also* Footbinding
Woodblock prints, 70, 143
Workers' organizations, 50. *See also* Labor

Writers, 68
Writing, 91
Wu Jingzi, 67–68
Wujiang, Jiangsu, 104

Xi'an, Shaanxi, 192
Xiangtan, Hunan, 161
Xiedou, 157, 174
Xinjiang, 29, 76, 188–90

Yan Ruoju, 65
Yangzhou, Jiangsu, 57, 69, 70, 152
Yao people, 160, 177. *See also* Non-Han
    minorities
Yiyang style, 61. *See also* Drama
Yongzheng emperor, 6, 19, 117, 173
Yuan Mei, 53, 68

Zhangzhou, Fujian, 211
Zhili famine, 25
Zhu Xi, 9–10, 65, 66
Zhu Yun, 144
Zunghars, 29, 188